OBBLIGATI

Essays in Criticism

Anthony Hecht

OBBLIGATI

Essays in Criticism

Atheneum   *New York*

1986

ACKNOWLEDGMENTS

SHADES OF KEATS AND MARVELL—*Hudson Review*, Spring 1962

THE RIDDLES OF EMILY DICKINSON—*TV Guide*, December 18, 1976, and *New England Review*, Autumn 1978

RICHARD WILBUR—*TLS*, May 20, 1977

ELIZABETH BISHOP—*TLS*, August 26, 1977

ON W. H. AUDEN'S "IN PRAISE OF LIMESTONE"—*New England Review*, Autumn 1979

ROBERT LOWELL—Lecture given at the Library of Congress, May 2, 1983; *Grand Street*, Spring 1983; and published by the Library of Congress

THE PATHETIC FALLACY—Lecture given at the Library of Congress, May 7, 1984; *The Yale Review*, Summer 1985; and published by the Library of Congress

OTHELLO—Lecture given at Georgetown University, March 6, 1986

HOUSES AS METAPHORS: THE POETRY OF ARCHITECTURE—Lecture given at The Folger Shakespeare Library, January 13, 1985

PAGE 329 CONSTITUTES A CONTINUATION OF THIS COPYRIGHT PAGE

Library of Congress Cataloging in Publication Data

Hecht, Anthony, ———
    Obbligati : essays in criticism.

    1. English literature—History and criticism—Addresses, essays, lectures. 2. American literature—History and criticism—Addresses, essays, lectures. I. Title.
    PR403.H42   1985   820'.9   84-45707
    ISBN 0-689-11570-9

TO EVAN
with Love and Admiration

Preface

MY TITLE refers to a complex set of obligations undertaken by these essays—obligations to the works and poets they deal with, as well as to the editors, teachers, and administrators who offered me their pages and podia. I also mean to affirm what I conceive to be the proper role of criticism as a musical obbligato: that is, a counterpart that must constantly strive to move in strict harmony with and intellectual counterpoint to its subject, and remain always subordinate to the text upon which it presumes to comment.

The essays vary strikingly in length, from the shortest, those brief reviews of Elizabeth Bishop (here somewhat expanded) and Richard Wilbur that were budgeted to the frugal spaces of the *Times Literary Supplement*, to the longest, on *The Merchant of Venice*, composed without restrictions of space and appearing here for the first time. There is a good deal of latitude as well in the time of composition, the earliest essay, on Keats and Marvell, having been published in 1962, and the latest making their first appearances in this volume.

A book of poems is sent forth nowadays with an unwritten

envoy ("Goe, little Booke: thy selfe present") as a silent prayer and invisible amulet against the dangers it must encounter; while a critic is allowed a preface in which to try to forestall and disarm the attacks he imagines may be levelled against him. Critics are permitted and expected to employ prolepsis, while poets must abide in silence until a sympathetic expositor comes along to serve them. And I have wondered what shall be made (if anything) of this curious assortment of pieces. I envision the enemy approaching on both flanks. To the right they declare that so heterogeneous a collection, written off and on over so long a span of time, cannot hope for unity of vision, nor any kind of intellectual coherence. To the left they proclaim that the volume suffers from a narrow set of concerns, a limited sensibility, a fixed and unchanging view, repetitive and everywhere to be anticipated.

I confront this grim vision with my own, no doubt self-serving, view of the book as it stands. I am pleased to discover here what I think of as an unexpected coherence, the more surprising in that it was not planned. As to what this coherence consists in, I had better leave it to others to say. In any case I don't mean to use my preface defensively. There are those to whom I owe very warm and heartfelt thanks for help and encouragement. Among these are the editors of journals who generously allowed my essays to make their first appearances—Frederick Morgan, editor of *The Hudson Review*; Sydney Lea, editor of *New England Review* (now *New England Review & Bread Loaf Quarterly*); Ben Sonnenberg, editor of *Grand Street*; Kai Erikson, editor of *The Yale Review*; and John Gross, formerly editor of the *TLS*. I owe a special debt of gratitude to Daniel Aaron, who, as Director of the Seminars in the History of American Civilization at Harvard, invited me to lecture there on Emily Dickinson on April 24, 1975. The essay on Dickinson that appears here is a conflation of that lecture, originally printed in *New England Review*, with a brief commentary, written for *TV Guide*, commissioned by

Preface

one of its editors, John Weisman, for appearance in the December 18, 1976, issue, just before the telecast of "The Belle of Amherst," with Julie Harris. I owe very special debts to the Library of Congress, and more particularly to Daniel Boorstin, Librarian of Congress, and to John C. Broderick, Assistant Librarian for Research Services, who not only were responsible for my appointment as Consultant in Poetry, but afforded me the opportunity for my lectures on Robert Lowell and The Pathetic Fallacy. The Lowell lecture first appeared as a review of Ian Hamilton's biography of the poet in the Spring 1983 issue of *Grand Street*, and was then enlarged by half again its original length. But perhaps my most extensive thanks must go, with a keen and lasting sense of gratitude, to Joseph H. Summers and Rabbi Abraham Karp, colleagues of mine at the University of Rochester, for their generous and valuable advice and encouragement during the early stages of my venture into Shakespearean criticism. They are not to be held accountable for any errors I may have insinuated into the essay on *The Merchant* after they lost sight of it. I have singled out this essay for dedication, with love, to Irma Brandeis, a colleague of mine when I taught at Bard College. I am indebted to the administration of the University of Rochester for giving me the opportunity to accept the Consultantship in Poetry at the Library of Congress, during which appointment a large part of this book was written. In addition I acknowledge with warmest thanks the support and helpful comments of William Arrowsmith, John Hollander, Cyrus Hoy, David Kalstone, Bernard M. W. Knox, William MacDonald, Jonathan Post, Mary Jo Salter, and Jon Stallworthy. But no one encouraged and aided me more than my dear Helen.

Contents

OBBLIGATI

Essays in Criticism

The Pathetic Fallacy

Un paysage quelconque est un état de l'âme.
HENRI-FRÉDÉRIC AMIEL

The world is a fair field fresh with the odor of Christ's name.
SAINT AUGUSTINE

M Y T I T L E is a famous coinage of John Ruskin's, and comes from his five-volume study called *Modern Painters*. I want to begin this evening by quoting Ruskin at some length, intruding an occasional impertinent interruption, as a way of recalling to you his original and provocative formulation, while permitting myself an obbligato of comment. I begin with a sentence of his full of high disdain and mockery.

German dulness, and English affectation, have of late much multiplied among us the use of two of the most objectionable words that were ever coined by the troublesomeness of metaphysicians,—namely, "Objective," and "Subjective."

A promising beginning, and Ruskin proceeds with a brisk and touching confidence that these philosophic muddles can be laid to rest once and for all.

Now, therefore, putting these tiresome and absurd words quite out of our way, we may go on at our ease to examine

3

the point in question,—namely, the difference between the ordinary, proper, and true appearances of things to us; and the extraordinary, or false appearances, when we are under the influence of emotion, or contemplative fancy; false appearances, I say, as being entirely unconnected with any real power or character in an object, and only imputed to it by us. . . . What is more, if we think over our favorite poetry, we shall find it full of this kind of fallacy, and that we like it all the more for being so.

It will appear also, on consideration of the matter, that this fallacy is of two principal kinds. Either . . . it is the fallacy of wilful fancy, which involves no real expectation that it will be believed; or else it is a fallacy caused by an excited state of the feelings, making us, for the time, more or less irrational.

I interrupt here to remark that Ruskin was no slouch at employing the fallacy when he cared to. Here, for example, is a fragment of description from *Modern Painters*:

Such precipices are . . . dark in color, robed with everlasting mourning, for ever tottering like a great fortress shaken by war, fearful as much in their weakness as in their strength, and yet gathered after every fall into darker frowns and unhumiliated threatening . . .

That sentence continues for another two hundred and eight words. Of the two kinds of fallacy he distinguishes, the first (that of the "wilful fancy, which involves no real expectation that it will be believed") is characteristic of the poetry of wit both of the Renaissance and of the eighteenth century, and of poetry that adopts conventions meant to be recognized as conventional, and tradition that is consciously traditional. It is this kind for which Ruskin feels the easiest and most derisive contempt. The other kind (the fallacy caused by excited and irrational feelings) enlists his deeper and more serious consideration.

4

The Pathetic Fallacy

All violent feelings have the same effect. They produce in us a falseness in our impressions of external things, which I would generally characterize as the "pathetic fallacy."

Now we are in the habit of considering this fallacy as eminently a character of poetic description, and the temper of mind in which we allow it, as one eminently poetical, because passionate. But I believe, if we look well into the matter, that we shall find the greatest poets do not often admit this kind of falseness,—that it is only the second order of poets who much delight in it.

And by way of explaining this distinction, he adds an important footnote:

I admit two orders of poets, but no third; and by these two orders I mean the Creative (Shakespeare, Homer, Dante), and the Reflective or Perceptive (Wordsworth, Keats, Tennyson). But both of these must be *first*-rate in their range, though their range is different; and with poetry second-rate in quality no one ought to be allowed to trouble mankind.

There is enough in that note to make almost any modern poet tremble; but I ask you please to observe, before Ruskin proceeds, that he has neatly arrogated the three poets of the first rank to his side as being virtually guiltless of the fallacy. Having divided poets conveniently into two ranks, only a moment later he adds another:

So, then, we have the three ranks: the man who perceives rightly, because he does not feel, and to whom the primrose is very accurately the primrose, because he does not love it. Then, secondly, the man who perceives wrongly, because he feels, and to whom the primrose is anything else than a primrose: a star, or a sun, or a fairy's shield, or a forsaken maiden.

The Pathetic Fallacy

I interrupt to intrude as an example D. H. Lawrence's statement, "The perfect rose is only a running flame," the sort of statement that in all likelihood prompted Gertrude Stein's famous reflection, "A rose is a rose is a rose." But to return to Ruskin's third rank:

> And then, lastly, there is the man who perceives rightly in spite of his feelings, and to whom the primrose is forever nothing else than itself—a little flower apprehended in the very plain and leafy fact of it, whatever and how many soever the associations and passions may be that crowd around it. And in general, these three classes may be rated in comparative order, as the men who are not poets at all, and the poets of the second order, and the poets of the first; only however great a man may be, there are always some subjects that ought to throw him off his balance. . . .

So, having begun with two ranks, and moved onward to three, Ruskin now advances to four, though only two, properly speaking, are poets:

> And thus, in full, there are four classes: the men who feel nothing, and therefore see truly; the men who feel strongly, think weakly, and see untruly (the second order of poets); the men who feel strongly, think strongly, and see truly (the first order of poets); and the men who, strong as human creatures can be, are yet submitted to influences stronger than they, and see in a sort untruly, because what they see is inconceivably above them. This last is the usual condition of prophetic inspiration.

You will not have failed to notice how central is the notion of "strength" to Ruskin's formulation, and how for him the ideal poet of the first rank enjoys a neatly symmetrical balance of strong mind and strong feeling perfectly matched. There is, in any case, no question in his mind (nor, he assumes, in the reader's) that strong feeling, all other considerations apart, is essential to poetry. He declares quite flatly:

> A poet is great, first in proportion to the strength of his passion, and then, that strength being granted, in proportion to his government of it; there being, however, always a point beyond which it would be inhuman and monstrous if he pushed this government, and, therefore, a point at which all feverish and wild fancy becomes just and true.

That point, for Ruskin, is the acknowledgment of the divine order and divinity itself, which, according to him, would seem to permit any kind of rant and raving whatever. For him, the forces of mind and of feeling are pitted against each other in exhausting contest, the mind obliged to govern the feelings, but the feelings determined to make it as difficult as possible for the mind to do so; and the quality of the poetry, according to this combative metaphor, will be determined by the ferocity, the persistence and inconclusiveness of the antagonism. It is, quite clearly, a distinctly romantic description of the problem, and it should come to us as no surprise that Ruskin is as loftily dismissive of Alexander Pope as he is of Claude Lorrain. He exhorts us sneeringly to "hear the cold-hearted Pope say to a shepherd girl—" and then quotes the lovely lines that Handel set so beautifully to music:

> Where'er you walk, cool gales shall fan the glade;
> Trees, where you sit, shall crowd into a shade;
> Your praise the birds shall chant in every grove,
> And winds shall waft it to the powers above.

Of these lines Ruskin writes contemptuously, "This is not, nor could it for a moment be mistaken for, the language of passion. It is simple falsehood, uttered by hypocrisy," and one cannot help feeling that there speaks the voice of the complete prig. The entire genre of the pastoral, which presupposes a sympathetic relationship between nature and rustic humanity, is here dismissed. So much for "Lycidas." Falsehood is charged, we may suppose, because we don't for a minute believe Pope (in eighteenth-century London) is really addressing a genuine shepherdess; and hypocrisy because a compliment involving the universal obeisance of nature to the young lady presents us with a pathetic fallacy so hyperbolic, so extravagant and beyond the limits of credence, that it ceases to be a compliment, and proves itself mere artifice and empty flattery. But Pope and his century ought not to be spurned quite so easily. Paul Fussell has observed that even when poetry of this period

> has not been specifically dismissed on charges of artifice and conventionality, it has been benignly neglected in favor of the sort which seems to reflect back onto us those extreme emotional states made peculiarly our own by modern history—strain, personal and collective guilt, hysteria, madness.

He proceeds to remind us that "any kind of art, just because of its conspicuous distinction from the natural and the accidental, is much more conventional and institutionalized than we may have imagined."*

Ruskin, however, turns from what he regards as the cold-heartedness of Pope to the ungoverned passion of a poem by Wordsworth, and concludes:

> I believe these instances are enough to illustrate the main point I insist upon respecting the pathetic fallacy,—that so far as it *is* a fallacy, it is always the sign of a morbid state of mind, and comparatively of a weak one.

And he adds that it is "eminently characteristic of the modern mind."

His eagerness to find this morbidity distinctly modern may perhaps be an attempt to protect a badly exposed flank. You

* Paul Fussell, Introduction to *English Augustan Poetry*.

The Pathetic Fallacy

will recall that he numbered among his poets of the first order both Homer and Shakespeare. And Ruskin is eager to forestall the charge that the earliest of the great poets was liberal in his use of the fallacy. So to anticipate our objections, he himself raises the question in regard to the famous passage in the *Iliad* in which Achilles and the river Scamander argue and fight with one another. One would suppose this was the *locus classicus* of the pathetic fallacy. But Ruskin is concerned to claim all the Greeks, and Homer as their representative, for the camp of clear-sighted realism, and he insists that the deification or personification of the river—which allows it to remonstrate, and petition, and express all manner of feeling in human language—is not to impute human feelings to the world of nature, but is the Greeks' pious deification, not of the river itself, but of the power behind and within it. There is something unnervingly question-begging about how he makes this obscure and not altogether convincing distinction, but I had best let him make it in his own words.

> With us, observe, the idea of the Divinity is apt to get separated from the life of nature; and imagining our God upon a cloudy throne, far above the earth, and not in the flowers or waters, we approach those visible things with a theory that they are dead; governed by physical laws, and so forth. But coming to them, we find the theory fail; that they are not dead; that, say what we choose about them, the instinctive sense of their being alive is too strong for us; and in scorn of all physical law, the wilful fountain sings, and the kindly flowers rejoice. And then, puzzled, and yet happy; pleased, and yet ashamed of being so; accepting sympathy from nature, which we do not believe it gives, and giving sympathy to nature, which we do not believe it receives,—mixing, besides, all manner of purposeful play and conceit with these involuntary fellowships,—we fall necessarily into the curious

9

web of hesitant sentiment, pathetic fallacy, and wandering fancy, which form a great part of our modern view of nature. But the Greek never removed his god out of nature at all; never attempted for a moment to contradict his instinctive sense that God was everywhere. "The tree *is* glad," he said, "I know it is; I can cut it down: no matter, there is a nymph in it. The water *does* sing," said he; "I can dry it up; but no matter, there was a naiad in it."

Ruskin's position here is predicated on what he seems to posit as the incontestable sincerity of Hellenic pantheism, a very doubtful and certainly unprovable ground. But Homer is not as neat in his distinctions as Ruskin, and he not only exhibits to us the deity that animates the river but presents a Trojan named Asteropaeus, a valiant mortal, whose mortality is put beyond question when Achilles kills him, but who identifies himself as the son of a river. So the genetics of divinity begin to thin out a little. But Homer carries the matter further still. When Asteropaeus and Achilles were engaged in their duel, the Trojan let fly one of his spears, which grazed Achilles, drawing blood. Homer then declares, "The spear passed over him and stuck in the ground, still hungering for flesh." This locution of the hunger of the spear for flesh comes up again and again in the *Iliad*, and it has no bearing upon Greek piety or pantheism. It is a straightforward imputation of human feelings to an inanimate object. As for Shakespeare, another of Ruskin's poets of the first order, he elects to put into the mouth of Hotspur, a professed hater of poetry, what amounts to a very deliberate imitation of these very passages from the twenty-first book of the *Iliad*, when Hotspur commends Mortimer, and rises hotly to his defense before King Henry IV.

> He never did fall off, my sovereign liege,
> But by the chance of war. To prove that true
> Needs no more but one tongue for all those wounds,
> Those mouthed wounds, which valiantly he took

The Pathetic Fallacy

When on the gentle Severn's sedgy bank,
He did confound the best part of an hour
In changing hardiment with great Glendower.
Three times they breathed, and three times did they drink,
Upon agreement, of swift Severn's flood;
Who then, affrighted with their bloody looks,
Ran fearfully among the trembling reeds
And hid his crisp head in the hollow bank,
Bloodstained with these valiant combatants.

                    (*Henry IV*, Part I: I, iii)

Shakespeare, of course, *pace* Ruskin, is a mine and fund of instances of the fallacy, of which Duke Senior's famous speech
in the Forest of Arden is a useful example.

Now, my co-mates and brothers in exile,
Hath not old custom made this life more sweet
Than that of painted pomp? Are not these woods
More free from peril than the envious court?
Here feel we but the penalty of Adam;
The seasons' difference, as the icy fang
And churlish chiding of the winter's wind,
Which, when it bites and blows upon my body
Even till I shrink with cold, I smile and say
'This is no flattery'; these are counsellors
That feelingly persuade me what I am.
Sweet are the uses of adversity,
Which, like the toad, ugly and venomous,
Wears yet a precious jewel in his head;
And this our life, exempt from public haunt,
Finds tongues in trees, books in the running brooks,
Sermons in stones, and good in everything.

                    (*As You Like It*: II, i)

This speech may be taken as representing the anagogic or
emblematic mode of viewing nature that was nearly a com-

monplace from the Middle Ages up to at least the seventeenth
century. It is a mode characteristically religious, beautifully
stated in the epigraph I have used from Saint Augustine, and
premised on the conviction that the whole purpose and majesty
of God is made legible in the most minute, as well as the most
stunning and conspicuous, parts of his creation; that attentive
contemplation of any single part will reveal in code but with
clarity the whole glory and intent of the Creator. This conviction is based on biblical texts as well as theological argument, and one of the best known of the texts is the Nineteenth
Psalm.

> The heavens declare the glory of God;
> and the firmament sheweth his handywork.
> Day unto day uttereth speech,
> and night unto night sheweth knowledge.
> There is no speech nor language,
> where their voice is not heard.

This eloquence of the physical universe, this demonstration
on the part of the natural world, amounts to a revelation to all
who are not blind and deaf. "He that hath ears to hear, let him
hear; and who hath eyes to see, let him see." The world as holy
cipher and mute articulator can be found not only in medieval
texts and Shakespeare but in those emblematic or symbolic
poems by Herbert and Donne and Herrick that are among the
great achievements of their age, and for which I will let the
less well-known poem by Henry King, called "A Contemplation Upon Flowers," stand as an instance.

> Brave flowers, that I could gallant it like you
> And be as little vain;
> You come abroad, and make a harmless shew,
> And to your beds of earth again;
> You are not proud, you know your birth,
> For your embroidered garments are from earth.

The Pathetic Fallacy

You do obey your months, and times, but I
Would have it ever spring;
My fate would know no winter, never die
Nor think of such a thing;
Oh, that I could my bed of earth but view
And smile, and look as cheerfully as you.

Oh, teach me to see death, and not to fear,
But rather to take truce;
How often have I seen you at a bier,
And there look fresh and spruce;
You fragrant flowers, then teach me that my breath
Like yours may sweeten, and perfume my death.

From such grave counsellors as these let me ask you to shift
your attention abruptly to the world of fiction. Novelists were
not slow to make use of strategies that Ruskin discovers in the
works of poets and painters. Merely to propose to you such
diverse authors as Dickens, Conrad, Dostoyevski, Hawthorne,
Joyce, and Mann may suggest without further elaboration the
various ways in which a "setting" is made to bear a significant
burden of meaning and a virtual role in a story. But let me use
Hardy's *Return of the Native* as an example. The first chapter
of that novel is given over entirely to the description of a landscape, a landscape not only bleak in itself but here, in its initial
appearance, devoid of human life and habitation.

A Saturday afternoon in November was approaching the
time of twilight, and the vast tract of unenclosed wild
known as Egdon Heath embrowned itself moment by
moment.

That's Hardy's first sentence, and I invite you to notice that his
chief verb, "embrowned," is not only active, suggesting that
the landscape is purposively engaged in its own transmuta-
tions, but that the word is richly Miltonic, coming straight
from a landscape in *Paradise Lost*:

13

Both where the morning sun first warmly smote
The open field and where the unpierced shade
Embrowned the noontide bowers. . . .

and it bears, in consequence, the omen of a landscape shadowed by doom. I continue to quote selectively from Hardy's chapter.

The face of the heath by its mere complexion added half an hour to the evening; it could in like manner retard the dawn, sadden noon, anticipate the frowning of storms scarcely generated, and intensify the opacity of a moonless midnight to a cause of shaking and dread. . . . The spot was, indeed, a near relation of night. . . . The sombre stretch of rounds and hollows seemed to rise and meet the evening gloom in pure sympathy, the heath exhaling darkness as the heavens precipitated it. And so the obscurity of the air and the obscurity of the land closed together in a black fraternization towards which each advanced half-way. . . . It was at present a place perfectly accordant with man's nature—neither ghastly, hateful, nor ugly: neither commonplace, unmeaning, nor tame; but, like man, slighted and enduring; and withal singularly colossal and mysterious in its swarthy monotony. As with some persons who have lived long apart, solitude seemed to look out of its countenance. It had a lonely face, suggesting tragical possibilities.

The point is not merely that Hardy gives a countenance and human quality to his landscape, as might the composer of a *paysage moralisé*, but that he gives to it a dimension we may call superhuman: as *mise en scène* it becomes the destiny and fate, tragic in character, of all those who there inhabit. Hardy, of course, did much the same thing in his best lyrics, but I should like to give you instead another poetic example, one that when I was a college student in the forties was still able to

confound, bewilder, and even enrage a large number of readers. By now, of course, most of you will know these lines by
heart.

> Let us go then, you and I,
> When the evening is spread out against the sky
> Like a patient etherised upon a table; . . .

There was in those days a certain splenetic sort of reader who
never got beyond this point in the poem. Red-faced and apo-
plectic, he would ask explosively, "How can an evening be
like a patient? How can similes be used with so little regard
for visual accuracy or plain intelligibility? This is just modern hokum." But Eliot is really doing pretty much the same
thing Hardy did in the passage I quoted; instead of a landscape, he presents a skyscape that shall serve as the presiding
fate and destiny of the chief characters who inhabit beneath its
crepuscular dimness.

Let me detain my splenetic reader in the witness box for yet
a moment longer. There is so much in modern poetry that
sends him into paroxysms of fury. Think of the fulminations
engendered by his reading of William Carlos Williams's "The
Red Wheelbarrow."

> so much depends
> upon
>
> a red wheel
> barrow
>
> glazed with rain
> water
>
> beside the white
> chickens.

If I may be allowed to eliminate my witness's characteristic
expletives, expressions of repugnance at omissions of capital-

ization, and his blank incomprehension about the division of lines (though syllabically they form a handsome and symmetrical pattern), his central complaint comes to this: What is the thing that so much depends; and how much is "so much"? To which we may respond that the "so much" does not require measurement, being part of what is an exclamatory statement, implying astonishment at how very much indeed is concerned in this dependency. And what, finally, is the dependency but the intimate and indissoluble relationship of the inner and outer worlds, the "subjective" and "objective" states that Ruskin was so eager to eliminate. The objective is straightforward, factual, visual; the subjective is evaluative, secret and interior. The objective world is nothing but random data without the governing subjective selection and evaluation; the two are halves of a single act of cognition. So there is mystery to the poem, but it is the common mystery of our moment-to-moment existence. Thus stated, it would seem that the pathetic fallacy was almost unavoidable, however condemnatory Ruskin felt about it. And, indeed, as a puzzle, it has fascinated modern poets, who have even written about the possibility of trying to avoid it. Can it be avoided? The topic was famously addressed by Ortega y Gasset in his essay "The Dehumanization of Art," from which I want to quote selectively:

> What is it the majority of people call aesthetic pleasure? What happens in their minds when they "like" a work of art; for instance, a theatrical performance? The answer is easy. A man likes a play when he has become interested in the human destinies presented to him, when the love and hatred, the joys and sorrows of the personages so move his heart that he participates in it as though it were happening in real life. And he calls a work "good" if it succeeds in creating the illusion necessary to make the imaginary personages appear like living persons. In poetry he seeks the passion and pain of the man behind the

poet. Paintings attract him if he finds in them figures of men and women whom it would be interesting to meet. A landscape is pronounced "pretty" if the country it represents deserves for its loveliness or its grandeur to be visited on a trip. . . . Now . . . not only is grieving and rejoicing at such human destinies as a work of art presents or narrates a very different thing from true artistic pleasure, but preoccupation with the human content of a work of art is in principle incompatible with aesthetic enjoyment proper. . . . I will not now discuss whether pure art is possible. Perhaps it is not; but as the reasons that make me inclined to think so are somewhat long and difficult the subject better be dropped. Besides, it is not of major importance for the matter in hand. Even though pure art may be impossible, there doubtless can prevail a tendency toward a purification of art. Such a tendency would effect a progressive elimination of the human, all too human, elements predominant in romantic and naturalistic production. And in this process a point can be reached in which the human content has grown so thin that it is negligible. We then have an art which can be comprehended only by people possessed of the peculiar gift of artistic sensibility—an art for artists and not for the masses, for "quality" and not for hoi polloi.

The masses, who would include my splenetic commentator of a moment ago, can point contemptuously to what they regard as elitist paintings wherein, in Ortega's words, "the human content has grown so thin that it is negligible." In Mondrian, for example. And they are not likely to be persuaded otherwise even by so eloquent a spokesman for the opposition as is Meyer Schapiro in his fine essay "On the Humanity of Abstract Painting." But is such purity possible in a *poem*? Is it even imaginable? The puzzle lies at the center of Wallace Stevens' celebrated poem "The Snow Man."

The Pathetic Fallacy

One must have a mind of winter
To regard the frost and the boughs
Of the pine-trees crusted with snow;

And have been cold a long time
To behold the junipers shagged with ice,
The spruces rough in the distant glitter

Of the January sun; and not to think
Of any misery in the sound of the wind,
In the sound of a few leaves,

Which is the sound of the land
Full of the same wind
That is blowing in the same bare place

For the listener, who listens in the snow,
And, nothing himself, beholds
Nothing that is not there and the nothing that is.

The poem projects a kind of mind that out of either numbness or a gritty and stoical courage can set itself apart from every chilling fact of its existence, a chill which is thermal and metaphysical at once, accepting both the coldness and the nothingness for what they are and apart from any human valuation. As a poem it is wonderful and harrowing; as a strategy to circumvent the pathetic fallacy it almost works. Almost, except that it claims of the wind that it blows "in the same bare place/For the listener," thereby attributing a motive and purpose, a curiously human attribute, either to the wind, or to some fateful agency that presides over wind and listener. But in any case the poem suggests that "objectivity" is a condition that can be approached only by cancelling our humanity, and by advancing toward a state that strongly resembles insensibility or death. Stevens is continuously concerned in his work with the peculiar relations between "subjective" and "objective" reality, and returns to the puzzle again and again in such poems as "Esthétique du Mal" and "Extracts from Addresses to the Academy of Fine Ideas."

Though Stevens and Frost used to taunt one another about being antipodal and polar opposites in their poetic concerns (Stevens said that Frost's poetry was full of "subjects," by which he seemed to mean the sort of human interest topics that belonged to a classroom assignment; while Frost said that Stevens' poems were "full of bric-a-brac"), Frost nevertheless addressed the same puzzle so continuously in successive poems that the two poets seem curiously allied. I have had some diffi- culty deciding which poem of Frost's I could best employ here, having given serious consideration to "Directive," "The Need of Being Versed in Country Things," "For Once, Then, Some- thing," and "The Most of It," and I've settled on "The Wood Pile."

> Out walking in the frozen swamp one gray day,
> I paused and said, "I will turn back from here.
> No, I will go on farther—and we shall see."
> The hard snow held me, save where now and then
> One foot went through. The view was all in lines
> Straight up and down of tall slim trees
> Too much alike to mark or name a place by
> So as to say for certain I was here
> Or somewhere else: I was just far from home.
> A small bird flew before me. He was careful
> To put a tree between us when he lighted,
> And say no word to tell me who he was
> Who was so foolish as to think what *he* thought.
> He thought that I was after him for a feather—
> The white one in his tail; like one who takes
> Everything said as personal to himself.
> One flight out sideways would have undeceived him.
> And then there was a pile of wood for which

The Pathetic Fallacy

I forgot him and let his little fear
Carry him off the way I might have gone,
Without so much as wishing him good-night.
He went behind it to make his last stand.
It was a cord of maple, cut and split
And piled—and measured, four by four by eight.
And not another like it could I see.
No runner tracks in this year's snow looped near it.
And it was older sure than this year's cutting,
Or even last year's or the year's before.
The wood was gray and the bark warping off it
And the pile somewhat shrunken. Clematis
Had wound strings round and round it like a bundle.
What held it though on one side was a tree
Still growing, and on one a stake and prop,
These latter about to fall. I thought that only
Someone who lived in turning to fresh tasks
Could so forget his handiwork on which
He spent himself, the labor of his ax,
And leave it there far from a useful fireplace
To warm the frozen swamp as best it could
With the slow smokeless burning of decay.

Like countless other Frost poems, this one insists upon the solitariness and isolation of the speaker, involved in some sort of
quest or pilgrimage, and the opening lines cannot fail to remind us of

> Nel mezzo del cammin di nostra vita
> mi ritrovai per una selva oscura
> che la diritta via era smarrita.
>
> (When I had journeyed half of our life's way,
> I found myself within a shadowed forest,
> for I had lost the path that does not stray.)

The Pathetic Fallacy

The journey is perilous, over unstable and uncharted terrain, by one so lonely and uncertain that he talks to himself, as the lonely do, positing an alter ego, a companion and dialectical double, with whom to debate the wisdom of going on, and with whom to join ranks in "we shall see." The role of Doppelgänger is then taken over by the bird, onto which the speaker projects thoughts, fears, all manner of human attitudes, not least of them paranoia, which is itself an illness consisting of projecting baseless feelings upon others. It is an illness from which Frost himself was not immune, and here he is trying to make light of it with a jest that has its deeply touching aspect. That bird is clearly part of his own psyche, and, though troubled, he is also wise enough to acknowledge this. The bird may be governed chiefly by fear; the man seems directed wholly by chance (as are most of us in the main matters of our lives) and it is chance that brings him to the wood pile. As in many another Frost poem, like "After Apple Picking," "Two Tramps in Mud Time," or "The Tuft of Flowers," in which well and patiently performed manual labor symbolizes the craft of writing poetry, the wood pile is the symbol once again of accomplished craftsmanship, a human opus, a body of work, here inexplicably lost from common sight or practical utility, a carefully composed effort that has come to nothing. And what do most of our lives come to after all? Dante, of course, attained Paradise within his poem, and even worldly immortality by means of it. In this pilgrimage poem the poet, who is still as lost at the end of the poem as at the beginning, tries to put a cheerful face on a situation that looked bleak right from the start, by saying, "I thought that only/Someone who lived in turning to fresh tasks/Could so forget his handiwork on which/He spent himself. . . ." But surely we are allowed to consider the possibility that the speaker is trying to cheer himself up, since other possibilities present themselves to explain the odd abandonment of that wood pile, only the most obvious of which is that the man who cut and stacked it has died. And if his labor decays unnoticed, how much more likely is this to be the case with the work of poets, whose audiences are not inclined to be large, whose work is quickly forgotten after their deaths, if it was ever noticed in their lifetimes, unless it were to be stumbled upon by some total and unexpected stranger. The poet composes his world in solitude and anxiety, for which Frost has here found what Eliot called an "objective correlative," and he has done this, as I think, with stunning success. The poem appeared in 1914, when the poet was by no means confident he would ever be famous or remembered, and much inclined to question his entire goal and purpose.

The poet's digression into paranoia and related psychic states, the critic's coinage of "objective correlative," invite further inspection. George Steiner has remarked that "the primary thrust of all libido is towards injection of all realities into the self . . ." and in *Crime and Punishment* we are witness to a dream of Svidrigailov's in which he cunningly transforms his lust for a child by turning her into a six-year-old prostitute, and making himself her helpless victim. As for the strategies of the critic, things have come a long way since the comparative critical innocence of Mr. Eliot. Here, from an essay that appeared in the Winter 1983 issue of *Daedalus*, is Eugene Goodheart commenting upon and quoting from the work of Roland Barthes.

For Roland Barthes, the pleasure of the text is in the making of one's own text at the expense of another's. "Thus begins at the heart of the critical work the dialogue of two histories and two subjectivities, the author's and the critic's. But this dialogue is egotistically shifted toward the present: criticism is not an homage to the truth of the past or to the truth of 'others'—it is a construction of the intelligibility of our own time." In shamelessly confessing the egotism of the critical act, Barthes casts doubt upon the objective existence of "others." . . . His motive is to make the "other" vulnerable and defenseless, so that he can appropriate the text to his own purpose: Barthes speaks of the critical act as theft. Interpretation, in this transvalued sense, is not obliged to represent the text, which is, rather, broken up so that it can fill the critic's subjectivity. In declaring "the death of the author," Barthes eliminates interference from an author's intention. The critical reader's access to the text is immediate, dominant, and impermanent. The critic's text is always provisional, his relationship to the text of the other in constant change. The critic need be faithful only to his own changing, desiring subjectivity.

It was not Eliot, of course, but W. K. Wimsatt who long ago pointed out the dangers of the "intentional fallacy," i.e., limiting the meaning of a text to either what the author thought it meant (since, as Freud has told us, we can often mean more than we are aware of) or what the critic posits as the author's intention. But it is a giant step, a seven-league stride, from Wimsatt to Barthes and others of the current French School of Decomposition so favored these days in certain circles. And so, by an easy exchange of critic for lover, the modern reader, paraphrasing Theseus, may conclude that "The lunatic, the critic and the poet/Are of imagination all compact." But might not the reader also assume that however screwy the literary types might be, however lost in their subjective mists, their solipsisms, their blind self-absorption, at least the scientist, the physicist, could be appealed to as clear-headed defender of "Objectivity"? This would be rash. Listen to Werner Heisenberg: "What we observe is not nature itself but nature exposed to our method of questioning." So much for Ruskin's easy dismissal of the terms "subjective" and "objective." But I dare not end my lecture in a celebration of chaos and confusion. And by way of rescuing myself from that peril, I turn with pleasure to one more poem, this one by Richard Wilbur, and called, "Advice to a Prophet."

When you come, as you soon must, to the streets of our city,
Mad-eyed from stating the obvious,
Not proclaiming our fall but begging us
In God's name to have self-pity,

Spare us all word of the weapons, their force and range,
The long numbers that rocket the mind;
Our slow, unreckoning hearts will be left behind,
Unable to fear what is too strange.

Nor shall you scare us with talk of the death of the race.
How should we dream of this place without us?—
The sun mere fire, the leaves untroubled about us,
A stone look on the stone's face?

Speak of the world's own change. Though we cannot
conceive
Of an undreamt thing, we know to our cost
How the dreamt cloud crumbles, the vines are blackened
by frost,
How the view alters. We could believe

If you told us so, that the white-tailed deer will slip
Into perfect shade, grown perfectly shy,
The lark avoid the reaches of our eye,
The jack-pine lose its knuckled grip

On the cold ledge, and every torrent burn
As Xanthus once, its gliding trout
Stunned in a twinkling. What should we be without
The dophin's arc, the dove's return,

24

The Pathetic Fallacy

These things in which we have seen ourselves and spoken?
Ask us, prophet, how we shall call
Our natures forth when that live tongue is all
Dispelled, that glass obscured or broken

In which we have said the rose of our love and the clean
Horse of our courage, in which beheld
The singing locust of the soul unshelled,
And all we mean or wish to mean.

Ask us, ask us whether with the worldless rose
Our hearts shall fail us; come demanding
Whether there shall be lofty or long standing
When the bronze annals of the oak-tree close.

My motives in reading that poem here in Washington tonight
are by no means confined to their pertinence to my topic,
thought that pertinence is of a rich and complex kind. In his
reference to Xanthus, another name for the River Scamander,
Wilbur returns me to my beginnings with the *Iliad*, and in
his beautiful and intricate weavings of the imagery of speech
and sight, his protracted braiding of "These things in which
we have seen ourselves and spoken," he recapitulates the very
means and methods of the Nineteenth Psalm: "The heavens declare the glory of God; and the firmament showeth his handiwork. Day unto day uttereth speech, and night unto night
showeth knowledge." But in addition to all these important
resonances, there is the beautiful and undoubted fact that
metaphor is our mode not merely of expressing *ourselves* but
of expressing the world, or what we are able to know of it. And
metaphor is not merely the gadget of poets; it is virtually unavoidable as an instrument of thought. Here is Ruskin himself
upon the topic.

Will you undertake to convey to another person a perfectly distinct idea of any single emotion passing in your

own heart? You cannot—you cannot fathom it yourself—
you have no actual expression for the simple idea, and are
compelled to have instant recourse to metaphor.

The very act of description is in some degree metaphoric, and
when Socrates tries to say what the Good is, the nearest he can
come is to say that it is like Light. In Wilbur's rich inter-
twining of voice and image, of sight and sound, he asks,

> . . . how shall we call
> Our natures forth when that live tongue is all
> Dispelled, that glass obscured or broken
>
> In which we have said the rose of our love . . .
> . . . in which beheld
> The singing locust of the soul. . . .

That glass of Wilbur's is not only the lens or prism of the
sciences but also the infinitely lavish hall of mirrors, the Ver-
sailles of facets and reflections, in which wherever we look
we see, as we must, unfailingly, some unexpected aspect of
ourselves.

On W. H. Auden's
"In Praise of Limestone"

IN PRAISE OF LIMESTONE

If it form the one landscape that we the inconstant ones
    Are consistently homesick for, this is chiefly
Because it dissolves in water. Mark these rounded slopes
    With their surface fragrance of thyme and beneath
A secret system of caves and conduits; hear these springs
    That spurt out everywhere with a chuckle
Each filling a private pool for its fish and carving
    Its own little ravine whose cliffs entertain
The butterfly and the lizard; examine this region
    Of short distances and definite places:
What could be more like Mother or a fitter background
    For her son, for the nude young male who lounges
Against a rock displaying his dildo, never doubting
    That for all his faults he is loved, whose works are but
Extensions of his power to charm? From weathered outcrop
    To hill-top temple, from appearing waters to

On W. H. Auden's "In Praise of Limestone"

Conspicuous fountains, from a wild to a formal vineyard,
    Are ingenious but short steps that a child's wish
To receive more attention than his brothers, whether
    By pleasing or teasing, can easily take.

Watch, then, the band of rivals as they climb up and down
    Their steep stone gennels in twos and threes, sometimes
Arm in arm, but never, thank God, in step; or engaged
    On the shady side of a square at midday in   .
Voluble discourse, knowing each other too well to think
    There are any important secrets, unable
To conceive a god whose temper-tantrums are moral
    And not to be pacified by a clever line
Or a good lay: for, accustomed to a stone that responds,
    They have never had to veil their faces in awe
Of a crater whose blazing fury could not be fixed;
    Adjusted to the local needs of valleys
Where everything can be touched or reached by walking,
    Their eyes have never looked into infinite space
Through the lattice-work of a nomad's comb; born lucky,
    Their legs have never encountered the fungi
And insects of the jungle, the monstrous forms and lives
    With which we have nothing, we like to hope, in common.
So, when one of them goes to the bad, the way his mind works
    Remains comprehensible: to become a pimp
Or deal in fake jewelry or ruin a fine tenor voice
    For effects that bring down the house could happen to all
But the best and the worst of us . . .
                That is why, I suppose
    The best and worst never stayed here long but sought
Immoderate soils where the beauty was not so external,
    The light less public and the meaning of life
Something more than a mad camp. "Come!" cried the granite
    wastes,
    "How evasive is your humor, how accidental

On W. H. Auden's "In Praise of Limestone"

Your kindest kiss, how permanent is death." (Saints-to-be
    Slipped away sighing.) "Come!" purred the clays and
        gravels,
"On our plains there is room for armies to drill; rivers
    Wait to be tamed and slaves to construct you a tomb
In the grand manner: soft as the earth is mankind and both
    Need to be altered." (Intendant Caesars rose and
Left, slamming the door.) But the really reckless were fetched
    By an older colder voice, the ocean whisper:
"I am the solitude that asks and promises nothing;
    That is how I shall set you free. There is no love;
There are only the various envies, all of them sad."

They were right, my dear, all those voices were right
And still are; this land is not the sweet home that it looks,
    Nor its peace the historical calm of a site
Where something was settled once and for all: A backward
    And delapidated province, connected
To the big busy world by a tunnel, with a certain
    Seedy appeal, is that all it is now? Not quite:
It has a worldly duty which in spite of itself
    It does not neglect, but calls into question
All the Great Powers assume; it disturbs our right. The poet,
    Admired for his earnest habit of calling
The sun the sun, his mind Puzzle, is made uneasy
    By these solid statues which so obviously doubt
His antimythological myth; and these gamins,
    Pursuing the scientist down the tiled colonnade
With such lively offers, rebuke his concern for Nature's
    Remotest aspects: I, too, am reproached, for what
And how much you know. Not to lose time, not to get caught,
    Not to be left behind, not, please! to resemble
The beasts who repeat themselves, or a thing like water
    Or stone whose conduct can be predicted, these
Are our Common Prayer, whose greatest comfort is music

On W. H. Auden's "In Praise of Limestone"

Which can be made anywhere, is invisible,
And does not smell. In so far as we have to look forward
  To death as a fact, no doubt we are right: But if
Sins can be forgiven, if bodies rise from the dead,
  These modifications of matter into
Innocent athletes and gesticulating fountains,
  Made solely for pleasure, make a further point:
The blessed will not care what angle they are regarded from,
  Having nothing to hide. Dear, I know nothing of
Either, but when I try to imagine a faultless love
  Or the life to come, what I hear is the murmur
Of underground streams, what I see is a limestone landscape.

I N   P R A I S E   O F   L I M E S T O N E is by more or less common consent regarded as one of Auden's finest poems, and there are even those who grant this with a special emphasis by insisting that after *Nones*, the volume in which this poem first appeared, the poet's career and talent slipped into detectable decline. I am not one who concedes anything of the sort, but that is beside my point. What I want to do is to offer a commentary on this poem, a commentary composed of related texts, both in prose and in poetry, many by Auden himself though a few by persons who knew neither him nor his poem, not one of them specifically undertaken for the light it might shed on the poem, all of them arranged by me in a sort of collage, and in the hope that, by offering mutual comment upon one another, and upon the poem especially, something useful might appear. So I begin, perhaps as remotely as possible from the poem, with a piece of prose, a piece, moreover (though here translated), of eighteenth-century French prose, from which I take the liberty of quoting somewhat *ad libitum*:

On W. H. Auden's "In Praise of Limestone"

Cold air constringes the extremities of the external fibres of the body; this increases their elasticity, and favors the return of the blood from the extreme parts to the heart. It contracts those very fibres; consequently it increases their force. On the contrary warm air relaxes and lengthens the extremes of the fibres; of course it diminishes their force and elasticity.

People are, therefore, more vigorous in cold climates . . . the heart has more power. This superiority of strength must produce various effects, a greater boldness, more courage; a greater sense of superiority, that is, less desire for revenge; a greater opinion of security, that is, more frankness, less suspicion, policy and cunning. . . . The inhabitants of warm countries are, like old men, timorous; the people of cold countries are, like young men, firm.

In cold countries they have very little sensibility for pleasure; in temperate countries, their sensibility is exquisite. . . . I have been at the opera in England and in Italy, where I have seen the same pieces and the same performers; and yet the same music produces such different effects on the two nations: one is so cold and phlegmatic, and the other so lively and enraptured, that it seems almost inconceivable.

It is the same with regard to pain . . . You must flay a Muscovite alive to make him feel.

In northern climates scarcely has the animal part of love a power of making itself felt. In temperate climates, love, attended by a thousand appendages, endeavors to please by things that have at first the appearance, though not the reality, of this passion. In warmer climates it is liked for its own sake, it is the only cause of happiness, it is life itself.

In southern countries a machine of delicate frame but strong sensibility resigns itself either to a love which rises

31

and is incessantly laid in a seraglio, or to a passion which leaves women in a greater independence, and is consequently exposed to a thousand inquietudes. In northern regions a machine robust and heavy finds pleasure in whatever is apt to throw the spirits into motion, such as hunting, travelling, war and wine. If we travel towards the north, we meet people who have few vices, many virtues, and a great share of frankness and sincerity. If we draw near the south, we fancy ourselves entirely removed from the verge of morality; here the strongest passions are productive of all manner of crimes, each man endeavoring, let the means be what they will, to indulge his inordinate desires.

We do not find in history that the Romans ever killed themselves without a cause; but the English are apt to commit suicide most unaccountably.

This passage is from the *Esprit des Lois*, by Montesquieu, and from a particular section of that work called, "Of Laws in Relation to the Nature of the Climate." The work has been called "certainly one of the greatest of the French eighteenth century," though perhaps to modern ears the little fragment I have quoted will sound like provincial bigotry, parlor sociology, irresponsible anatomy, and reckless generalization. But I offer it here, not for the soundness of its judgments but rather because, quite aside from whether it is right or wrong on any particular point, it represents an imaginative attitude or posture of the mind which lies very conspicuously behind the idea of the *paysage moralisé*: it presents to us a climate, and, by extension, its characteristic landscape, which corresponds to, or even induces, certain moral qualities of human behavior, personality or character traits. And clearly this poem of Auden's is a particularly handsome example of the genre, the "conceit" of the *paysage moralisé* which fascinated him

On W. H. Auden's "In Praise of Limestone"

throughout his literary career. It figures not only in the sestina "Hearing of Harvests," which he later retitled "*Paysage moralisé*," but in the group of poems called Bucolics, in the allegorical Part III of *Age of Anxiety*, even, I would want to argue, in "The Fall of Rome." And here, in the poem under consideration, we have not only the central moralized landscape that dominates the poem, the Parthenopean landscape of Ischia and the Siren Isles of Odyssean temptation, of Mediterranean warmth and sunlight, but within that large view three other and alternative moralized landscapes. But let us return to the beginning of the poem.

> If it form the one landscape that we the inconstant ones
>   Are consistently homesick for, this is chiefly
> Because it dissolves in water.

One might reasonably begin by asking, Who are "we the inconstant ones"? And a case could be made for 1) homosexuals, who are often thought compulsively promiscuous, as Auden has noted in essays on Wilde and Ackerly, and as Isherwood has recorded in his autobiography, 2) tourists, northerners, come to bask in this temperate, gentle climate—Gothic invaders brought south by all the Nordic longings of Thomas Mann's early heroes into a strange and alien culture. (Here, for example, is Mann's narrator in "Mario and the Magician" doing a little landscape moralizing of his own, in speaking of the atmosphere of an Italian summer resort:

> ... classic weather, the sun of Homer, the climate wherein human culture came to flower—and all the rest of it. But after a while it is too much for me, I reach a point where I begin to find it dull. The burning void of the sky, day after day, weights one down; the high coloration, the enormous naiveté of the unrefracted light—they do, I dare say, induce lightheartedness, a carefree mood born

33

of immunity from downpours and other meteorological caprices. But slowly, slowly, there makes itself felt a lack: the deeper, more complex needs of the northern soul remain unsatisfied.

Before we have done I shall ask you to recall Mann's familiar antithetical or antipodal confrontation of North and South when Auden himself takes it up.) Then, finally, there is a third gloss on "we the inconstant ones": 3) all mortals, exiled since Adam's Fall from the ideal Eden, but yearning for its likeness if that likeness is to be found at all on earth. We the inconstant ones are at least consistent about one thing—our homesickness. And though Auden was actually born in a limestone region of England it seems clear that in this poem homesickness is more than simple *Heimweh*. All the religious aspects of this poem—and there are a number of them, quite aside from the mention of "the blessed" and "the life to come" near the end—suggest a double sense of Eden as both the earliest state of Creation and the innocent joys of an individual childhood.

Since the landscape reflects by its dissolution (mark that, if you please) in water a kind of fickleness, or a physical frailty in "us" (which is to say, we are homesick for it because it is like us: it dissolves as we become dissolute), might it not therefore seem a constant form of reproach, or, at the very least, a constant reminder of our mortality, and therefore a place to be fled? Perhaps, but we can bear the reproach and the reminder because limestone is *human* in several special ways. If it is frail like us it is also especially adaptable to being turned into palaces and monuments—everything especially noble and handsome in worldly terms. And limestone is "double" like humans, having a surface beauty, and a hidden, arterial life, not only like the human body, but like the human psyche. Secret systems of caves and conduits. Unplumbed meanings

and depths. A doubleness Auden remarked on in Part V of
Age of Anxiety as follows:

> Human beings are, necessarily, actors who cannot become
> something before they have pretended to be it; and they
> can be divided, not into the hypocritical and the sincere,
> but into the sane who know they are acting and the mad
> who do not.

No doubt some of the palaces and monuments embodied in
limestone are not so much beautiful as they are expressions
of human vanity, or empty postures of greatness, modes of
hypocrisy, manifest fakes, "a mad camp" (which is homosexual *patois* for comic exaggeration or parody). But that is a
part of the human dilemma: our beauties and our virtues slip
so easily and "naturally" into cognate forms of corruption and
dissolution; this instability is, at least here, endearingly human, and it is only the fanatics (the saints and dictators) who
find it either uncongenial or terrifying, who long for a fixed,
unchanging landscape consistent with their own terrible fixity.

> What could be more like Mother or a fitter background
>   For her son, for the nude young male who lounges
> Against a rock displaying his dildo, never doubting
>   That for all his faults he is loved, whose works are but
> Extensions of his power to charm?

Here we have a particularly secular madonna and child, both
of whom are "like" the landscape, beautiful, with the woman's
softness and depth, and the male's external sexuality. If the
"nude young male" is an exhibitionist, we should remember
that ". . . The blessed will not care what angle they are regarded from,/ Having nothing to hide." The desire to excel
("From weathered outcrop/ To hill-top temple, from appearing waters to/Conspicuous fountains, from a wild to a formal
vineyard,/ Are ingenious but short steps that a child's wish/

On W. H. Auden's "In Praise of Limestone"

To receive more attention than his brothers, whether/ By pleasing or teasing, can easily take")—this desire to excel, which is almost instinctive in children and which accounts for all that is best in culture, including agriculture, and the artful ordering of nature into fountains and temples, is both good and bad in us: bad as a symptom of pride, good as a symptom of a love of excellence, including that special excellence which is divine and beyond us. The people and the landscape of this poem are constantly exhibiting this doubleness; and both are frankly pagan—the god who can be "pacified by a clever line/ Or a good lay" might easily be Zeus or Apollo, but is certainly not the God either of Moses or of Milton. Despite this, there follows immediately a covert but very important reference to one of the gospels, which should be cited here.

> And Jesus being full of the Holy Ghost returned from Jordan, and was led by the Spirit into the wilderness, being forty days tempted of the devil. And in those days he did eat nothing: and when they were ended, he afterwards hungered.
> And the devil said unto him, If thou be the Son of God, command this stone that it be made bread.
> And Jesus answered him, saying, It is written, That man shall not live by bread alone, but by every word of God.
> And the devil, taking him up into an high mountain, shewed unto him all the kingdoms of the world in a moment of time.
> And the devil said unto him, All this power will I give thee, and the glory of them: for that is delivered unto me; and to whomsoever I will give it.
> If thou therefore wilt worship me, all shall be thine.
> And Jesus answered and said unto him, Get thee behind me, Satan: for it is written, Thou shalt worship the Lord thy God, and him only shalt thou serve.
> And he brought him to Jerusalem, and set him on a pin-

nacle of the temple, and said unto him, If thou be the
Son of God, cast thyself down from hence:
For it is written, He shall give his angels charge over
thee, to keep thee:
And in their hands they shall bear thee up, lest at any
time thou dash thy foot against a stone.
And Jesus answering said unto him, It is said, Thou shalt
not tempt the Lord thy God.
And when the devil had ended all the temptation, he
departed from him for a season.

(Luke 4: 1–13)

In this poem, the three invitations addressed to the saints-to-
be, the intendant Caesars, and the really reckless, correspond
rather clearly to the three temptations of Christ in Saint Luke.
There is first the temptation of spiritual pride, the performing
of an overt miracle (turning stones into bread) which will
elicit awe and worship but not that true faith which demands
effort and initiative on the part of the believer. The temptation
to other-worldly powers to deal with or overcome the poverty
of this world through miracles or a sublimated asceticism are
both of them rejections of the God-created universe, and therefore forms of pride. They are the First Temptation. The voice
that speaks is that of the "granite wastes," unyielding, inhuman, and unpitying. The voice of the Second Temptation is
malleable, clays and gravels, something that can be pushed
around and improved. It speaks, both in the Bible and in the
poem, of worldly power; and it whispers the heresy that all of
mankind's ills are susceptible of correction by mankind itself,
which needs only to find the right program and to furnish the
totalitarian power to put it into effect. The Third Temptation
is the temptation of suicide as the ultimate act of freedom, a
demonstration that one is free from all the bonds and demands
and needs of this world. The ultimate existential freedom is to
have no ties. Fittingly, the voice that whispers this invitation,

37

an older, colder voice, is "the oceanic whisper," the voice of unbridled chaos. "And the earth was without form, and void; and darkness was upon the face of the deep. And the Spirit of God moved upon the face of the waters."

Auden had used this same device, a parody of the temptations of Christ, on other occasions, most especially in the libretto of *The Rake's Progress*, the opera text he wrote for Stravinsky.

After the three Siren voices of the Temptations, calling Odysseus, the wanderer, the inconstant one, to various delusions of *soi-disant* "constancy," the poem continues,

> They were right, my dear, all those voices were right
> And still are; this land is not the sweet home that it looks,

which is to say, though the Sirens delude, and would lure us into the dangers of pride and death, this land we inhabit is not the Eden we like to think it is or remember from the Bible or childhood. It is the fallen world, "a backward/ And dilapidated province," yet it performs a necessary moral and spiritual function. First, by its flux and changeableness, its capacity to dissolve in water, it "calls into question/ All the Great Powers assume," that things can somehow be made stable. It makes the poet, who would interpose no deity between the outward universe and the mind that re-creates it, uneasy, suggesting that there are depths beyond the poet's designs or discoveries. As for the scientist, we will come to him in a moment.

The poem concludes:

> Dear, I know nothing of
> Either, but when I try to imagine a faultless love
> Or the life to come, what I hear is the murmur
> Of underground streams, what I see is a limestone
> landscape.

I take it that "Either" refers ahead to the "faultless love" or "the life to come," and admits that the poet knows nothing of either, that he is, like us, a fallen man, who can imagine Paradise, if not "know" it. This surely reflects back on "we the inconstant ones." The water and the stone are both here in the last line, as they are in the "Innocent athletes" (obviously referring to statues here) and "gesticulating fountains," as they were in the weathered outcrop transformed to hilltop temple and the appearing waters piped into conspicuous fountains, and as they first were in the curious and arresting paradox of the first sentence.

Let me return both to the doubleness of people and of landscapes mentioned earlier, and to the poet and scientist, discomfited by the landscape itself. In Part V of *Age of Anxiety* Auden writes,

> Had they been perfectly honest with themselves, they would have had to admit that they were tired and wanted to go home alone to bed. That they were not [perfectly honest] was in part due, of course, to vanity, the fear of getting too old to want fun or too ugly to get it, but also to unselfishness, the fear of spoiling the fun of others.

Note especially how the vice of vanity becomes indistinguishable among our motives from the virtue of unselfishness. The passage continues,

> Besides, only animals who are below civilization and angels who are beyond it can be sincere. Human beings are, necessarily, actors who cannot become something before they have pretended to be it; and they can be divided, not into the hypocritical and the sincere, but into the sane who know they are acting and the mad who do not.

With regard to the animals who are "below civilization" and to the scientist's concern with "Nature's remotest aspects," as well as to the poet's, especially the Romantic poet's, temptation

39

On W. H. Auden's "In Praise of Limestone"

to dehumanize both the cosmos and the world itself, here is
Auden in 1936 in "A Letter to Lord Byron."

'I hate a pupil-teacher,' Milton said,
    Who also hated bureaucratic fools;
Milton may thank his stars that he is dead,
    Although he's learnt by heart in public schools,
    Along with Wordsworth and the list of rules;
For many a don while looking down his nose
Calls Pope and Dryden classics of our prose.

And new plants flower from that old potato.
    They thrive best in a poor industrial soil,
Are hardier crossed with Rousseaus or a Plato;
    Their cultivation is an easy toil.
    William, to change the metaphor, struck oil;
His well seems inexhaustible, a gusher
That saves old England from the fate of Russia.

The mountain-snob is a Wordsworthian fruit;
    He tears his clothes and doesn't shave his chin,
He wears a very pretty little boot,
    He chooses the least comfortable inn;
    A mountain railway is a deadly sin;
His strength, of course, is as the strength of ten men,
He calls all those who live in cities wen-men.*

I'm not a spoil-sport, I would never wish
    To interfere with anybody's pleasures;
By all means climb, or hunt, or even fish,
    All human hearts have ugly little treasures;
    But think it time to take repressive measures
When someone says, adopting the 'I know' line,
The Good Life is confined above the snow-line.

Besides, I'm very fond of mountains, too;
    I like to travel through them in a car;

---

* Cobbett calls the Metropolis "The greatest wen of all."

On W. H. Auden's "In Praise of Limestone"

I like a house that's got a sweeping view;
    I like to walk, but not to walk too far.
I also like green plains where cattle are,
And trees and rivers, and shall always quarrel
With those who think that rivers are immoral.

Not that my private quarrel gives quietus to
    The interesting question that it raises;
Impartial thought will give a proper status to
    This interest in waterfalls and daisies,
    Excessive love for the non-human faces,
That lives in hearts from Golders Green to Teddington;
It's all bound up with Einstein, Jeans, and Eddington.

It is a commonplace that's hardly worth
    A poet's while to make profound or terse,
That now the sun does not go round the earth,
    That man's no centre of the universe;
    And working in an office makes it worse.
The humblest is acquiring with facility
A Universal-Complex sensibility.

For now we've learnt we mustn't be so bumptious
    We find the stars are one big family,
And send out invitations for a scrumptious
    Simple, old-fashioned, jolly romp with tea
    To any natural objects we can see.
We can't, of course, invite a Jew or Red
But birds and nebulae will do instead.

The Higher Mind's outgrowing the Barbarian,
    It's hardly thought hygienic now to kiss;
The world is surely turning vegetarian;
    And as it grows too sensitive for this,
    It won't be long before we find there is
A Society of Everybody's Aunts
For the Prevention of Cruelty to Plants.

On W. H. Auden's "In Praise of Limestone"

I dread this like the dentist, rather more so:
  To me Art's subject is the human clay,
And landscape but a background to a torso;
    All Cezanne's apples I would give away
    For one small Goya or a Daumier.
I'll never grant a more than minor beauty
To pudge or pilewort, petty-chap or pooty.

Art, if it doesn't start there, at least ends,
    Whether aesthetics like the thought or not,
In an attempt to entertain our friends;
    And our first problem is to realize what
    Peculiar friends the modern artist's got;
It's possible a little dose of history
May help us in unravelling this mystery.

This rather amusing mockery of Romantic nature-poetry, this
jest at the expense of "the sublime," centers on the absence
of human actors and the visible features of civilization, the
cultivated field, the man-made house, the ordered garden
and governed city. Nothing is allowed to interpose between
"This interest in waterfalls and daisies" and the sensitive,
self-absorbed mind of the poet, who is, himself, his "antimythological myth." But for Auden the landscape is human-
ized by local habitation, and humane in its appearance. Here,
for instance, is a fragment from Part II of *Age of Anxiety*.

> So it was now as they sought that state of prehistoric
> happiness [for prehistoric we could properly read pre-
> lapsarian] which, by human beings, can only be imag-
> ined in terms of a landscape bearing a symbolic resem-
> blance to the human body. . . .

In our poem this appears as "this region/ Of short distances
and definite places:/ What could be more like Mother . . ." So
it appears in the end that it is Mother we are homesick for, the
comforts of the womb, short distances and definite places, that

On W. H. Auden's "In Praise of Limestone"

Mother towards whom Michael Ransom yearned and ascended in "The Ascent of F6," the womb created and hymned in what may have been Auden's very last poem, "Lullaby," from which these fragments are excerpted.

> Now you have license to lie,
> naked, curled like a shrimplet,
> jacent in bed, and enjoy
> its cosy micro-climate:
> *Sing, Big Baby, sing lullay.*
>
> . . . . . .
>
> now you fondle
> your almost feminine flesh
> with mettled satisfaction,
> imagining that you are
> sinless and all-sufficient,
> snug in the den of yourself,
> *Madonna* and *Bambino*:
> *Sing, Big Baby, sing lullay.*
>
> . . . . . .
>
> Now for oblivion: let
> the belly-mind take over
> down below the diaphragm,
> the domain of the Mothers,
> They who guard the Sacred Gates,
> without whose wordless warnings
> soon the verbalising I
> becomes a vicious despot,
> lewd, incapable of love,
> disdainful, status-hungry.
>
> . . . . . .

"In Praise of Limestone" combines rather curiously (and rather like Michelangelo's famous tondo, or round painting of the Holy Family, with young male nude athletes lounging

43

around in the background) a serious religious concern, indicated at the very least by references to "the blessed" and "the life to come," with a particularly worldly sensuality. And in this it resembles a good deal of Italian baroque and mannerist art. Both that art and this poem envision an antipuritanical ideal, and the art was part of the deliberate achievement of the Counter Reformation. It had been the Reformers, of course, who so violently divided pleasure from piety; and here in this poem, as in those paintings of Michelangelo, those statues and buildings of Borromini and Bernini, we have "modifications of matter into/ Innocent athletes and gesticulating fountains,/ Made solely for pleasure. . . ."

Indeed, in an essay that opens a volume of Auden's prose, *The Dyer's Hand*, we have an explicit description of his personal Eden.

LANDSCAPE—Limestone uplands like the Pennines plus a small region of igneous rocks with at least one extinct volcano. A precipitous and indented sea-coast.

CLIMATE—British.

ETHNIC ORIGIN OF INHABITANTS—Highly varied as in the United States, but with a slight nordic predominance.

LANGUAGE—Of mixed origins, like English, but highly inflected.

WEIGHTS AND MEASURES—Irregular and complicated. No decimal system.

RELIGION—Roman Catholic in an easygoing Mediterranean sort of way. Lots of local saints.

FORM OF GOVERNMENT—Absolute monarchy, elected for life by lot.

SOURCES OF NATURAL POWER—Wind, water, peat, coal. No oil.

MEANS OF TRANSPORT—Horses and horse-drawn vehicles, canal barges, balloons. No automobiles or airplanes.

ARCHITECTURE—State: Baroque. Ecclesiastical: Roman-

On W. H. Auden's "In Praise of Limestone"

esque and Byzantine. Domestic: Eighteenth Century
British or American Colonial.

FORMAL DRESS—The fashions of Paris in the 1830's and
'40's.

SOURCES OF PUBLIC INFORMATION—Gossip. Technical and
learned periodicals but no newspapers.

PUBLIC STATUES—Confined to famous defunct chefs.

PUBLIC ENTERTAINMENTS—Religious processions, brass
bands, opera, classical ballet. No movies, radio or
television.

This is clearly an Eden of sophisticated and unmechanized
pleasure—pleasure, moreover, with religious sanction; and
with characteristic baroque and mannerist embellishments
that keep mankind centrally placed and grandly proportioned
in his universe; and which personalize and humanize the
world of nature which is never allowed to become more than
a suitable background to the human stage. It is perfectly in
keeping with the general "decor" of "In Praise of Limestone,"
and so I turn to a commentary on that style by the architectural historian Vincent Scully, who, in his book, *Modern
Architecture*, chooses as his point of departure a famous baroque instance, the Spanish Steps in Rome, constructed in the
mid-eighteenth century by Specchi and De Sanctis. Here is
Scully's formulation.

. . . The Spanish Stairs in Rome, of 1721–25, embody the
character of the Baroque. . . . All movement is around
fixed points. It is a union of the opposites of order and
freedom. The order is absolutely firm, but against it an
illusion of freedom is played. Secondly, for all the sculp-
tural plasticity and humanistic imagery of the solids, it is
in fact the space that governs the design, and the solids
are entirely at the service of its dramatization. It is therefore an architecture that is intended to enclose and shelter
human beings in a psychic sense ["this region of short

45

distances and definite places"], to order them absolutely
so that they can always find a known conclusion at the
end of any journey, but finally to let them play at freedom and action all the while. Everything works out; the
play seems tumultuous but nobody gets hurt and everybody wins. It is a paternal or, perhaps better, maternal
architecture, and creates a world with which, today, only
children, if they are lucky, could identify. This may be
one reason why, since the Second World War, Baroque
Rome has become a Mecca for some literati who would
escape maturity. . . .

The very features of the Baroque that Scully singles out for
opprobrium—those spaces which give the illusion of freedom
while really serving as protections and safeguards—are in fact
exactly the ones that Auden means to embrace. But while
Scully, with the contemptuous tone of a very superior adult
admonishing a backward and regressive child, can see in a
modern person's taste for this period style only some immature
perversity, some unwillingness to grow up and face facts,
Auden very explicitly selects the style as "edenic," as part of
a mythic and psychic landscape of our own licensed invention,
not meant to correspond to any harsh realities of this world,
but, on the contrary, to evoke some prehistorical perfection. In
addition to the essay in *The Dyer's Hand* to which I have just
referred there is another in the same volume that takes up
the same theme, and in which, in his fourth axiom, Auden
deliberately adopts the terms that Scully so emphatically
reprehends.

The psychological difference between the Arcadian
dreamer and the Utopian dreamer is that the backward-
looking Arcadian knows that his expulsion from Eden is
an irrevocable fact and that his dream, therefore, is a
wish-dream which cannot become real. . . . How any
individual envisages Eden is determined by his tempera-

ment, personal history and cultural milieu, but to all dream Edens the following axioms, I believe, apply.

1) Eden is a world of pure being and absolute uniqueness. Change can occur but as an instantaneous transformation, not through a process of becoming. Everyone is incomparable.

2) The self is satisfied whatever it demands; the ego is approved whatever it chooses.

3) There is no distinction between the objective and the subjective. What a person appears to others to be is identical to what he is to himself. His name and his clothes are as much *his* as his body, so that, if he changes them, he turns into someone else.

4) Space is both safe and free. There are walled gardens but no dungeons, open roads in all directions but no wandering in the wilderness.

We may, if we wish, ignore the psychological and sexual slur of Mr. Scully's conclusion here, or else set it down to the fact that he has chosen the Spanish Steps to contrast it unfavorably with Le Corbusier's High Court in Chandigarh, India, a spectacular "modern" instance that leaves us full of existential unease, and in which the vast, inhuman scale of plain and mountain against which the building is set seems to assert all the frightening remoteness and impersonality of an alien and possibly hostile universe, unpeopled, uninhabited. Howsoever that may be, Auden does not require my defense, since, after all, he consciously and deliberately gave up the Parthenopean setting and all its trappings, and instead made himself a home in Austria. And in celebration of that choice and that departure he wrote a poem called "Goodbye to the Mezzogiorno," with which I conclude, only asking you to remember Thomas Mann's antipodal climates and cultures alluded to earlier.

On W. H. Auden's "In Praise of Limestone"

Out of a gothic North, the pallid children
    Of a potato, beer-or-whiskey
Guilt culture, we behave like our fathers and come
    Southward into a sunburnt otherwhere

Of vineyards, baroque, *la bella figura*,
    To these feminine townships where men
Are males, and siblings untrained in a ruthless
    Verbal in-fighting as it is taught

In Protestant rectories upon drizzling
    Sunday afternoons—no more as unwashed
Barbarians out for gold, nor as profiteers,
    Hot for Old Masters, but for plunder

Nevertheless—some believing *amore*
    Is better down South and much cheaper
(Which is doubtful), some persuaded exposure
    To strong sunlight is lethal to germs

(Which is patently false) and others, like me,
    In middle-age hoping to twig from
What we are not what we might be next, a question
    The South seems never to raise. Perhaps

A tongue in which Nestor and Apemantus,
    Don Ottavio and Don Giovanni make
Equally beautiful sounds is unequipped
    To frame it, or perhaps in this heat

It is nonsense: the Myth of an Open Road
    Which runs past the orchard gate and beckons
Three brothers in turn to set out over the hills
    And far away, is an invention

Of a climate where it is a pleasure to walk
    And a landscape less populated
Than this one. Even so, to us it looks very odd
    Never to see an only child engrossed

On W. H. Auden's "In Praise of Limestone"

In a game it has made up, a pair of friends
    Making fun in a private lingo,
Or a body sauntering by himself who is not
    Wanting, even as it perplexes

Our ears when cats are called *Cat* and dogs either
    Lupo, Nero or *Bobby*. Their dining
Puts us to shame: we can only envy people
    So frugal by nature it costs them

No effort not to guzzle and swill. Yet (if I
    Read their faces rightly after ten years)
They are without hope. The Greeks used to call the Sun
    He-who-smites-from-afar, and from here, where

Shadows are dagger-edged, the daily ocean blue,
    I can see what they meant: his unwinking
Outrageous eye laughs to scorn any notion
    Of change or escape, and a silent

Ex-volcano, without a stream or a bird,
    Echoes that laugh. This could be a reason
Why they take the silencers off their Vespas,
    Turn their radios up to full volume,

And a minim saint can expect rockets—noise
    As a countermagic, a way of saying
Boo to the Three Sisters; "Mortal we may be,
    But we are still here!"—might cause them to hanker

After proximities—in streets packed solid
    With human flesh, their souls feel immune
To all metaphysical threats. We are rather shocked,
    But we need shocking: to accept space, to own

That surfaces need not be superficial
    Nor gestures vulgar, cannot really
Be taught within earshot of running water
    Or in sight of a cloud. As pupils

On W. H. Auden's "In Praise of Limestone"

We are not bad, but hopeless as tutors: Goethe,
  Tapping Homeric hexameters
On the shoulder blade of a Roman girl, is
  (I wish it were someone else) the figure

Of all our stamp: no doubt he treated her well,
  But one would draw the line at calling
The Helena begotten on that occasion,
  Queen of his Second *Walpurgisnacht*,

Her baby: between those who mean by a life a
  Bildungsroman and those to whom living
Means to-be-visible-now, there yawns a gulf
  Embraces cannot bridge. If we try

To "go southern," we spoil in no time, we grow
  Flabby, dingily lecherous, and
Forget to pay bills: that no one has heard of them
  Taking the Pledge or turning to Yoga

Is a comforting thought—in that case, for all
  The spiritual loot we tuck away,
We do them no harm—and entitles us, I think
  To one little scream at *A piacere!*,

Not two. Go I must, but I go grateful (even
  To a certain *Monte**) and invoking
My sacred meridian names, *Pirandello*,
  Croce, Vico, Verga, Bellini,

To bless this region, its vendages, and those
  Who call it home: though one cannot always
Remember exactly why one has been happy,
  There is no forgetting that one was.

---

* The name of Auden's Ischian landlord who avariciously raised the
rent as soon as he heard that the poet had won a large monetary award
from the Austrian government.

Othello

I FIRST READ T. S. Eliot's essay "Shakespeare and the Stoicism of Seneca," with its, as I then thought, dismissive comment on Othello's final speech, when I was an undergraduate more than forty years ago. I found Eliot's remarks provoking, as I have no doubt they were meant to be, and I was able to distill them in my memory to the terse phrase that what Othello was doing in that speech was "cheering himself up." My regard for Shakespeare in those days was limitless; and in some ways, of course, thoughtless, being unwittingly a trusting veneration of the editors and textual scholars who certified the texts for me, and, without my having to do so much as trouble myself with doubt or thought, furnished me with perfect, completely coherent, intricately knit poetic dramas by a matchless author who always did everything right, who, above all, was never guilty of any lapse of dramatic intelligence, never given to literary sloth, and whose texts arrived unimpaired as from his pen.

Since those days of happy innocence I have come to recognize that I was unjust both to Eliot and Shakespeare. The problems and puzzles in the texts are enormous, and in all likelihood beyond the possibility of definitive solution. And Eliot's actual position was not quite so flat-footed as I had gotten into the habit of declaring. In fact, George K. Hunter's opinion of the passage in question is that Eliot's remarks may be taken as wholly admiring. In his essay on "T. S. Eliot and the Symbolist Shakespeare" he writes, "The famous passage in which Eliot describes Othello 'cheering himself up' in his final speech is presented as if it is praise: 'I do not believe that any writer has ever exposed this *bovarysme*, the human will to see things as they are not, more clearly than Shakespeare.'" Well, if this is praise on Eliot's part, it is given with one hand while the other has been busily employed in furtive and less generous ways. It would be best, I think, to give Eliot's view in a fuller context.

That Shakespeare deliberately took a "view of life" from Seneca there seems to be no evidence whatever.

Nevertheless, there is, in some of the great tragedies of Shakespeare, a new attitude. . . . It is the attitude of self-dramatization assumed by some of Shakespeare's heroes at moments of tragic intensity. It is not peculiar to Shakespeare; it is conspicuous in Chapman; Bussy, Clermont and Biron, all die in this way. Marston—one of the most interesting and least explored of all the Elizabethans—uses it; and Marston and Chapman were particularly Senecan. But Shakespeare, of course, does it very much better than any of the others, and makes it somehow more integral with the human nature of his characters. It is less verbal, more real. I have always felt that I have never read a more terrible exposure of human weakness—of universal human weakness—than the last great speech of Othello. I am ignorant of whether anyone else has ever adopted this view, and it may appear subjective and fantastic in the extreme. It is usually taken on its face value, as expressing the greatness in defeat of a noble but erring nature.

> Soft you; a word or two before you go.
> I have done the state some service, and they know't,—
> No more of that.—I pray you, in your letters,
> When you shall these unlucky deeds relate,
> Speak of me as I am; nothing extenuate,
> Nor set down aught in malice: then must you speak
> Of one that loved not wisely, but too well;
> Of one not easily jealous, but, being wrought,
> Perplex'd in the extreme; of one whose hand,
> Like the base Indian, threw a pearl away
> Richer than all his tribe; of one whose subdued eyes,
> Albeit unused to the melting mood,
> Drop tears as fast as the Arabian trees
> Their medicinal gum. Set you down this;
> And say, besides,—that in Aleppo once,
> Where a malignant and a turban'd Turk
> Beat a Venetian and traduced the state,
> I took by the throat the circumcised dog,
> And smote him—thus.

What Othello seems to me to be doing in making this speech is *cheering himself up*. He is endeavoring to escape reality, he has ceased to think about Desdemona, and is thinking about himself. Humility is the most difficult of all virtues to achieve; nothing dies harder than the desire to think well of oneself. Othello succeeds in turning himself into a pathetic figure, by adopting an *aesthetic* rather than a moral attitude, dramatizing himself against his environment. He takes in the spectator, but the human motive is to take in himself. I do not believe that any writer has ever exposed this *bovarysme*, the human will to see things as they are not, more clearly than Shakespeare.

Othello

Soft you; a word or two before I proceed. Eliot begins his essay by taking exception to what he viewed as partial and lopsided books on Shakespeare by Lytton Strachey, Middleton Murry and Wyndham Lewis. He finds these critics more up-to-date and sympathetic "in the year 1927" than Coleridge, or Swinburne, or Dowden, and continues, with a sort of mock-generosity: "If the only way to prove that Shakespeare did not feel and think exactly as people felt and thought in 1815, or in 1860, or in 1880, is to show that he felt and thought as we felt and thought in 1927, then we must accept gratefully that alternative." And after long consideration it seems to me that Eliot in his turn is doing in his essay pretty much what he reprehended Strachey, Murry, and Lewis for doing: he is putting Othello up against personal strictures of his own. Othello is to be rebuked for giving no thought to Desdemona, exhibiting neither remorse nor humility, for adopting an aesthetic rather than a moral attitude to his situation; and Shakespeare is to be congratulated on revealing this particular weakness.

If, in Eliot's words, Strachey gave us "the fatigued Shakespeare, a retired Anglo-Indian," Murry the "messianic" Shakespeare, and Lewis the Shakespeare dominated by the influence of Machiavelli, or an Elizabethan caricature of the Italian, Eliot himself says here that what Shakespeare offers is not what the "face value" of this speech seems to declare; it does not express "the greatness in defeat of a noble but erring nature," but is rather "a terrible exposure of human weakness."

I think Eliot is wrong here, and that his search for, and inability to find, humility is misplaced; and I also believe there is real evidence of remorse, which Eliot either fails to see or ignores. There is no doubt that Othello is "playing a role" in this last speech, as he does often in the course of the play. Robert Heilman and others, including Eliot, have pointed to his dramatizing proclivities. But the role he plays in his final speech is not the role Eliot casts him in. It is a more complex role than the one of evading reality, soothing his own ego, exculpating himself. But to try to define it will require some considerations of a general sort, a view of the whole play, and some of the puzzles that it presents.

Let me enumerate a few of these puzzles. To begin with, there are the various lections of the play: passages that appear only in the quarto, others that appear only in the folio. The same problem arises, of course, in many other plays, and has drawn special attention in recent studies of *King Lear*. The problem is serious and important not only because we would like, if we could, to be sure what it was that Shakespeare meant his actors to say, but because different readings give rise to interpretive confusion, even, sometimes, by an individual critic.

For example, Stanley Edgar Hyman has written a brilliantly ingenious book called *Iago*, illustrating what he calls "pluralist criticism." Concentrating entirely on one character, Mr. Hyman presents in sequence five interpretations: Genre Criticism (in which Iago is a traditional Stage Villain); Theological Criticism (Iago as Satan); Symbolic Action Criticism (Iago and Prospero: two contrasting portraits of the artist); Psychoanalytic Criticism (Iago as latent homosexual); and History of Ideas Criticism (Iago as Machiavel.) He made interesting and persuasive cases for each of these interpretations, though of course they are not consistent with one another. But his ability to pull so many rabbits out of his hat was based in part on his use of any lection he wished for his purposes at the moment; and this is not quite straightforward. The playwright did not write several versions of the play; and though compositors, transcribers, and editors have created problems even as they've tried to solve them, one is not free to treat the text as if it were multiple.* Mr. Hyman, for instance, uses

---

* I have been cautioned that "several versions" is just what scholars are now convinced Shakespeare *did* write in the case of *King Lear*, or if not several at least two. And so many are the discrepancies between the texts

"base Iudean" alternately with "base Indian" according to the dictates of the mode of criticism he is discussing.

Secondly, the Time Scheme. Ever since at least the mid-nineteenth century critics have been aware that the play produces a curious and illusory sense of time that under scrutiny makes no sense. Briefly, if Othello is jealous of Cassio and suspicious of Desdemona, his feelings must be based on such grounds as would be provided after the arrival at Cyprus. Othello is not concerned about the possibility that Cassio may have had relations with Desdemona before her marriage; that contingency is never considered. Since everyone departs for Cyprus on Othello's wedding night, and since Cassio is not on the same ship as Desdemona, the only opportunities that might offer must be placed in Cyprus. All parties arrive within half an hour of one another, and the subsequent action of the play, during a good part of which time Othello and Desdemona are in one another's company, takes place in the course of some thirty-three hours, which is certainly not enough for Cassio to compass the ends Iago attributes to him, and which drive Othello to his fury and his crime, along with his claim that

> ... she with Cassio hath the act of shame
> A thousand times committed.

We are not, of course, once we notice this discrepancy, invited to think of Othello as a still greater gull than Roderigo, though

---

of *Othello* that no Alexandrian solution to their composite and Gordian complexities is possible. The first quarto was published in 1622, and the First Folio in 1623. A second quarto, including elements of both previous versions, appeared in 1630. There are more than a thousand verbal variants between the first two versions, and the Folio contains about 160 lines which are absent from the quarto, while the quarto exhibits some 13 lines absent from the Folio. These numerical differences do not seem to me sufficient to make a claim for two independent acting texts designed by the author, though I would have to confess immediately that this is no more than unsupported conjecture on my part. At the two cruxes where in this essay I make a decisive choice among variant readings, I have tried to justify them both by local context and by what I conceive to be a general design of the play as I try to outline it here.

"gull" is just what Emilia calls him. As audience and readers we ourselves have been "taken in," persuaded by the sheer force of the drama. And we exonerate Othello even as we exonerate ourslves, setting the whole puzzle down to "the illusory magic of Shakespeare."

Third, while admittedly Roderigo is credulous, dim-witted, and a gull, he is not without serious feelings with regard to Desdemona. He was once suitor for her hand in marriage (one among many of the "curled darlings," we may suppose) and his anxiety when the play opens has to do with the news of Desdemona's elopement. Anxiety is certainly what he feels because there is a chance she is not married yet, and that the marriage can be forestalled; and if not forestalled, then possibly annulled. And this is the reason for the awakening of Brabantio. But after the Duke confirms the legitimacy of the marriage, and Brabantio has been obliged to give his consent, and Othello and Desdemona are firmly a matrimonial couple, Roderigo is close enough to despair to declare, "I will incontinently drown myself." He is restrained from this course by Iago on the crude and simple basis of a promise that "thou shalt enjoy her." It is bewildering to find a man who, having thought of himself as potentially the legitimate husband of an admirable woman, and given to suicidal impulses when she chooses another, elects immediately to settle for a (questionable) promise of illicit sexual favors from her, especially since, in the following act, he speaks of her as "full of most blessed condition."

Fourth, if Roderigo's "psychology" puzzles, Brabantio's does so even more. He had originally forbidden Roderigo to pay court to his daughter, or even to approach his house ("I have charged thee not to haunt about my doors"). When he finds that Desdemona has eloped with Othello he completely changes his attitude and says to Roderigo, "O would you had had her." His revulsion at the notion of Othello as a mate for his daughter is stated in the most emphatic terms and several times.

Othello

For I'll refer to all things of sense,
If she in chains of magic were not bound,
Whether a maid so tender, fair, and happy,
So opposite to marriage that she shunned
The wealthy curled darlings of our nation,
Would ever have, t'incur a general mock,
Run from her guardage to the sooty bosom
Of such a thing as thou—to fear, not to delight.

And,

She is abused, stol'n from me, and corrupted
By spells and medicines bought of mountebanks;
For nature so prepost'rously to err,
Being not deficient, blind, or lame of sense,
Sans witchcraft could not.

And yet again,

A maiden never bold;
Of spirit so still and quiet that her motion
Blushed at herself; and she—in spite of nature,
Of years, of country, credit, everything—
To fall in love with what she feared to look on!

He makes it eminently clear that Othello is repugnant to him, and must be equally repugnant to his daughter. But when Othello speaks in his own defense he begins, "Her father loved me, oft invited me. . . ." What, then, are we to make of a Brabantio who "loved" Othello at least enough to invite him often to his home, from which Roderigo was banned, and who then decides he would rather have Roderigo as son-in-law, and that Othello is after all repugnant?

Fifth: how could Emilia have lived with her husband for any length of time without suspecting what sort of man he was?

There are, of course, many other puzzles, including those

that have to do with the interpretation of individual lines or passages, even when they are not in dispute as regards their textual authority. For example, in connection with Iago's delphic comment, "Were I the Moor, I would not be Iago," M. R. Ridley, editor of the Arden edition, comments,

> This is not, I think, such plain sailing as the silence of most commentators suggests. To say "If I were the master, I would not be the man" sounds an oddly feeble remark from Iago. But it may be noticed that Shakespeare seems to have deliberately given Iago a trick of speech by which he makes remarks which appear at first hearing well-turned and significant, and on examination turn out to mean very little. Cf. "Men should be what they seem, Or those that be not, would they might seem none" (III.iii. 130), "He's that he is; I may not breathe my censure, What he might be, if, as he might, he is not, I would to Heaven he were!" (IV. i. 267).

This strikes me as a curiously odd and unsatisfactory comment, even when buttressed by the two examples offered in support of this sort of "meaninglessness," both of which are spoken in faux-naif parlance, as circumstances dictate, one addressed to Othello, the other to Lodovico. But in this instance Iago is not playing the naif; he is showing off his worldliness to Roderigo; and what he says may have a number of interpretations. 1) If I were the Moor, I would not keep my Iago in so base a position, but would promote him to the lieutenancy to which he is entitled; 2) Were I the Moor, I would not keep such a one as myself for a confidant; 3) Were I the Moor, I would not be the crafty fellow that I so evidently am.

Othello himself is an odd amalgam of not easily reconcilable traits, and this may be said to be one of the most conspicuous things about him. While everywhere it is noted that he is given to self-dramatization, Iago, who has no affection for him, admits that he "is of a free and open nature/That thinks men honest that but seem to be so." Which is to say, he is both guileless and guileful. There is no question of his courage, nor of his weakness. Some of the contradictions about him will evince themselves in the very style of his speech, but in general I think they may be divided under two headings: the Christianized Moor and the "Roman" General.

THE CHRISTIANIZED MOOR

It seems to me evident that an Elizabethan audience would not have been willing to grant Othello the unlimited admiration he receives from Cassio, Desdemona, the Duke, and his senate at the beginning of the play. He would have been recognized from the start as an anomaly, not only "an extravagant and wheeling stranger/Of here and everywhere," who has no real home, and therefore no civic allegiance, but, far more suspiciously, one who, had things only been slightly different (and perhaps more normal) would have been fighting on the enemy side, with the Turks and against the Venetians. Not only are we invited to share this edgy feeling, we are led to believe that Othello himself is not quite at ease in any society except that of military action, and his uneasiness is expressed, now and again, in a baroque and unnecessarily contorted syntax and diction. His manner of speech is remarked on within the first fifteen lines of the play by Iago, who speaks contemptuously of his "bombast circumstance/Horribly stuff'd with epithets of war." But it is not only to military matters that this eccentricity applies. Othello's first speech in the play (aside from a brief half-line) is an example of the sort of knotted constructions that stand out as ungainly and unnatural. In response to Iago's warning that Brabantio is rousing sentiments against Othello's marriage, Othello declares,

Othello

Let him do his spite.
My services, which I have done the signiory,
Shall out-tongue his complaints; 'tis yet to know—
Which, when I know that boasting is an honour,
I shall promulgate*—I fetch my life and being
From men of royal siege, and my demerits
May speak unbonneted to as proud a fortune
As this that I have reach'd; for know, Iago,
But that I love the gentle Desdemona,
I would not my unhoused free condition
Put into circumscription and confine
For the sea's worth.

I submit that this is far from straightforward speech, and in it is couched no mere self-respect, nor even boasting under the guise of refusing to boast, but what I think was meant to be immediately recognized as a ludicrous and nervous vanity. We get no more about Othello's genealogy, nor any glimpse of his family life, since by his own admission he was given over to the profession of war from the age of seven. But to claim that the cream of Moorish society was the equal of the best of Venetian nobility would probably have provoked the sort of smile based on racial and national snobbery that has a central place in this play. "Unbonneted" occurs nowhere else in the entire Shakespeare corpus, and would normally mean taking the bonnet *off* as a sign of obeisance before a superior. In the present context, as has been noted, it must mean *without* taking the bonnet off, since Othello is insisting that he need defer to no one. Either he is using an exoticism with which we are unfamiliar, or he is misusing the language. There is, in any case, a manifest self-consciousness about his speech, with its intricate pattern of " 'tis yet to know, . . which, when I know . . . for know, Iago," that marks it off from the speech of

* *Provulgate* is the other lection here.

61

all others in the play—except Iago's when, out of malicious pleasure and spite, he parodies Othello to his face in speeches Othello is too preoccupied to recognize as parody, but which we are free to notice. I shall take note of these in due course. We have the unassailable fact of Othello's Moorishness, a fact conventionally assimilated to negroid features, and undisguisedly identified with black skin ("an old black ram/Is tupping your white ewe") and about which, since it cannot be concealed, Othello appears to be defensively proud.

But Othello is not simply a Moor; he is a Christian, and the play abounds with imagery of Christian salvation and damnation, and in the almost continuous confrontation of heaven and hell. When Othello offers to tell the story of his courtship, and reveal what magic charms he has used to win Desdemona (a taunt he is delighted to prove baseless and show that he is more sophisticated than to dabble in such primitive rites) he sends Iago to bring Desdemona to testify for herself, and says,

> And till she come, as truly as to heaven
> I do confess the vices of my blood,
> So justly to your grave ears I'll present
> How I did thrive in this fair lady's love,
> And she in mine.

It had best be said immediately that the quarto substitutes "faithful" for "truly," and omits the entire line, "I do confess the vices of my blood." But that line is by no means the only index of Othello's Christian orientation. Addressing the Duke and senators he swears, "Vouch with me, heaven," and says to them, "heaven defend your good souls." Agreeing to Desdemona's prayer that their marital happiness may continue and grow, he declares, "Amen to that, sweet powers!" More explicitly still, when called from his marriage bed by the brawl of Cassio and Roderigo, he calls everyone to order in the following terms:

Why, how now, ho! From whence ariseth this?
Are we turned Turks, and to ourselves do that
Which heaven hath forbid the Ottomites?
For Christian shame put by this barbarous brawl!

There would, I venture to suppose, be something slightly galling to an Elizabethan audience in having a Moor lecture his gentile associates and subordinates on Christian behavior. If "turn Turk" means "turn renegade," one wonders what this might have meant, coming from the mouth of a Moor, since the Moor himself must have turned renegade to become a Christian. He is, in all probability, a Morisco, or New Christian, a breed regarded without much trust by the Christian community at that time. In this regard I should like to cite some passages from Henry Kamen's account of the Spanish Inquisition. In his chapter on the Moors he says,

> Charles V finally on 13 September 1525 issued orders that Moors were no longer to be tolerated in Spain except as slaves, and measures for their conversion were to be set on foot. This was followed on 25 November by a decree for the expulsion of all Moors from Valencia by 31 December, and from Catalonia and Aragon by 31 January 1526. The unfortunate Moors came forward in their thousands to accept a religion which they neither believed nor loved nor intended to practice. . . .
>
> In Valencia many Moriscos spoke only Arabic and knew no 'christianesch'; but even those who spoke Valencian considered Arabic their mother tongue. In addition to the widespread ignorance of Christianity, therefore, there existed a language problem. The Spanish priests spoke no Arabic and most of them were like the bishop of Orileula, who considered it the duty of the Moriscos, as subjects of the Spanish crown, to learn the Spanish tongue. In their communities the Moriscos still retained

all the practices of their old faith as well as the traditional social customs which set them apart from the Christian population. This distinctive existence made it impossible to assimilate them into the body of a religiously united Spain.

Professor Kamen goes on to list the impossible burdens placed not only upon Moors but even upon New Christian Moriscos both by the Spanish crown and by the Inquisition, and then he declares,

> Faced with Christianity of such a merciless nature they resorted inevitably to rebellion and flight. In the Cortes [or local parliament] at Monzón in 1542 it was stated categorically that Moriscos had been fleeing abroad to join the Turks, 'because of the fear they have of the Inquisition'. They returned to their friends abroad, to the Muslim kingdoms in north Africa and the near East, and to the Barbary pirates.

The Moors and the Turks were united in religion, and the traditional enemies of Christian Europe, having pressed as far as Tours from the south, and as near as Vienna from the east. It was against their heresy and their possession of the Holy Land that the Crusades were directed, and the Crusades are remembered in this play by the word "crusadoes," the name of a coin, uttered by Desdemona, and recalling inevitably the Christian campaign against infidels.

The treatment of the Moors as well as of the New Christian Moriscos in Spain was very much like the treatment of Jews and those converts among the Jews who became New Christians, *marranos* or *conversos*. The parallel has its relevance. Kamen writes,

> The converso was not simply a convert. Christian society was all too conscious that the converted Jews had in reality been forced unwillingly into their new faith: the

converso was, from the first, therefore, regarded with suspicion as a false Christian and a secret judaizer or practicer of Jewish rites. The conversos or New Christians soon came to be distrusted even more than the Jews, for they were considered to be a fifth column within the body of the Church. New words were coined to describe them, the most common being *marranos*, a word which probably derives either from the Hebrew *maranatha* (the Lord comes) or from a description of the Jews as those who 'marran' or mar, the true faith. The conversos were thus resented by the body of Old Christians, who distrusted the sincerity of their faith and objected to the prominent part they played in Christian society. Although no longer Jews in religion, they now began to be subjected to all the rigors of antisemitism.

Moors and Jews were, accordingly, in a logically hopeless position, and regarded as infidels whether they converted or not, because, in the words of Samuel Butler in *Hudibras*,

> He that complies against his will
> Is of his own opinion still.

Brents Stirling, in an introduction to *The Merchant of Venice* in the Penguin edition, writes,

> London playgoers of 1596–97 would have included many who jibed at Dr. Roderigo Lopez, the Christianized Portuguese Jew and royal physician, who in 1594 was convicted on doubtful evidence of plotting to poison Queen Elizabeth. As Camden tells the story, just before Lopez was publicly hanged and quartered at Tyburn he protested from the scaffold that "he had loved the Queen as he loved Jesus Christ," an appeal, Camden adds, "which from a man of Jewish profession was heard not without laughter."

Othello

The same Elizabethan audience that could laugh at Lopez would regard Othello's ostentatious Christianity as suspect, unctuous, and offensive. They might even expect that sooner or later this show of piety would break down under pressure because it was not "natural" or "normal" in a Moor. What we know of Othello's background is sketchy, but it involves "being taken by the insolent foe;/And sold to slavery. . . ." That foe is not identified, but it is likely to be the Christian opponent; and if Othello is now himself a Christian, he is likely to have become so under the duress of slavery, as was the case with many others. If there were those who felt that Othello was not truly entitled to his Christian posture, they would have heard the following speeches with mounting irritation and derision.

> This hand of yours requires
> A sequester from liberty, fasting and prayer,
> Much castigation, exercise devout;
> For here's a young and sweating devil here,
> That commonly rebels.

> Naked in bed, Iago, and not mean harm?
> It is hypocrisy against the devil:
> They that mean virtuously, and yet do so,
> The devil their virtue tempts, and they tempt heaven.

(The last line here recalls the temptation of Christ in the wilderness.)

> Come, swear it, damn thyself;
> Lest, being like one of heaven, the devils themselves
> Should fear to seize thee. Therefore be double-damned—
> Swear thou art honest.

> Had it pleased heaven
> To try me with affliction, had they rain'd
> All kinds of sores and shames on my bare head,
> Steep'd me in poverty to the very lips,
> Given to captivity me and my utmost hopes,

66

I should have found in some place of my soul
A drop of patience.

You, mistress,
That have the office opposite to Saint Peter,
And keep the gates in Hell. . . .

OTHELLO: Have you pray'd tonight, Desdemon?
DESDEMONA: Ay, my lord.
OTHELLO: If you bethink yourself of any crime
        Unreconciled as yet to heaven and grace,
        Solicit for it straight.
DESDEMONA: Alack, my lord, what may you mean by that?
OTHELLO: Well, do it, and be brief; I will walk by.
        I would not kill thy unprepared spirit.
        No, heaven forfend! I would not kill thy soul.

This is merely a representative selection of quotations, but enough, I think, to suggest that if an audience looks for, and hopes to find, any crack in Othello's moral armor—if that audience expects to congratulate itself on its Iago-like, cynical good sense in doubting the stamina and authenticity of this Christian stance—its meanest and crudest hopes will be more than realized.

In spite of his early irony in regard to Brabantio's accusation that he, Othello, would employ "magic" to win Desdemona, with all the lofty suggestions that he is above such primitive traffic and belief (though Brabantio appears to believe it enough to offer it as a charge), he nevertheless tells Desdemona, in regard to the handkerchief he gave her, that "There's magic in the web of it." It is irrelevant whether Othello himself believes this or not; he wants Desdemona to think he believes it, and so he is acting as if he thought it were true, and wished others to believe he thinks it true. It is a signal reversion to something explicitly un-Christian, and its disconnection with Christianity is made as clear as possible:

A sibyl that had number'd in the world
The sun to course two hundred compasses,
In her prophetic fury sewed the work;
The worms were hallowed that did breed the silk;
And it was dyed in mummy which the skilful
Conserved of maiden's hearts.

Within a short time he has turned overtly savage: "I'll tear her all to pieces!" and "I will chop her into messes!" And, finally, by way of clinching the matter, after having told Desdemona that he will not kill her soul, and that she will be allowed what the basest prisoner is allowed, the right to make her peace with God before execution, he ignores his promise, breaks his word, and murders her before she has had a chance to pray. In these telling speeches and acts he has behaved as if his Christianity were never deeply believed, and therefore all the more dishonorable and affected in retrospect.

THE "ROMAN" GENERAL

By this epithet I mean to suggest several things about Othello. There is the high premium he puts on "honour," in the Roman military tradition, and his deeply professional feeling about soldiery. In this he bears a resemblance to other Shakespearean figures in the Roman and History plays; and his concern with "honour" is one that preoccupies Shakespeare over a large part of his career. In this connection Othello makes use of classical imagery, and it is used about him by others. But most strikingly of all, he gives way to, or affects, a sort of rhetoric, a distortion or inflation of speech that particularly irritates Iago, and which we cannot fail to take notice of.

After the arrival in Cyprus of the main segment of the Venetian fleet, and of all the main characters but Othello himself,

Othello

Cassio makes an exhilarated and grateful prayer of welcome and protection for Othello and Desdemona:

> Great Jove, Othello guard,
> And swell his sail with thine own pow'rful breath,
> That he may bless this bay with his tall ship,
> Make love's quick pants in Desdemona's arms,
> Give renewed fire to our extincted spirits,
> And bring all Cyprus comfort!—

At which point Desdemona enters, and he continues,

> O, behold!
> The riches of the ship is come on shore!
> You men of Cyprus, let her have your knees.
> Hail to thee, lady! and the grace of heaven,
> Before, behind thee, and on every hand,
> Enwheel thee round!

Cassio is clearly devoted to his commander, and reverently courteous to his commander's wife, but it seems to me that we are entitled to notice the conspicuous difference between the prayers he offers in behalf of each, for one is pagan and one is Christian. As significantly as the recent storm, an omen of the chaos and storm to come, these prayers separate rather than unite husband and wife—though this is certainly not part of Cassio's intention. The prayer for Othello invokes not only Jove but also the four elements: earth, air, fire, and water; while the Christian prayer is no less universal, but distinctly different. We may also be reminded that Cyprus was sacred to Aphrodite (Venus was called the Cyprean Queen), goddess of Love, and we will be struck at how tragic a setting it will be for "the divine Desdemona," who has a supremely Christian, and not a pagan, nature.

But well before this, in the first act, Othello has exhibited that inflated speech and contorted syntax we identify with the most egregious kind of rhetoric and oratory:

Othello

> The tyrant custom, most grave senators,
> Hath made the flinty and steel couch of war
> My thrice-driven bed of down: I do agnize
> A natural and prompt alacrity
> I find in hardness.

"Alacrity" is used here in what can only be called an eccentric way, and differently from the way Shakespeare uses it anywhere else. But aside from that, the lines quite obviously instance the sort of "bombast circumstance" Iago mentioned at the start. Lest we think this a momentary lapse, Othello remarks only a few lines later,

> No, when light-wing'd toys
> Of feathered Cupid seel with wanton dullness
> My speculative and offic'd instruments,
> That my disports corrupt and taint my business,
> Let housewives make a skillet of my helm,
> And all indign and base adversities
> Make head against my estimation!

There are puzzles here that only begin with differing lections. The quarto has "foils" for "seel," "active instruments" for "offic'd instruments," and "reputation" for "estimation." The "speculative" instruments may be either the eyes or the meditative mind; the "offic'd" instruments are probably limbs, or those parts of the body obedient to the mind. If "seel" means "blind," as some have thought, it is hard to see how limbs can be blinded, though they can be foiled. If "seel" means "put to sleep," we are presented with a situation in which the supposedly soldierly faculties sleep while the libidinous ones are allowed full play. Presumably Cupid could manage this, but the phraseology is not of the clearest. The passage ends in a sort of boast or defiant taunt: if I should neglect my duties, let housewives domesticate to their "huswifery" the martial emblems of my male profession. And what happens in this play is that in fact the military calling is hideously domesticated; the fury and terror of the field, having no outlet in action, settle into the bedroom, and "honour" is grotesquely fought over, ambiguously won and lost.

Anyway, it is the baroque mode of expression that not only galls Iago (who regards himself as both cunning and as a plain speaker) but is the occasion of his mockery by parody. When the brawl between Cassio and Roderigo occurs, and Othello, having been called to the scene, inquires what happened, Iago declares,

> I do not know. Friends all, but now, even now,
> In quarter, and in terms like bride and groom
> Divesting them for bed; and then, but now—
> As if some planet had unwitted men—
> Swords out, and tilting one at other's breast
> In opposition bloody. I cannot speak
> Any beginning to this peevish odds,
> And would in action glorious I had lost
> Those legs that brought me to a part of it!

I wish to call attention merely to the last two lines of this speech, and suggest that they are nearly ludicrous. Their distorted and silly connection to military glory, their unnecessarily encumbered way of saying the simple "I wish I'd never seen this," their contrived way of blaming his legs for conveying him to the presence of this disagreeable sight, all these are a mockery of what by this time we can recognize as an idiosyncrasy of Othello's mode of expression. Othello is given to the use of the vocative, the apostrophe, all the rhetorical modes and formulas throughout the play.

> O, now for ever
> Farewell the tranquil mind! farewell content!
> Farewell the plumed troop, and the big wars
> That make ambition virtue! O, farewell!
> Farewell the neighing steed and the shrill trump,

Othello

The spirit-stirring drum, th'ear-piercing fife,
The royal banner, and all quality,
Pride, pomp, and circumstance of glorious war!
And, O you mortal engines, whose rude throats
Th'immortal Jove's dread clamors counterfeit,
Farewell! Othello's occupation's gone!

Perhaps the first thing that must be said about this speech is that G. Wilson Knight calls it noble; but I think it is a tainted nobility: studied, artful, self-conscious, and almost immediately provocative of a parody by Iago, thus:

O monstrous world! Take note, take note, O world,
To be direct and honest is not safe.

This is not the way Iago speaks to anyone else in the play. It should also be noted that Othello, now well advanced in the tragic process of disintegration, here speaks of himself for the first time in the third person, as if he stood apart from himself and were a divided consciousness. This process becomes more and more pronounced as the play continues, and we must return to it in due course. But for the present, we may remark upon the patterned repetitions, the orchestrated luxuriance of military pageantry, the "pomp and circumstance" not of glorious war alone but of this speech. And we may further note the specifically "classical" employment of "engines," (*exeuremata*) and the poetic periphrasis by which the vulgar word "cannon" is avoided (swords and spears being the only weapons suitable for naming, according to epic tradition). Jove is named, and the roar of the unmentionable artillery compared to the thunder of the god. It is hard to feel that this speech's passion is not colored by a self-regard and self-consciousness that a little compromises its "nobility."

There follows almost immediately an interesting, relevant, and curiously disputed passage. Othello insists,

Othello

I'll have some proof. My name, that was as fresh
As Dian's visage, is now begrimed and black
As mine own face.

The quarto has "Her name" for "My name," but I think I
prefer the folio version, though the choice is not based on anything demonstrable, but simply on my sense of what is wanted
here; though it may be added that Othello's earlier repudiation of Cupid is consistent with this identification with Diana.
There is, in fact, something very chaste about the way Othello
thinks of himself, even within the context of marriage, and
this may be one of the reasons he is so vulnerable to Iago. He
continues to be concerned with the purity of his own reputation as he compares it to the chastity and whiteness of the
moon goddess. The classical, the Roman strain, which dictates
that Caesar's wife must be beyond reproach, continues. As does
the use of apostrophe:

Arise, black vengeance, from the hollow hell!
Yield up, O love, thy crown and hearted throne
To tyrannous hate! Swell, bosom, with thy fraught,
For 'tis of aspics' tongues!

And when Iago ventures to test him with, "Patience, I say;
your mind perhaps may change," he responds with a nearly
Homeric, at least an epic, simile:

Never, Iago. Like to the Pontic sea,
Whose icy current and compulsive course
Ne'er feels retiring ebb, but keeps due on
To the Propontic and the Hellespont;
Even so my bloody thoughts, with violent pace
Shall ne'er look back, ne'er ebb to humble love,
Till that a capable and wide revenge
Swallow them up.

It is almost as if he were calling upon classical authority and classical modes of discourse to justify his fury as well as to articulate it. This extended maritime metaphor, with its appropriate qualities of icy coldness, irresistible force, and singleness of direction is all, of course, eminently suitable to his purpose, but we may yet comment that it seems contrived, and that the classicism seems at least as important to Othello as do its local details and the burden of its meaning.

But the meaning, in any case, is persuasive enough for Iago. Having prodded Othello through various stages of torment and desperation, he has by this time brought his commander to his knees, quite literally; and there he joins him in a grotesque travesty of marriage in which the two men exchange vows, Desdemona having been firmly eliminated. And in a curious, half-mocking, half-serious, but sinister parody of Othello's compulsive habit of apostrophe, Iago declares,

> Witness, you ever-burning lights above,
> You elements that clip us round about,
> Witness that here Iago doth give up
> The execution of his wit, hands, heart
> To wronged Othello's service! Let him command,
> And to obey shall be in me remorse,
> What bloody business ever.

It should be apparent that for Othello to think of himself as a classical hero on the one hand, and to think of himself as a pious Christian on the other, involves a painfully uncertain sense of himself, and even of how to "dramatize" himself. It is one of the indices of a very deep perplexity.

Othello's generalship is evidenced in his command of others, his clear impartiality:

> Hold your hands,
> Both you of my inclining and the rest.

He tries to apply these same methods to Iago's insinuations, and to his own fears:

> Think'st thou I'ld make a life of jealousy,
> To follow still the changes of the moon
> With fresh suspicions? No! To be once in doubt
> Is once to be resolved. Exchange me for a goat
> When I shall turn the business of my soul
> To such exsufflicate and blown surmises,
> Matching this inference.

(The O.E.D. remarks, regarding *exsufflicate*, "apparently an arbitrary formation on Exsufflate"; and the only instance is from this speech.) But of course the swift and objective decisions of a commander are not available to the subjective vacillations of a mind, or the interior torments to which he so much desires to apply them. In all these crises he is concerned with Justice and Honour, both of them conceived as Roman virtues. They are related, moreover, having to do with the preservation of purity from contamination—a species of chastity. And both are matters of public inspection. Justice is established by public evidence and general consent; honour, in both men and women, has to do with reputation, which is publicly assigned. Cassio holds the same Roman regard for Honour, or Reputation, as his commander; and Iago, addressing Othello, adopts the same attitude:

> Good name in man and woman, dear my lord,
> Is the immediate jewel of their souls.

OTHELLO DIVIDED AGAINST HIMSELF

Othello's torment and internal strife is like the war of heaven and hell that figures so prominently in the play's language.

It is a civil, or an "intestine," struggle, and only in part to be explained by the Christian-Moorish or the Christian-Roman oppositions. It begins with the implantation of the seeds of suspicion in Othello by Iago in Act III. The metaphor of planting a seed which is to bear the evil fruit of death is consistent both with the notion of Iago as Satanic, and with the passive role of Othello. In fact, it is Othello's passivity that in part enrages him, for his passivity is tied to his uncertainty. By the third scene in the act he is terribly divided:

> I think my wife be honest, and think she is not;
> I think that thou art just, and think thou art not.

Honesty, or Honour, and Justice are paralleled here, and the effect of this torment, from Iago's point of view at least, is emasculating, and he keeps pointing to this, not without some inward relish:

> Are you a man?

> Would you would bear your fortune like a man!

> Good sir, be a man.

> A passion most unsuiting such a man—

>   Marry patience!
> Or I shall say y'are all in all in spleen
> And nothing of a man.

The fiendishness of Iago during these scenes consists in provoking Othello's anxieties, frustrations, and furies, and then blaming him for not being able sufficiently to govern them. And Othello's torment arises precisely out of the conflict of the passions he feels and the genuine attempts he makes to govern them. The attempts at government are wholly connected with his role as "Roman" general. Early in the play he was supremely in command of himself and of others. And he never carried his authority with more magisterial effect than with the line, "Keep up your bright swords, for the dew will rust them." The commanding presence who speaks there continues in authority so secure that without discomfort he can show obeisance and obedience to the Duke and senate, though knowing, of course, as everyone seems to know, that in fact they depend wholly upon him. The protocols of mutual courtesy are smoothly and flawlessly observed. What wrecks this seemingly absolute poise is, after all, a change of setting or venue; the field of action shifts from war, where Othello is absolute, to the isle of the Cyprean Queen and the domain of Love in which Othello confesses his inexperience and inadequacy, and where the cynicism of Iago passes for worldly knowledge.

> IAGO: No, let me know;
> And knowing what I am, I know what she shall be.
> OTHELLO: O, thou art wise! 'Tis certain.

Othello has clearly indicated (or as clearly as a muddled text will allow) as early as the first act that he is very nearly disqualified, virtually *hors de combat*, in that field of carnal intimacy in which Iago claims expertise and subtle knowledge. Asking the senate permission to allow Desdemona to accompany him to Cyprus, Othello says,

> Let her have your voice.
> Vouch with me heaven, I therefore beg it not
> To please the palate of my appetite,
> Not to comply with heat—the young affects
> In me defunct—and proper satisfaction;
> But to be free and bounteous to her mind.

There are puzzles here I must pass over, but I would point out that the sort of chastity suggested here obsesses Othello throughout the play, and his mention of Desdemona's mind chimes with her comment, "I saw Othello's visage in his mind." Earlier in the same scene he had said of himself,

> For since these arms of mine had seven years' pith
> Till now some nine moons wasted, they have used
> Their dearest action in the tented field

If we may take these statements as true and accurate, we must assume that Othello's arms experienced no "dearer" action than warfare from the age of seven until nine months before he speaks here, at which time he declares himself past the age of strong sexual appetite. This means that he has interested himself in no one before Desdemona, and his interest in her is of an uncommon purity. Iago, brilliant opportunist that he is, affects to believe this or not to believe it as suits his various purposes. In his dealings with Brabantio and Roderigo, he strongly affirms the animality of Othello, and associates that animality with rampant sexual energy and with the black skin of a primitive man. Dealing, on the other hand, with Othello, he patiently acknowledges his commander's painful naiveté. Speaking to an utterly credulous Othello, he remarks of his nation's women,

> I know our country disposition well:
> In Venice they do let God see the pranks
> They dare not show their husbands; their best conscience
> Is not to leave't undone, but to keep't unknown.

The torment of division, or disintegration, from which Othello suffers, and which begins in Act III, continues in intensity and divisiveness until he falls into an epileptic seizure, and briefly passes out. One of the definitions of this malady in the O.E.D. quotes a 1658 text regarding "the Epilepsy that ariseth from the strangling of the Mother," in which "Mother," as it appears in *King Lear*, is hysteria.

> O, how this mother swells up toward my heart!
> Hysterica passio, down, thou climbing sorrow;
> Thine element's below.

We may take it, then, that Othello's epileptic swoon has re-
sulted from his attempt to "strangle" or govern his hysterical
passion, and that this is a symbol of his unresolved conflicts. If
they are unresolved at this point, they are cruelly revived by
Iago almost as soon as Othello comes to. And shortly thereafter
we witness an Othello so hideously divided, so totally un-
manned, that the spectacle comes as near to seeing protracted
and deforming torture on the stage as anything Shakespeare
has ever offered.

OTHELLO: O Iago!

IAGO: And did you see the handkerchief?

OTHELLO: Was that mine?

IAGO: Yours, by this hand! And to see how he prizes the foolish
woman your wife! She gave it him, and he hath giv'n it
his whore.

OTHELLO: I would have him nine years a-killing!—A fine
woman! a fair woman! a sweet woman!

IAGO: Nay, you must forget that.

OTHELLO: Ay, let her rot, and perish, and be damned tonight;
for she shall not live. No, my heart is turned to
stone; I strike it, and it hurts my hand.—O, the
world hath not a sweeter creature! She might lie by
an emperor's side and command him tasks.

IAGO: Nay, that's not your way.

OTHELLO: Hang her! I do but say what she is. So delicate with
her needle!—an admirable musician! O she will
sing the savageness out of a bear!—Of so high and
plenteous wit and invention!—

IAGO: She's the worse for all this.

OTHELLO: O, a thousand, thousand times! And then, of so
gentle a condition!

IAGO: Ay, too gentle.

OTHELLO: Nay, that's certain. But yet the pity of it Iago! O
Iago, the pity of it, Iago!

There are some who find this very nearly unendurable, and it is by no means the end of Othello's exhibition of his inner division. It poisons his interview with Desdemona in the next scene, and is yet present, in a somewhat crazed and hypnotized form, when he enters the last scene of the play.

CONCLUSION

When Othello enters the bedchamber in the last scene he has taken upon himself the role of justicer, though by no means for the first time. From the very beginning of the play he was cast as arbiter of all disputes. But here, in his almost dazed condition, he seems to feel himself an agent of the Supreme Law, or of the Roman virtue of Justice. Even in the insane calm of his opening speech he indicates his division from himself, posing in balance the demands of "duty" with his regret at having to perform it, like some deranged Aeneas. He is indeed very nearly demented, and his calm is the more awful for that. It ought to make us shudder as much as, though in a different way from, the spectacle of his symbolic castration. But the evidence of division only begins with this mad attempt at balance. It expresses itself in the patent degeneration of his speech, which already, under the torture of Iago had declined into expletives and groans. Here his vocatives become cries of feebleness:

> But O vain boast!
>
> O ill-starred wench!
>
> O cursed, cursed slave!

This last expression refers to himself, and seems an ironic fulfillment of Brabantio's early prediction:

> For if such actions may have passage free,
> Bondslaves and pagans shall our statesmen be.

The division is expressed in his references to himself again and again in the third person:

> Man but a rush against Othello's breast,
> And he retires. Where should Othello go?

And in response to the question Lodovico asks upon entering, "Where is this rash and most unfortunate man?" Othello responds, "That's he that was Othello. Here I am." There are clearly several ways to read that line. One way is to convey the sense that the speaker knows exactly what he is saying, and means that "Othello," an admirable, competent and decent man, existed in the past, but exists no more, and in his place stands the wreck of man that speaks. Another would suggest that the first part of the line, "That's he that was Othello," would be something like the equivalent of, "He must be talking about me."

In addition, as Wilson Knight has carefully indicated, Othello's long speech beginning, "Behold, I have a weapon," while achieving moments of genuine eloquence, slips suddenly into rant, like music into discord, or, perhaps equally aptly, like order into the chaos of apocalypse that seemed predicted almost from the start. Othello makes feeble attempts to recover himself, as, for example, in finding the concealed sword, but they collapse into nothing, as his speech collapses into raving. And therefore his final speech ought to astonish us as an achievement of unexpected strength and self-command, even as we are astonished to find an unexpected weapon in his possession.

The speech itself is a quite extraordinary piece of oratory. Since he has just been ordered to come away, his very first line is striking: "Soft you! a word or two before you go." Not "before we go," which would have been expected; nor "before I go."

> I have done the state some service, and they know't.
> No more of that.

This cannot be said in extenuation of his crime, since the punishment he will inflict cannot be mitigated. It is the beginning of his request that some balance sheet of his deeds may represent him properly to posterity. For this to be called purely self-regarding vanity is to miss its strong classical, its deliberately Roman component. Fame is desirable, and a proper, even a noble, ambition; and in this speech, with an astonishing summoning of final strength, Othello is exhibiting, without flinching, all his Roman virtues, and some others as well. If he makes no mention of Desdemona here (and he does indeed allude to her) it would be in keeping with the Duke's stoic advice to Brabantio at the beginning of the play:

> When remedies are past, the griefs are ended
> By seeing the worst, which late on hopes depended.

His balance sheet is not merely a plea for justice but a rhetorical feat of extraordinary skill, a speech which, considering all that he has had to face about himself, about Desdemona, about Cassio, about Iago, is nothing short of triumphant in its matched and mated parallelisms, its antiphonal pairings of thesis and antithesis, its decisively Ciceronian patterns of poised and balanced phrases. At no other point in the play does his rhetoric show itself to such advantage, unblemished by contortions or exoticisms. Neither is it merely self-exculpating, nor simply Roman in its courage, if one elects, as I do, for the reading of "base Iudean" rather than "base Indian," and thereby allows Othello, quite consistently with the Christian aspect of his speech, to identify himself with Judas Iscariot, and Desdemona, the pearl he throws away, with Christ. Desdemona not only has proven faultless, but has died refusing to accuse her murderer. And the speaker, as I think, means to convey his complete sense of this. He is therefore committing himself not only to the death by suicide that was the lot of Judas, but to hell and damnation. He had al-

ready hinted as much earlier when he said, addressing Desdemona's corpse,

> When we shall meet at compt,
> This look of thine will hurl my soul from heaven,
> And fiends will snatch at it.*

In other words, up to this point the speech has united the
Roman and the Christian aspects of Othello. And its conclusion will extirpate the Moor, and exhibit in definitive form
the absolute division within him. As both defender of the
Venetian cause and as the circumcised dog, as both Christian
and Muslim, Othello performs the last struggle of his inward
life; heaven and hell drive him to his end, and, without hope of
redemption in the next life, he asks for an accurate report of
this one. The judgment he passes upon himself is absolute and
remorseless, though this is not what Eliot meant in charging
that he exhibits no remorse. His performance is admittedly
theatrical, but it bears so heavy a spiritual penalty, and bears
it with such complete consciousness, that the theatrics, I maintain, cease to matter, and he attains a painful but undoubted
nobility. His self-inflicted death is the death not only of Judas
but of Brutus; it involves both Christian and Roman aspects,
which, admittedly, do not sit comfortably together. But that
has been part of Othello's drama from the first. And there is
a species of oratorical remorse, despite what Eliot says. There
are four main items in Othello's balance sheet, and all but the
last of them in the past tense. He loved; he was perplexed; he

---

* I do not mean that we, audience or reader, are to take the position that
this is a rather narrow and straightforward morality play, and that Othello
is indeed consigned to hell and damnation by universal consent as well as
by the playwright. And certainly there can be nothing in Desdemona's
looks that could so consign him, since she explicitly forgives his terrible
trespass. But I believe that Othello himself so views his situation, and what
he sees in the innocence and beauty of the dead Desdemona is a perfection
he has destroyed, and which therefore, in his own mind and soul, damns
him.

threw the pearl away; but he weeps. His ability to say this, without halting, without inflation or bombast, is in itself an accomplishment that has its spiritual dimension. And his suicide is offered as a Venetian-Christian-Roman victory over guileless trust and ignorance, over the barbarian-pagan innocence of a Moorish slave.

The Riddles of Emily Dickinson

L ET ME BEGIN by acknowledging how provisional and circumspect my commentary on Emily Dickinson's poetry is going to be. I present no better credentials than those of a poet who delights in poetry. But it would be dishonest of me if I did not confess to a sense of intimidation by the sheer volume of Emily Dickinson's poems—1775 of them in the splendid Thomas Johnson edition—upon which has been piled the excruciating weight of commentary too vast to contemplate, though I have contemplated parts of it with a suitable shudder. I can assert right at the beginning, however, that my title, which differs only by a single letter from the title of a book by Rebecca Patterson, *The Riddle of Emily Dickinson*, does not intend a resemblance to that study, which diligently discovers parental inadequacy, repressed homosexuality, and frustrated love. So perhaps I should also apologize for the conspicuous absence of scandal and gossip in what follows, though I do not mean to dismiss with a jest the very serious inquiries— biographical, psychological, and historical—that have been brought to bear on her poetry.

The Riddles of Emily Dickinson

Indeed there is a strong modern prejudice (strongly supported by a good deal of modern poetry) to the effect that it is impossible to talk about poetry without reference to the poet's life; that biography is the ultimate sanction and authentication of art. And I agree that in the case of Emily Dickinson it would be foolish to try to make sense of certain poems which are intelligible only if we know what gift they accompanied or to whom they were addressed. But criticism owes to her work a special gallantry and diffidence. Out of those 1775 poems only seven were published in her lifetime, and of those most came to print without her consent or supervision, sometimes altered and invariably for the worse, like the kindnesses performed by Mr. Tottel upon poems of Sir Thomas Wyatt.

About some of our greatest writers we in fact know very little of an intimate nature. In Shakespeare's case we have, besides the texts of his poems and plays (parts of them of doubtful authenticity), a number of legal documents, the brief and businesslike testimony of a few associates, some church records and very little else. Of John Webster and Cyril Tourneur we have even less. Of Emily Dickinson we have, by way of contrast, a good deal more: her poems and letters, to start with, and both are of inestimable value; but also a considerable knowledge of the society into which she was born; abundant details about all her family and many of their friends; as well as important reports, by kindly and interested witnesses, of the poet herself. And yet she was, like Hamlet, not one to let anybody pluck out the heart of her mystery. She was enigmatic even to those nearest to her, and she continues to be so for us today.

"Since knowledge of an artist's private life never throws any significant light upon his work, there is no justification for intruding upon his privacy," wrote W. H. Auden in regard to Vincent Van Gogh. And A. E. Housman, trying to avoid a newspaper interviewer, wrote to an intermediary, "Tell him that the wish to include a glimpse of my personality in a literary article is low, unworthy and American. Tell him that some men are more interesting than their books but that my book is more interesting than its man. Tell him that Frank Harris found me rude and William Blunt found me dull. Tell him anything else that you think will put him off."

And yet the world is unwilling to be put off when confronted, or, rather, when evaded, by such an undeniable genius as Emily Dickinson, who seems to us the more fascinating for the richness and abundance of an imagination sprung from a life that, to most of us, seems barren, constricted, and even hermetic. She never married, though her attachments to certain men and women were of an intensely passionate sort; and yet she nevertheless felt compelled to conceal, to cloak such feelings with an eccentric or cool behavior. Except for a few brief journeys to Boston, mostly for eye treatment, and a brief visit to Philadelphia and Washington, she never left her family home in Amherst, Massachusetts, where she lived in self-imposed, good-humored retirement, dressed almost always in a white dress, a "habit" of her own choice, and of which she writes in several of her poems.

Her mother has been described as "demure, submissive, domestic and deeply religious." Her father, a man with a stern and inflexible sense of duty, was a lawyer, a treasurer of Amherst College for thirty-eight years, and for two years a United States Congressman. There was a brother, Austin, also a lawyer, who, with his wife and sons, lived right next door, on the same property. There was a sister, Lavinia, called "Vinnie." The poet herself, second after her brother of the three siblings, was born on the tenth of December, 1830.

Her behavior with all but the most immediate members of her family was likely to be odd. Samuel Bowles, a distinguished journalist from Springfield, and only four years older than the poet, was well liked by the whole Dickinson family—a man of wide travel, broad acquaintance, and a frequent visitor to the Dickinson home. During his summer abroad in 1862 Emily wrote to him twice, saying in her second letter, "I tell you, Mr. Bowles, it is a suffering to have a sea—no care how blue—between your soul and you. . . . I've learned to read the steamer place in newspapers now. It's 'most like shaking hands with you, or more like your ringing at the door." And yet, for all the affectionate intimacy of those words, as well as others in the same two letters, when Bowles returned and visited the family in Amherst in November, she remained in her room and sent him a note: "Dear Friend,—I cannot see you. You will not believe me. That you return to us alive is better than a summer, and more to hear your voice below than news of any bird." Indeed, Dickinson not infrequently conducted interviews or took part in conversations while standing at the head of the stairs on the second floor, while her interlocutor sat in the parlor below, and raised his or her voice to carry up the stairwell.

There has been a good deal of speculation, much of it frivolous and irresponsible (some of it, in Housman's words, "low, unworthy and American") about what compelled Dickinson's strange retirement from a world she addressed so fervently in her poems. The simple truth is that we don't know, and that our guesses had better be discreet and without presumption.

I take that caveat as addressed first of all to myself, since I have chosen to broach this delicate and insoluble topic. For with what I hope is suitable diffidence I want to propose an answer to this riddle, and it is based in part upon another of the poet's letters, this one attempting further to explain to Samuel Bowles why she chose to remain invisible during his visit mentioned above; and in which letter she refers to her brother and sister, those stalwarts of religious orthodoxy, as, "Oh They of little faith!" It may be argued, of course, that the phrase was appropriated in jest, but not the least part of our problem in reading this poet lies in determining where jest leaves off and earnestness begins. In any case, if such as Austin and Vinnie were of "little faith," and if such as she, as she also claims in the letter, were a prophet unrecognized, then everything in the whole spiritual order, visible and invisible, would have to be revised and virtually inverted.

Her letters have much of the quality, even the rhythms, of her poetry; she must indeed have *thought* in this intense, elliptical way. Trying to explain to Bowles why she would not see him, and thanking him at the same time for a gift he had brought her from abroad, she wrote, "Dear Friend. I did not need the little Bat—to enforce your memory—for that can stand alone, like the best Brocade—but it was much—that far and ill, you recollected me—Forgive me if I prize the Grace—superior to the Sign. Because I did not see you, Vinnie and Austin, upbraided me—They did not know I gave my part that they might have the more—but then the Prophet had no fame in his immediate Town—My Heart led all the rest—I think that what we *know*—we can endure that others doubt, until their faith be riper. And so, dear friend, who knew me, I make no argument—to you—

"Did I not want to see you? Do not the Phebes want to come? Oh They of little faith! I said that I was glad you were alive—Might it bear repeating? Some phrases are too fine to fade—and Light but just confirms them—Few absences could seem so wide as yours has done, to us—if 'twas a larger face—or we a smaller Canvas—we need not know—now you have come—We hope often to see you—Our poverty—entitles us—and friends are nations in themselves—to supersede the Earth. . . ."

The New England to which she was native was still in the grip of a traditional Calvinist revivalism that could trace its way back over more than a hundred years to the fervors and terrors of Jonathan Edwards's time. As Thomas Johnson has written, "For an individual not to undergo conversion by physical sensation was almost a moral delinquency, more serious therefore, since it was not merely social, than would be today a failure to submit to a test if suspected of being a typhoid carrier." And so it came about that in her sixteenth year something took place that must have been crucial to her whole life, her vocation, her art and her soul.

She entered at that age—the age at which her mother's sister had been "converted"—a seminary for young ladies at Mount Holyoke. The 235 enrolled students in the fall of that year fell into three roughly equal categories: those who were professing Christians, those who "had hope," and those "without hope."

By December, exhortations and prayer meetings had reduced the last group to twenty-five. Dickinson wrote, "Christ is calling everyone. . . . All my companions have answered, even my darling Vinnie believes she loves, and trusts him, and I am standing . . . alone in rebellion. . . . How strange is this sanctification, that works such a marvelous change, that sows in such corruption, and rises in golden glory, that brings Christ down, and shews him, and lets him select his friends! . . . *I* am one of the lingering *bad* ones, and so do I slink away, and pause and ponder, and ponder and pause, and do work without knowing why, not surely, for this brief world, and more sure it is not for heaven, and I ask what this message *means* that they ask for so eagerly. . . ."

That year, in which she must have gone through agonies of self-inquisition, made the more terrible by the public disgrace in which she stood, she became so sick that her father brought her home, and except for the few journeys already mentioned, she never left home again. She had failed, she thought, to receive the message, and the light. And what she felt about this, her poems show, was a mixture of shame and pride. Shame at what she may have thought (and what others very likely did think) a wickedness that denied her the revelation vouchsafed to so many others. Pride in that strength and independence of mind which will not deceive itself nor bend with the winds of opinion; the pride of an inward integrity that prizes the Grace above the Sign, the invisible above the visible, the solitary pride of the prophet unrecognized in his immediate town. So she withdrew from what she called "the auction of the mind . . .

so foul a thing." She sewed the poems together into packets and stowed them away. In so large a body of work there are almost of necessity poems of a wide range of finish and accomplishment. Criticism is obliged to notice that some poems of hers are not very good, and for various reasons: some seem archly cute, some seem incomplete, some are manifestly drafts or merely notations to which she might have planned to return at some time. That they were preserved in a bureau in neat packets gives us no clue about her sense of their completion or her sense of satisfaction with them. And so to criticize her faults in the top-lofty tones of Yvor Winters, for example, is a little like criticizing the table manners of one who eats alone in the privacy of his home. Still, it in no way diminishes the greatness of her achievement (which, by my hesitant estimate, would number some three hundred superb poems) to notice some of her characteristic flaws.

There is, for example, her striking and often very effective use of abstraction, scarcely surprising in a poet so given to religious and moral speculation; but sometimes it runs away with her, as in these stanzas from a poem about a bobolink.

> Of impudent Habiliment
> Attired to defy,
> Impertinence subordinate
> At times to Majesty.
>
> Of Sentiments seditious
> Amenable to Law—
> As Heresies of Transport
> Or Puck's Apostacy
>
> 1279

What is being described here, under the rubric of the bird, is a psychological state, a youthful, admirable, and permissible impetuosity and independence. But we have lost track of what Professor I. A. Richards would call "the vehicle"; the bird has flown, and the notations are, I suggest, remote and unpersuasive. There are also occasional lapses into "cuteness," to which I react as to the squeak of hard chalk on a blackboard, but which others identify with a deliberate and conscious mask or persona that Emily Dickinson adopted as both a defensive and aggressive weapon, demanding the impunities and indulgences that we are prepared to grant to a child. But there are many ways of adopting the child's guise for the purposes of poetry, and William Blake, whose work I would shyly conjecture Emily Dickinson had read, has done it without creating the edgy discomfort aroused by these lines about the moon—

> Her Bonnet is the Firmament—
> The Universe—Her Shoe—
> The Stars—the Trinkets at her Belt—
> Her Dimities—of Blue—
>
> 737

—lines which succeed in translating the whole heavens, which were once said to declare the glory of God, into the cute dimensions of a doll. And here, to dismiss considerations of such lapses for good and all, is one more poem.

> Bee! I'm expecting you!
> Was saying Yesterday
> To Somebody you know
> That you were due—
>
> The Frogs got Home last Week—
> Are settled, and at work—
> Birds, mostly back—
> The Clover warm and thick—
>
> You'll get my Letter by
> The seventeenth; Reply
> Or better, be with me—
> Yours, Fly.
>
> 1035

The Riddles of Emily Dickinson

It is ungenerous, I suppose, to point out such faults of coyness
and girlishness, but I do so in part to show that at times, under
the dramatic impulse of the poem, she can redeem them with
an astonishing success, and make us feel that even the gambit
of childishness has been employed for wholly justifiable and
effective purposes. In the following poem, for example, the
first three and a half stanzas are written in what might be
described as the cool and somewhat arch language of an idle
and cold-blooded child. But in the middle of the fourth stanza
a miracle occurs: a bird takes flight. And the effect of this upon
the child and on the child's language is astonishing, and con-
vinces us of a genuine experience of awe.

> A Bird came down the Walk—
> He did not know I saw—
> He bit an Angleworm in halves
> And ate the fellow, raw,
>
> And then he drank a Dew
> From a convenient Grass—
> And then hopped sidewise to the Wall
> To let a Beetle pass—
>
> He glanced with rapid eyes
> That hurried all around—
> They looked like frightened Beads, I thought—
> He stirred his Velvet Head
>
> Like one in danger, Cautious,
> I offered him a Crumb
> And he unrolled his feathers
> And rowed him softer home—
>
> Than Oars divide the Ocean,
> Too silver for a seam—
> Or Butterflies, off Banks of Noon
> Leap, plashless as they swim.
>   328

The Riddles of Emily Dickinson

To identify the miracle in this poem by the crude statement, "a bird takes flight," was purposely to conceal its mystery by the use of emphatically plain terms, which often disguise more than they reveal. The truth is more nearly as follows. The first fourteen lines of the poem describe the familiar world of the natural predator, ruthlessness quite unconcealed by nice conventions of etiquette. Here is the world we all know, in which not only beasts prey upon each other, but some men live at the expense of other men, upon the labors, pains, the life-blood of others—facts especially visible in a society that, for all its polite pretensions, tolerated slavery—a matter about which Emily Dickinson and many of her friends had very strong feelings. This world is governed by Darwinian laws of fear and aggression, superficially disguised and domesticated by norms of a social order so well established, and so much taken for granted, that none of us finds it shocking in the least. It would brand us as sentimental to do so. And while slavery now is gone, the laws of that world are still our laws. We all know, and even admit, in candor and in our cups, that the world is a matter of "dog eat dog," that everyone looks out for "Number One," that respect for others is purely a prudential or conventional consideration, and that, as even children know, "losers are weepers." Those are the blunt facts that "realists" keep telling us, telling those of us especially who cherish the childish notion that the world might be otherwise. Even those of us who accept this world with reluctance must admit to our daily familiarity and commerce with it. We have been inured by its terrible forces into taking it for granted. So that any change from it seems stunning and improbable. And the change magnificently takes place in the last six lines of this poem. We move literally to a higher world. An ascension takes place. And what had been a carnivore is translated to a species of angel, as the air becomes a metaphoric ocean in which all capable and harmless creatures bathe and play and are cleansed. And might not this be a shy and modest allegory of human possibility? There

94

The Riddles of Emily Dickinson

are other poems by Emily Dickinson that could support such a construction.

Let me turn briefly to her metrics and prosody, which are considerably more various and interesting than has been commonly allowed. Anyone who has read through the entire body of her work can testify that she by no means confined herself to the tetrameter quatrains of the standard anthology pieces. And I am convinced that one of the commonplaces that is due for serious revision is her supposedly narrow indebtedness to the hymnals, and to Dr. Watts in particular. Dr. Watts, at one of his pinnacles of eloquence wrote,

> Hark! She bids all her friends adieu;
> Some angel calls her to the spheres;
> Our eyes the radiant saint pursue
> Through liquid telescopes of tears.

To be sure, Watts was not always up to that level, as his parodists have suggested; but I delight to think how well and comfortably that stanza of his might have appeared among Samuel Johnson's anthology of the blemishes of metaphysical poetry. Watts, as I say, was not always so inspired and adventurous. Like most of the hymnodists his stanzas were mostly short, singable quatrains, with a syntax that perfectly conformed to the simplicity of the verse: the full stops always at the end of the stanza, and often of the individual line—a simple necessity for the untrained voices of a congregation. But Emily Dickinson did not work under those particular compulsions, and she did some violence to them. Here, for example, is a poem about a butterfly, composed to be sure, in quatrains, but with some telling surprises for all that.

> He parts himself like leaves,
> And then he closes up,
> Then stands upon the bonnet
> Of any buttercup,
> And then he runs against

95

And oversets a Rose,
And then does nothing.

                 Then away
Upon a jib he goes,
And dangles like a mote
Suspended in the noon,
Uncertain to return below
Or settle in the moon.
What come of him at night
The privilege to say
Be limited by ignorance.

What come of him that day
The frost possess the world,
In cabinets be shown:
A sepulchre of quaintest floss—
An abbey—a cocoon.

         517

The first full stop here comes in what is metrically (for this is poulter's measure) the midst of the seventh line with "And then does nothing." Or another way to describe the effect is to say that the first sentence runs to six and one-half lines, the next five and one-half, the next three, and the last five; so that nowhere in the poem does the syntax conform to the quatrain. I have not found a comparable freedom among the hymns. In addition to poulter's measure, the measure of

        I lothe that I did love,
        In youth that I thought swete:
        As time requires for my behove
        Me thinkes they are not mete,

and the familiar tetrameter quatrains, Emily Dickinson employed various other stanza forms and line lengths. There is one stanzaic pattern she uses a number of times that interests me especially.

Bring me the sunset in a cup,
Reckon the morning's flagons up
And say how many Dew,
Tell me how far the morning leaps—
Tell me what time the weaver sleeps
Who spun the breadths of blue!

128

Into this Port, if I might come,
Rebecca, to Jerusalem,
Would not so ravished turn—
Nor Persian, baffled at her shrine
Lift such a Crucifixial sign
To her imperial Sun.

506

I am obliged to admit that the hymnals, and Dr. Watts himself, exhibit this form; but I prefer to think that Emily Dickinson might have come upon it in an anthology of religious poetry, and in the incarnation of a poem of which these are two stanzas.

Rich almonds colour to the prime
For adoration; tendrils climb,
And fruit trees pledge their gems:
And Ivis with her gorgeous vest
Builds for her eggs a cunning nest
And bell-flowers bow their stems.

. . . .

But stronger still, in earth and air,
And in the sea, the man of prayer;
And far beneath the tide;
And in the seat to faith assigned
Where ask is have, where seek is find,
Where knock is open wide.

(Christopher Smart, "A Song to David")

97

The Riddles of Emily Dickinson

There has, of course, been a good deal of investigation into, and speculation upon, her reading; and a number of influences upon her work now seem almost inarguable. Of these, one of the strongest and most recognizable is George Herbert.

> Where Thou art—that—is Home—
> Cashmere—or Calvary—the same—
> Degree—or Shame—
> I scarce esteem Location's Name—
> So I may Come—
>
> What Thou dost—is Delight—
> Bondage as Play—be sweet—
> Imprisonment—Content—
> And Sentence—Sacrament—
> Just We Two—meet—
>
> Where Thou art not—is Wo—
> Tho' Bands of Spices—row—
> What Thou dost not—Despair—
> Tho' Gabriel—praise me—Sir—
>
> 725

The carefully balanced rhetorical and syntactical structure of this poem is far nearer Herbert's practice than Emily Dickinson's. The two initial five-line stanzas, each beginning with its topic phrase—"Where Thou art"; "What Thou dost"—followed in each case by a series of paradoxes; the inverted or negative versions of the topic phrases—"Where Thou art not"; "What Thou dost not"—each followed by a noun that represents the opposite of the corresponding noun in the positive version—for Home, Wo; for Delight, Despair—compressed into a quatrain, this neatness and intricacy of form, together with the intimacy of address, strongly suggests the Herbert influence. And her poem " 'Unto Me?' I do not know you—" (968) seems to me directly indebted to Herbert's "Love."

From her antecedents let me turn to her descendants, who

are more numerous and various than you might at first think.
Richard Wilbur has honorably confessed to burglaries from
her work. And it is hard for me to believe that the following,
by Theodore Roethke, would have been written without her
practice to emulate.

> Thought does not crush to stone.
> The great sledge drops in vain.
> Truth never is undone;
> Its shafts remain.
>
> The teeth of knitted gears
> Turn slowly through the night,
> But the true substance bears
> The hammer's weight.
>
> Compression cannot break
> A center so congealed;
> The tool can chip no flake;
> The core lies sealed.

I think I detect in some of her comic and ironic poetry (in
1461 and 1207) notes of impertinence and attitudes that I encounter also in the work of Robert Frost. But I should like to
make the claim for a couple of even unlikelier candidates:
W. H. Auden and E. E. Cummings. We have the testimony of
Christopher Isherwood that some of Auden's early poetry was
influenced by hers, and I find these lines of hers strikingly like
some of Auden's early work. This is about a child.

> Credits the world—
> Deems His Dominions
> Broadest of Sovereignties—
> And Caesar—mean—
> In the Comparison—
> . . . . . .
> Grown bye and bye
> To hold mistaken

The Riddles of Emily Dickinson

> His pretty estimates
> Of Prickly Things
> He gains the skill
> Sorrowful—as certain—
> Men to anticipate
> Instead of Kings—
>
> 637

The dimeter line, the widely spaced rhymes, elision of articles, inversions, these were all early Auden trademarks. And as for Cummings, hear this:

> Love—is that later Thing than Death—
> More previous than life
> Confirms it at it's entrance—And
> Usurps it—of itself
>
> 924

Surely there is an intimate connection between these lines of Emily Dickinson's and the following by Cummings.

> love is more thicker than forget
> more thinner than recall
> more seldom than a wave is wet
> more frequent than to fail

I adduce these foster children with no litigious motives, but merely to demonstrate that her own work was far more various in its styles and forms than is commonly supposed. And even with regard to her regular tetrameter quatrains, I would claim, with Robert Frost, that "The possibilities for tune from the dramatic tones of meaning struck across the rigidity of a limited meter are endless."

Her vocabulary. I have already alluded to the grand abstractions which so often appear in her work. In addition there is a gorgeous display of the exotic, balanced with or contrasted to the domestic and homely. Her exotic treasures come under the headings of jewels, cloths, colors, geography, cartography, military and buccaneer adventure, the great hierarchy of heavenly and earthly nobility, marine and maritime imagery, and the enormous presence of the sea in the work of a poet who hardly ever saw it—a sea laden with argosies, armadas, navies and pirates, galleons and treasures, and catastrophic death. The domestic would include nineteenth-century colloquial diction, such as "don't" for "doesn't," houses, rooms, clothing, sewing, planting, harvesting, legal phraseology, seasons, weather, and, in far greater abundance than almost any poet I can think of, money; money as reward, investment, mortgage, tax, gain and loss at the hands of that "Burglar, Banker, Father," who, in the words of the liturgy, giveth and taketh away.

And now let me address my topic a little more narrowly. In a letter to Thomas Wentworth Higginson, dated April 25, 1862, Emily Dickinson, undertaking, rather evasively and with a modesty not easy to evaluate, to describe herself, to give some personal characteristics, to identify herself to a correspondent she had never met, wrote that "for several years my lexicon was my only companion." This is the letter in which she identifies her "books": Keats, Mr. & Mrs. Browning, Ruskin, Sir Thomas Browne, and the Revelations. We know that her reading was far wider, and not always so high-class; Harvard has her annotated books, and a good deal of study has, very fittingly, gone into them.

But it is to that lexicon of hers I wish to return. For it seems to me that one of her characteristic poetic strategies is the poem conceived of as "definition," as a lexicographic undertaking which formulates and identifies.

A fascination with words, with assemblages of words, with the dictionary process of "definition," that attempt at precision and uniqueness which must sometimes acknowledge the equivocal and the moot, these are scarcely remarkable in a poet. Nor does it require an unusual imagination to conceive

of "definition" as metaphor, as metonymy, the giving or
changing of names, an equation of which one part is the name
for something, and the other part the solution to its mystery
and identity, to see the dictionary as itself a kind of poetry,
perhaps a very fundamental kind. Think for example of such
poems of hers as "Hope is a strange invention" (1392); "Faith
is the pierless bridge" (915); "Remorse is memory" (744).
These are what I should call exemplary poems of definition:
they are solutions to problems of scrutiny or meditation, the
answers to riddles, attempts to identify things, and to give
those things their identities, as Emily Dickinson was undertaking to do for herself in her letter to Higginson. "Identity"
is a complicated word in any case, and particularly so in connection with Emily Dickinson. It means either something singular, "intrinsic," unique and irreplaceable, as is, for example,
the human soul in the sight of God or of Love; or it means precisely the opposite—things are identical that can stand for or
replace one another. Masks, in fact. Personae. Emily Dickinson used not a few of them, and the voice or the guise of a small
girl was only one. There are a number of her poems in which
the speaker is obviously male, and a certain group of critics
have elected to make much of this. There is a poem in which I
think the speaker is Christ, and the speaker of another is God.

In preparation for this paper I have devoted my attention
almost entirely to Emily Dickinson's poems. I made a personal
selection of those I liked best, as well as those that might best
serve the topic's purposes, and the two groups coincided in a
sufficiently reassuring way. For it became increasingly my
conviction the more I read that "riddles" of identity, of voice,
of definition, abounded in her work as almost a technique.
And whatever psychological gratifications they may have had
for her, they had the sanction not only of her dictionary but of
her Bible.

The grand one is, of course, the Bible, not only for many an
ultimate riddle, but containing many diverse riddles, them-

selves richly compounded by controversies of doctrine and commentary, of which Emily Dickinson seems to have been sufficiently aware. A second and humbler one is that body of children's fairy tales and verse which we also know her to have had some acquaintance with, for she refers to some of it in her letters. And I should like to deal with the humbler one first.

The best known verses of "Mother Goose" date from the eighteenth century and before. It is a literature that abounds in riddles, and for my present purposes I wish to do no more than recall some characteristic examples. There are explicit riddles, formulated as questions to which answers are expected.

> As I was going to St. Ives
> I met a man with seven wives,
> Each wife had seven sacks,
> Each sack had seven cats,
> Each cat had seven kits;
> Kits, cats, sacks, and wives,
> How many were going to St. Ives?

To which, of course, the answer is, "one," the speaker. But not all such riddles take the shape of questions; they are preponderantly enigmatic statements, requiring interpretation. Were Tenniel's drawings not so familiar to all of us, it might not be so utterly transparent that Humpty Dumpty, whom all the king's horses and all the king's men could not reassemble, was a broken egg.

> How many miles to Babylon?
> Three score miles and ten.
> Can I get there by candle-light?
> Yes, and back again.

As soon as we recognize that Babylon is "baby-land," and that the three score and ten miles are the three score and ten years biblically allotted to the lifespan of man, the enigma disappears, and we have a little runic statement about the pilgrimage of life from the first childhood to the second, with a strong memento mori flavor of life's brevity. And here is another which might, superficially, appear to be about the same topic.

> Solomon Grundy,
> Born on Monday,
> Christened on Tuesday,
> Married on Wednesday,
> Took ill on Thursday,
> Worse on Friday,
> Died on Saturday,
> Buried on Sunday,
> And that was the end of
> Solomon Grundy.

Commentators have remarked that this verse is no more than a mnemonic device to teach small children the names of the days of the week. But I am inclined to suspect that it is something more; that it is in fact an account of the diet of a poor family, obliged to budget out carefully over the space of a whole week a single salmagundi stew.

Let me turn now to the Scriptures; specifically to the fourteenth chapter of the book of Judges.

And Samson said unto them, I will now put forth a riddle unto you. . . . And he said unto them, Out of the eater came forth meat, and out of the strong came forth sweetness. And they could not in three days expound the riddle.

That riddle of the lion and the honeycomb was more subtle and complicated than even Samson knew at the time he asked it. It was a riddle he was to solve for good and all only at the end of his life, through pain, humiliation and self-sacrifice. It may be the most famous of biblical riddles, yet it is only one of many, and of many biblical references to riddles.

> Son of man, put forth a riddle, and speak a parable unto the house of Israel; . . .
>
> (Ezekiel 17:2)

> I will open my mouth in a parable: I will utter dark sayings of old:
> Which we have heard and known, and our fathers have told us.
>
> (Psalms 78:2–3)

The Queen of Sheba apparently tested the wisdom of Solomon by means of riddles which are not recorded (I Kings, 10) but the book of Proverbs contains a good number of riddles, along with the answers to them. These appear not infrequently as paradoxes, (common enough in Emily Dickinson's poetry) and as answers to such questions as "What is like X?" or "Why is X like Y?" Such questions are, by their very nature, near the heart of metaphor, implying, as they do, correspondences that we are challenged to recognize, or that we are urged to meditate upon.

> The Horseleach hath two daughters, crying, Give, give.
> There are three things that are never satisfied, yea,
> four things say not, It is enough.
> The grave; and the barren womb; the earth that is not
> filled with water; and the fire that saith not, It is enough.
>
> (Proverbs 30:18–19)

> There be four things which are little upon the earth,
> but they are exceeding wise.
> The ants are a people not strong,
> yet they prepare their meat in the summer;
> The conies are but a feeble folk,
> yet they make their houses in the rocks;

The locusts have no king,
yet they go forth all of them by bands;
The spider taketh hold with her hands,
and is in kings' palaces.

(Proverbs 30:24–28)

I close this brief list with a paradox.

Answer not a fool according to his folly,
lest thou also be like unto him.
Answer a fool according to his folly,
lest he be wise in his own conceit.

(Proverbs 26:4–5)

Let me point directly at two poems of Emily Dickinson's that seem, at least to me, to bear intimate family resemblances to the two models I have posited.

Who is the East?
The Yellow Man
Who may be Purple if He can
That carries in the Sun.
Who is the West?
The Purple Man
Who may be Yellow if He can
That lets Him out again.

1032

This is neither a compelling poem nor a very complex riddle, but I submit that in its formal and personified presentation of sunrise and sunset it might easily be mistaken for a "Mother Goose" rhyme. And here is a poem which imitates, as I think, some of the formal principles of the riddles in the Book of Proverbs that I just cited.

Some things that fly there be—
Birds—Hours—the Bumblebee—
Of these no Elegy.

The Riddles of Emily Dickinson

> Some things that stay there be—
> Grief—Hills—Eternity—
> Nor this behooveth me.
>
> There are that resting, rise.
> Can I expound the skies?
> How still the Riddle lies!
>   89

Let me labor, for a moment, the parallels to the Proverbs: the general statement that there are certain unnamed "things" that share a common characteristic, that are never satisfied or that fly; that statement stands for the "question" which will be answered by the list, the discontinuous series, which will not only satisfy the conditions of the so-called question, or initial statement, but redefine it—sometimes through puns or double meanings. So "fly" in the first line means both "perish" and "take wing." But the first two tercets about things impermanent and permanent, riddling and surprising as they are, are merely preliminary riddles to contrast with the insoluble paradox of the last stanza, which I presume refers to the souls who have seen "salvation." The last line is a riddle all by itself, and may refer either to the soul or to God. In either case, it seems to insist that the living are denied any sure sign of their own salvation.

The word "Riddle" itself appears in some four or five of her poems, but rather than discuss those, let me turn instead to her more familiar riddling practice. These are poems which either provide their own surprising answers, or in which we are challenged to identify a thing metaphorically described. Most commonly the "answer" was omitted altogether, though sometimes the poems accompanied gifts (a cocoon, a pine needle, some apples) which were themselves the subject of the poem and the answer to its riddle. So abundant are examples of this kind of poem in her work that I shall do no more than list a few representative ones and their answers.

The Riddles of Emily Dickinson

It sounded as if the Streets were running (1397)—a gale
She slept beneath a tree (25)—a flower
It sifts from Leaden Sieves (311)—snow
The Guest is gold and crimson (15)—sunset
A route of Evanescence (1463)—a hummingbird
A Narrow Fellow in the Grass (986)—a snake
A Visitor in Marl (391)—frost
He fumbles at your Soul (315)—the wind

Lovely as some of these poems are, ingenious or powerful in their descriptive or imaginative language as they may be, I wish instead to examine a few others that seem to me both more puzzling and more interesting.

> The Soul selects her own Society—
> Then—shuts the Door—
> To her divine Majority—
> Present no more—
>
> Unmoved—she notes the Chariots—pausing—
> At her low Gate—
> Unmoved—an Emperor be kneeling
> Upon her Mat—
>
> I've known her—from an ample nation—
> Choose one—
> Then—close the Valves of her attention—
> Like Stone—

303

This poem is not usually conceived of as a riddle, but rather as a description of those instinctive preferences and choices, those defiantly nonrational elections and allegiances, like love, that we all make, without regard to personal advantage, to rank or to estate. To the degree that the poem has been construed as a private and guarded revelation of the poet's emotional life, and to some circumstantial events in it, there is a dispute about whether the choice of "one" means someone else or the poet herself; whether she is electing the solitude of a society of one, or committing herself to another. And it is not out of place, I think, to construe the poem as being about love. The mixed metaphor of the last two lines ("Then close the valves of her attention/Like stone") could be rather comfortably resolved if we substituted "heart" for "soul," since hearts can be "stony" and they have valves.

But I suggest that the power of this poem derives from a suppressed riddle, an unstated but implied parallel. As the soul is to its society (absolute, arbitrary, ruthless) so is God in His election and salvation of souls. Moreover, it seems to me that the second stanza not improbably suggests the adoration of the Magi, though I have no care to press that point. Still, the ominous quality of the final words is considerably amplified when the ultimate mystery of election is taken into account. We play at being God; it is characteristically human of us to do so.

> Tell all the Truth but tell it slant—
> Success in Circuit lies
> Too bright for our infirm Delight
> The Truth's superb surprise
> As Lightning to the Children eased
> With explanation kind
> The Truth must dazzle gradually
> Or every man be blind—
>
> 1129

Again, this poem has been read as an instance of Emily Dickinson's deliberate tact and poetic strategy "in a generation which did not permit her, without the ambiguity of the riddle, to 'tell all the truth' . . . she early learned that 'success in circuit lies.' " I cannot disprove that notion, nor do I feel obliged to; but the poem seems to me to have a good deal of

religious significance that such a statement inclines altogether
to flout.

> And it came to pass on the third day in the morning, that
> there were thunders and lightning and thick clouds upon
> the mount. . . . And the Lord said unto Moses, Go down,
> charge the people, lest they break through unto the Lord
> to gaze, and many of them perish.
>
> (Exodus 19:16–21)

The blinding effect of direct access to the Godhead, which is
to say the Truth (except in the case of selected few, and Moses
one of them), has been a commonplace of religious poetry from
long before Emily Dickinson to our own century. And there is
what might be called a New Testament version of the same
idea. Jesus has just told his followers the parable of the sower
and the seed:

> And he said unto them, He that hath ears to hear,
> let him hear. And when he was alone, they that
> were about him with the twelve asked of him the
> parable.
> And he said unto them, Unto you is given to know
> the mystery of the kingdom of God: but unto them
> that are without, all these things are done in
> parables.
>
> (Mark 4:9–11)

Christ himself has been seen as that human manifestation of
the Godhead which allows all men to look upon that Truth
which would otherwise be blinding. Milton clearly has such a
meditating notion in mind in the "Nativity Ode."

> That glorious form, that light unsufferable,
> And that far-beaming blaze of majesty,
> Wherewith he wont at Heaven's high council-table
> To sit the midst of Trinal Unity,

He laid aside; and here with us to be,
Forsook the courts of everlasting day,
And chose with us a darksome house of mortal clay.

The same idea is, as I understand it, somewhat blasphe-
mously paralleled by John Donne in "The Extasie," in which,
like Christ undergoing human incarnation, the Truth and the
Word becoming flesh, so must the pure lovers' "souls descend/
T'affections and to faculties," and he continues, "To our bodies
turne we then, so that/Weak men on love revealed may look."
   I am not asserting an influence of either Milton or Donne on
Emily Dickinson. I am, however, convinced that the success
that lies in circuit, that dictates that all the truth must be told,
but told slant, has behind it the authority of both the Old and
New Testament: that parables, riddles, the Incarnation itself
are but aspects of a Truth we could not comprehend without
their mediation.

> As if some little Arctic flower
> Upon the polar hem—
> Went wandering down the Latitudes
> Until it puzzled came
> To continents of summer—
> To firmaments of sun—
> To strange, bright crowds of flowers—
> And birds, of foreign tongue!
> I say, As if this little flower
> To Eden, wandered in—
> What then? Why nothing,
> Only, your inference therefrom!
>
> 180

"All virtue in 'as if,' " wrote Robert Frost, in parody of
Falstaff, and about some lines by Edward Arlington Robinson.
And here the same words shyly amplify, or multiply, the in-
ferences that might be drawn from this curious, cryptic little

poem. Half of a comparison has been omitted, and we are invited to supply the missing part by careful attention to what is given. Yet we are on very uncertain ground: the poem is conversationally casual, reticent, and daring in the double sense of boldness and challenge.

I find at least two ways to read the poem, which are not mutually exclusive, and which may neither of them be right. One may suppose, to begin with, that "Arctic flower" is itself a metaphoric description for something like an Indian Pipe, one of those curious white plants or flowers that have no chlorophyl or pigmentation, that are identifiable interlopers among the more familiar plants of summer, and that are, as it happens, rather rare. One may further surmise that Emily Dickinson, who had adopted a white habit, who had written of her "white election," who was "different" from virtually everyone she knew, could, without great strain, have identified with such a flower. In which case, the poem appears to be about a state of beatitude on the part of one who might have thought herself exempt from it, given the outward signs. And the daring consists in the almost explicit claim to having found salvation. So daring a boast would that be that it would have to be said circumspectly. And the poem is all innuendo. All virtue in "as if."

Let me now propose a radically different reading. Thomas Johnson dates the poem "about 1860." This is only a year after the publication of *The Origin of Species*, and I have no safe grounds to suppose that Emily Dickinson entertained any notions whatever about theories of evolution at this stage of her life, though she clearly knew of Darwin and his work at some point. But let us suppose that the poem is in fact about the evolutionary process of survival with regard to the flower. How but by chance, patience, strength and mystery has it persisted to arrive at last in an alien, Edenic climate? And if a single human soul were like that flower, how uncertain its election to God's grace, how mysterious and chancy its survival, how very long and ruthless is the process by which many might be called but few are chosen. This second reading is far less complacent than the first. But Emily Dickinson was capable of adopting so many attitudes and tones toward her immortal longing that we cannot confirm or deny anything by appealing to other poems of hers.

> I read my sentence—steadily—
> Reviewed it with my eyes,
> To see that I made no mistake
> In its extremest clause—
> The Date, and manner, of the shame—
> And then the Pious Form
> That "God have mercy" on the Soul
> The jury voted Him—
> I made my soul familiar—with her extremity—
> That at the last, it should not be a novel Agony—
> But she, and Death, acquainted—
> Meet tranquilly, as friends—
> Salute, and pass, without a Hint
> And there, the Matter ends.
>
> 412

We have here a small drama, with its peripeteia, and with a surprisingly large cast, all of whom but one are versions or facets or personae of the poet. There is a judge, an Accused, a clergyman, the soul of the Accused, and Death. And all of them but the soul are male. Moreover, it is the soul and Death who, in the course of the drama, overturn the entire "official" proceedings, and turn out to be cooperative friends, when the mortal and judicial world had counted upon them to be enemies. I take the first eight lines to be spoken by the persona as judge pronouncing sentence on the Accused (who is, of course, part of the same person) and pronouncing that sentence with a chilling jest which seems to doubt that the malefactor could possess such a thing as a soul, though one must ceremoniously take account of the jury's expression of compassion ("and may God have mercy on his soul")—much as officers in the United States Army are made "gentlemen" by an act of Congress. The tone is lofty, inflexibly cool, and slightly jesting. I take the next lines to be no more unbending but clearly more compassionate.

> I made my soul familiar—with her extremity—
> That at the last, it should not be a novel Agony—

This is the office of the clergyman, to prepare the Accused to face the inevitable, and at least to spare him the additional terror of uncertainty or the unexpected. It is a more charitable tone than the judge's, and altogether lacking in his judicial contempt. But these two, the judge and the clergyman, are mere mortals. The immortals have an understanding which makes a mockery of the trial. As such, it is a little allegorical pageant, but it also clearly speaks of a mind frighteningly divided, without an external orthodoxy to appeal to or to judge by, the nightmarish solipsism of the lonely who must work out their salvation without help or tradition. And the light-hearted comradeship of the soul and Death at the end may not be so light-hearted after all.

I want to deal with one more poem (568) and I beg leave to approach it slowly, stanza by stanza. Here is the first of the three stanzas.

> We learned the Whole of Love—
> The Alphabet—the Words—
> A Chapter—then the mighty Book—
> Then—Revelation closed—

There will be nothing to come in the poem that will firmly determine for us whether the first word here, "We," refers to two people or to a larger group, a community, a congregation. And I want to suggest that part of the excitement of the poem resides precisely in this uncertainty. In any case, it appears that in this first stanza, "the Whole of Love" may be read as either sexual or spiritual, and that the stanza presents us with an experience of education, of maturation and of growing up, beginning with the most elementary units and graduating from alphabet to words to chapter to book. The last line, "Then—Revelation closed," is ambiguous, depending on whether we suppose the poet to have used an inversion or not—and inversions are common enough in her practice. The difference, though slight, seems important. If the word order is inverted, then the subject of the verb, "closed," is the "We" of the first line; and the sense is that "We" have completed a sort of education from beginning to end. But if the word order is "normal," there is a far more moot and edgy sense to the stanza: we read through the great book, or we grew up, or we made discovery upon discovery, and then revelation ceased. These two alternatives, which, in a rough way, incline to exclude each other, are maintained in the second stanza.

> But in Each Other's eyes
> An Ignorance beheld—
> Diviner than the Childhood's—
> And each to each, a Child—

If we conceive the first stanza to be about a species of education, the second stanza seems to suggest that the "We" who were educated either learned and understood or did not learn and understand. It seems to me very probable that a reference is intended here to a familiar passage in the Gospels.

> Suffer the little children to come unto me, and forbid them not: for of such is the kingdom of God.
> Verily I say unto you, Whosoever shall not receive the kingdom of God as a little child, he shall not enter therein.
>
> (Mark 10:14–15)

The Riddles of Emily Dickinson

The Christian and pastoral paradox is well known: children, in their sublime innocence and ignorance, are "wiser" than the rest of us, who have been corrupted by worldly wisdom. In order to attain to that original purity, which would allow us to enter into the kingdom of God, or to experience true love, we would have to go through a process of education which would uneducate us, and return us to a perfect state of ignorance. This state is "Diviner than the Childhood's" because consciously and deliberately sought for and attained with the careful patience that begins with the alphabet, instead of being the natural condition of infancy. Still, the poem is playing powerfully with the paradox that the infinitely painstaking efforts of education serve to uneducate. The last stanza:

> Attempted to expound
> What Neither—understood—
> Alas, that Wisdom is so large—
> And Truth—so manifold!

I should guess that a good deal of the tension and success of the poem derives from the double sense of the word "love" in the first line as both eros and agape. And the further paradoxical feeling that the growth or maturation of one of these senses is the necessary annihilation of the other. It is not only that, in the terms of this poem, divine love unfits us for worldly love; it is the further paradox that a perfect understanding of love (which is ignorance) makes love inexpressible, an ineffable mystery, a riddle. In this sense, such "ignorant knowledge" is not unlike, perhaps, the Book of Revelations, which, despite its name, is revelation in the ambiguous sense that what was revealed to Saint John is not absolutely intelligible to us; it is a complicated revealing with its mystery somehow intact. And coming, as it does, at the end of the Bible, as the last chapter of the Book of Love, it both reveals and conceals at once, educates us to ignorance, and leaves us incapable of articulating

The Riddles of Emily Dickinson

the ambiguous love we have striven toward from childhood. The poem seems to me full of awe; and full of frustration.

The scope of these remarks may seem modest or narrow, given the enormous volume and range of Emily Dickinson's work, and might suggest that any grandiose conclusions on my part would be ludicrously out of place. And no doubt the reader will be grateful, in these painful days, to someone who will go out of his way to avoid inflation. But I would want, even minimally, to urge the idea that it was not nineteenth-century debased puritan gentility, nor "tact" as the word is commonly employed, nor lonely eccentricity that accounts for Emily Dickinson's use of riddles. Not ladylike reticence, but rather a religious seriousness, however unorthodox, and a profound sense that neither life itself nor the holy text by which we interpret it is altogether intelligible, and both require a riddling mind or interpretive skill. And that "identity" has something to do with "certainty," in a world where certainties are hard to come by.

Elizabeth Bishop

POETS ARE NOT noticeably free from small envies and petty jealousies, and since, in the United States, they commonly review one another's books, the clannishness of schools and armed camps shows up in reviews that all too often vibrate with snide condescensions, grudging praises, as well as trumpet blasts of embattled wrath. So much is this the rule with us that any exception to it, as in the case of Elizabeth Bishop, is unsettling and not altogether easy to explain. The mystery is not that she should have established her own indisputable independence as a poet who belongs to no school and subscribes to no manifesto, but rather that other poets who never believed they had any common ground whatever are prepared to set aside their small parochialisms in admiration for her art. It is not easy to sort out the qualities in her poetry that call up such uncharacteristic sympathy and generosity from the barbarian hordes. Indeed, so diverse have been the praisers and the grounds of their praise that Miss Bishop has appeared to be all things to all poets.

She has rightly been praised for an eye that misses no detail of the soiled and modest furniture of our lives:

Meanwhile the eighty-watt bulb
   betrays us all,

discovering the concern
within our stupefaction;
lighting as well on heads
of tacks in the wallpaper,
on a paper wall-pocket,
violet-embossed, glistening
   with mica flakes.
     ("Faustina, or Rock Roses")

I looked into his eyes
which were far larger than mine
but shallower, and yellowed,
the irises backed and packed
with tarnished tinfoil
seen through the lenses
of old scratched isinglass.
     ("The Fish")

Or misses very seldom; there are no eighty-watt bulbs. She has
rightly been praised for a Veronese amplitude: all light, color,
and bustle. She has been rightly praised for a Shaker plainness: a strict, almost moral, unwillingness to exaggerate. And
this grandeur and plainness seem vaguely associated—but in
no fixed or exact way—with her settings of "North and South,"
her scenes of Canada and Worcester, Massachusetts, contrasted
with views of the lushness, the sometimes dirty and unkempt
lushness, of Florida and Brazil. Or perhaps the grandeur, the
spaciousness, is nothing but the perfectly natural property of
metaphor, of any straightforward and literal imagination that
could envision the ceiling, for example, as a Place de la Con-
corde, a large, white, cheerful place to sleep beside the central
fountain of the chandelier—a quality of vision that, as in
"Roosters," can move from the homely to the magnificent:

Elizabeth Bishop

A rooster gloats

over our beds
from rusty iron sheds
and fences made from old bedsteads

· · · · ·

glass-headed pins,
oil-golds and copper greens,
anthracite blues, alizarins,

· · · · · ·

Old holy sculpture
could set it all together
in one small scene, past and future:

Christ stands amazed,
Peter, two fingers raised
to surprised lips, both as if dazed.

But in between
a little cock is seen
carved on a dim column in the travertine,

explained by *gallus canit*;
flet Petrus underneath it.
There is inescapable hope, the pivot;

yes, and there Peter's tears
run down our chanticleer's
sides and gem his spurs.

with its surprising formal echoes of Crashaw's:

Who ere she bee,
That not impossible shee
That shall command my heart and mee;

Where ere she lye,
Lock'd up from mortal Eye,
In shady leaves of Destiny

120

Elizabeth Bishop

For Miss Bishop, the homely and the grand are quite simply obvious extensions of one another. Maps are themselves a species of metaphor, and in Miss Bishop's cartography the familiar pastels of pink and green and yellow that indicate different nations are at the same time stunningly adequate and colloquial metaphors for the slums and cathedrals, the poverty and the art galleries, the grime, the pain, and the triumphs that inhabit down there next to the surface, if we will but use her magnifying lens. Her language is so natural and unforced that her immense skill is all the more astonishing in its apparent effortlessness.

But while happily conceding all these claims, I should still want to attribute the particular spell of her work to another grace. Hers is a poetry, though in no very obvious way, of isolation and loneliness, without either the stoicism and desolation of Hardy or the wistfulness and self-mockery of Philip Larkin. Instead, there is an infinitely touching valor, a gallantry that is the more impressive because it is maintained in full knowledge of the odds against it, and with a breath-taking cheerfulness. In fact, one of her poems concludes:

> All the untidy activity continues,
> awful but cheerful.

It is a poem subtitled "On my birthday," all sight and sound, bristling with vivid tones and activities of machines and creatures, but without a single human except the viewer-narrator. Once, with a levity it was difficult to gauge, Miss Bishop remarked that "awful but cheerful" may have been the best line she ever wrote. Many of her poems, in any case, are about the isolated ("The Unbeliever," "The Weed," "The Fish," "The Burglar of Babylon," and "The Prodigal" are only conspicuous examples) and there are poems, like "Faustina," in which the poet speaks remotely about herself in the third person as "the visitor." Or in which ("Sestina" is an example) *absence* is the very center of the poem. Finally, there are poems in which she shyly identifies with crowds or groups of total strangers, as in "A Miracle for Breakfast," "Squatter's Children," and "Filling Station."

I suspect that she would firmly repel any suggestion that she was a "religious" poet, though it is worth pointing out that she was devoted to and influenced by the poetry of George Herbert, and when she was invited, in an anthology called *Preferences*, edited by Richard Howard, to select one representative poem of her own and to match it with a poem she admired by some poet of the past, she chose Herbert's "Love Unknown." The poem of her own for this anthology was "In the Waiting Room," a superb work, possibly picked because it was a recent accomplishment, as well as the fact that it did not resemble Herbert's poem in any very obvious or direct way. But the Herbert influence is detectable when her language is at its most simple, and the explicit influence of "Love Unknown" is virtually undeniable in her poem "The Weed."

The *religious* preoccupation is to be found in such poems as "The Unbeliever," "Roosters," "The Prodigal" (with its detectable influence of the early Lowell), perhaps "Night City," surely "Twelfth Morning; or What You Will," and "A Miracle for Breakfast." This last Miss Bishop wryly secularized by calling it (in an interview, I think) "my Depression, or Bread Line Poem." But however much it may bear on the social calamities of the 'thirties, the central metaphor is clearly that of the Eucharist and the Feeding of the Multitudes. There is, admittedly, a puzzle about just what constitutes the "miracle" in that sestina, and in fact the poem itself seems to repudiate anything miraculous, and do so right at the crucial moment when the miracle is supposed to take place: "I can tell what I saw next; it was not a miracle." What immediately follows has bewildered some readers, for it is, after all, a sudden and unexpected apparition:

Elizabeth Bishop

A beautiful villa stood in the sun
and from its doors came the smell of hot coffee.
In front, a baroque white plaster balcony
added by birds, who nest along the river,
—I saw it with one eye close to the crumb—

and galleries and marble chambers. My crumb
my mansion, made for me by a miracle,
through ages, by insects, birds, and the river
working the stone.

The miracle here I take to be engendered by the minute, close-up inspection of a crumb of bread, handed out in the Bread Line. The complex intricacies of the "architecture" of the risen dough, its baroque perforations, corridors, its struts, ribs and spans of support, all form the "beautiful villa" with its "white plaster balcony." And this bread, and the vision it provides, have come into existence by the miraculous and infinitely patient workings of that evolutionary process that Darwin (one of Miss Bishop's favorite writers) and other naturalists have so painstakingly recorded. The process itself is awesome enough to be characterized, not improperly, as a "miracle," and Miss Bishop is not the only poet to have felt as much.

No less miraculous, I think, is the later poem with a Brazilian setting called "Twelfth Morning; or What You Will."

Like a first coat of whitewash when it's wet,
the thin gray mist lets everything show through:
the black boy Balthazár, a fence, a horse,
    a foundered house,

—cement and rafters sticking from a dune.
(The Company passes off these white but shopworn
dunes as lawns.) "Shipwreck," we say; perhaps
    this is a housewreck.

Elizabeth Bishop

The sea's off somewhere, doing nothing. Listen.
An expelled breath. And faint, faint, faint
(or are you hearing things), the sandpipers'
    heart-broken cries.

The fence, three-strand, barbed-wire, all pure rust,
three dotted lines, comes forward hopefully
across the lots; thinks better of it; turns
    a sort of corner . . .

Don't ask the big white horse, *Are you supposed*
to be inside the fence or out? He's still
asleep. Even awake, he probably
    remains in doubt.

He's bigger than the house. The force of
personality, or is perspective dozing?
A pewter-colored horse, an ancient mixture,
    tin, lead, and silver,

he gleams a bit. But the four-gallon can
approaching on the head of Balthazár
keeps flashing that the world's a pearl, *and I,*
    I am

its highlight! You can hear the water now,
inside, slap-slapping. Balthazár is singing.
"Today's my Anniversary," he sings,
    "the Day of Kings."

This is a stunning poem, set on the Feast of the Epiphany,
which is to say, of Revelation, and like so much of Miss Bishop's poetry, it is concerned with the revelations apprehended
through *seeing* and *hearing.* We see at first as through a
gauze, dimly: through the gray mist, which is like a whitewash, but which eventually, as we, under the guidance of the
poet, persist in looking, lets everything show through. The
poem is, among other things, a *tour de force* of muted tones,

a Whistlerian excursion into the palest spectrum of the palette, Balthazár, of course, excepted. It might even be conceived of as a sort of "Study in Black and White," such as Miss Bishop offered in a quite different form much earlier in her career in the poem called "Cootchie."

Like many another of her poems, this one leaves us uncertain just who is being addressed. Though the command to "Listen" might be taken to be addressed to one or several who are in the company of the poet as she inspects this scene, we know from other poems that she is quite capable of admonishing herself in just such terms, and instructions about not asking questions of the horse are just the sort she inclines to give herself. Part of the intimacy of her tone comes from our sense of these poems as very nearly conversations that she has with herself, and which we are privileged to overhear. This is especially evident in her little asides, usually contained inside parentheses, but not always. They are "second thoughts," self-doubts, and, often, the eruption of a wry humor, as when, in the grease-stained scene of the "Filling Station," she observes that "Somebody waters the plant,/or oils it maybe." In this poem we have the "shipwreck-housewreck" aside, the, as it seems, *self*-inquiry, "are you hearing things," and the comment on "The Company's" practice of passing off dunes under the guise of lawns, a practice that may remind us not only of actual real estate experiences of our own but of that celebrated "development" described in Dickens's *Martin Chuzzlewit*, and called, with simple eloquence, "Eden."

Miss Bishop's strategy, in employing these sometimes light-hearted asides, allows her to mute a tone that may seem to her in danger of becoming too desperate, or to change course to avoid a too explicit emotional crux. For example, in the third stanza, when the admonition comes to "Listen," all we are privileged to hear is "An expelled breath." Is it our own? Is it the poet's? Is it all that can be heard of the distant and silent sea? Whatever it is, it is faint enough to match all the other faintnesses, especially faintnesses of color, that have made up the poem thus far, and it matches the faint (is this really what we are hearing?) "heart-broken cries" of the sandpipers. That tiny note of heart-break is the only intrusion of any such powerful and grievous feeling into the poem; and I think it is not out of place to recall that Miss Bishop's poem called "Sandpiper" describes that bird, with its insistent, narrowly focused attention to the grain of sand right before its beak (not unlike the practice of the poet), as exhibiting "a state of controlled panic." Anyway, immediately after those "heart-broken cries," the tone emphatically becomes jocular, as the fence is described pursuing its capricious and uncertain course—as though that slight approach to deep feeling had better be set aside, avoided as a matter of common courtesy. The heart-break, however, is not out of place in this, as it appears, pale and sterile landscape, with its seeming absence of promise. And yet slowly we come to recognize that the accumulation of pale, bleached, washed-out colors—the mist, the whitewash, the pewter-colored horse, the dunes and foundered house—are, as it were, the muted tones of the palette of a *pearl*, of which the gleaming highlight is the four-gallon can that has been gradually approaching. This can "keeps flashing" a signal, a revelation, that the world itself (in all its pale colorations) is a pearl, and it seems hard to believe we are not expected to recall Matthew 13:45–46,

> Again, the kingdom of heaven is like unto a merchantman seeking goodly pearls:
> Who, when he had found one pearl of great price, went and sold all that he had and bought it.

Moreover, I think we are meant to recall that in many paintings of the Adoration of the Magi, one of the kings is traditionally represented as being black. In this poem, out of the indistinctness, poverty and aridity of the beginning, the king himself, the pearl of great price, and the very sound of the sea (inside the can) arrive, come forward, like an epiphany. It is a beautiful poem.

In *Geography III* all the virtues of eye and ear, of speech and reticence, and of lonely courage are superbly, beautifully in evidence. "In the Waiting Room," for example, is a child's revelatory discovery, made while reading the *National Geographic* magazine in a dentist's office, of the common bond of humanity, pain and death that she shares with everyone in the world. And the discovery is simultaneously a discovery of her identity, her separateness, her isolation. In "Crusoe in England," the hero, home after all his adventures and privations, misses his loneliness, his shipwrecked existence:

> The books
> I'd read were full of blanks;
> the poems—well, I tried
> reciting to my iris-beds,
> "They flash upon that inward eye,
> which is the bliss . . ." The bliss of what?
> One of the first things that I did
> when I got back was look it up.

And there is a wonderful, long poem called "The Moose," which describes a bus trip, a hegira, south from Canada as the light of evening fades upon the decent, impoverished countryside; and, as darkness envelopes the bus, the half-heard voices of soft-spoken strangers become the reassuring sounds of the speaker's, the poet's, settled and imagined past, all the good and all the bad long since assimilated and accepted:

> Talking the way they talked
> in the old featherbed,
> peacefully, on and on,
> dim lamplight in the hall,
> down in the kitchen, the dog
> tucked in her shawl.

The topics covered in that talk in the old featherbed, the faint, distanced conversation, going "peacefully, on and on," only now dimly heard or understood, include all the major calamities (and a few of the triumphs) of human life.

> Grandparents' voices
>
> uninterruptedly
> talking, in Eternity:
> names being mentioned,
> things cleared up finally;
> what he said, what she said,
> who got pensioned;
>
> deaths, deaths and sicknesses;
> the year he remarried;
> the year (something) happened.
> She died in childbirth.
> That was the son lost
> when the schooner foundered.
>
> He took to drink. Yes.
> She went to the bad.
> When Amos began to pray
> even in the store and
> finally the family had
> to put him away.
>
> "Yes . . ." that peculiar
> affirmative. "Yes . . ."
> A sharp, indrawn breath,
> half groan, half acceptance,
> that means "Life's like that.
> We know *it* (also death)."

Miss Bishop's best poems (and she scarcely seems capable of writing any inferior ones) are all utterances of a peculiar affirmative, one that takes into account all the griefs and terrors of existence. *Geography III* as a book contains only ten poems, none unusually long. But ten new poems by Elizabeth Bishop are enough to make a good-sized readership in the United States rejoice in gratitude and pride. Hers is about the finest product our country can offer the world; we have little by other artists that can match it; and it beats our cars and films and soft drinks hollow.

Richard Wilbur

L ET ME TRY to list some of the virtues that distinguish the poetry of Richard Wilbur. First of all, a superb ear (unequalled, I think, in the work of any poet now writing in English) for stately measure, cadences of a slow, processional grandeur, and rich, ceremonial orchestration. His "musicianship" is of so fine and conspicuous a kind that it has often been ignored, and sometimes even mocked by those who are militantly tone-deaf. Next, a philosophic bent and a religious temper, which are by no means the same thing, but which here consort comfortably together. Wit, polish, a formal elegance that is never haughty or condescending, though, again, by those unimpressed by or envious of his skills it is taken for a chilling frigidity. And an unfeigned gusto, a naturally happy and grateful response to the physical beauty of the world, of women, of works of art, landscapes, weather, and the perceiving, constructing mind that tries to know them. But in a way I think most characteristic of all, his is the most kinetic poetry I know: verbs are among his decisively important tools, and his poetry is everywhere a vision of *action*, of motion and performance.

That this is no casual habit but instead deliberate policy can be shown, I think, by the fact that pivotal and energetic verbs so often are placed in a rhyming position, and by that slight but potent musical device call some measured attention to themselves.

> We could believe,
>
> If you told us so, that the white-tailed deer will slip
> Into perfect shade, grown perfectly shy,
> The lark avoid the reaches of our eye,
> The jack-pine lose its knuckled grip
>
> On the cold ledge, and every torrent burn
> As Xanthus once, . . .
>
> ("Advice to a Prophet")

> Or brewed in gulleys, steeped in wells, they spend
> In chilly steam their last aromas, yield
> From shallow hells a revenance of field
> And orchard air. . . .
>
> ("In the Elegy Season")

> For all they cannot share,
> All that the world cannot in fact afford,
> Their loft premises are floored
> With the massed voices of continual prayer.
>
> ("Altitudes")

> Sweet water brims a cockle and braids down
>
> Past spattered mosses, breaks
> On the tipped edge of a second shell, and fills
> The massive third below. It spills
> In threads then from the scalloped rim, and makes

Richard Wilbur

A scrim or summery tent. . . .
> ("A Baroque Wall-Fountain
> in the Villa Sciarra")

remembering how the bed
Of layered rock two miles above my head

Hove ages up and broke
Soundless asunder, when the shrinking skin
Of Earth, blacked out by sun and smoke,
Gave passage to the muddled fire within,
Its crannies flooding with a sweat of quartz,
And lathered magmas out of deep retorts

Welled up, as here, to fill
With tumbled rockmeal, stone-fume, lithic spray,
The dike's brief chasm and the sill.
Weathered until the sixth and human day
By sanding winds and water, scuffed and brayed
By the slow glacier's heel, these forms were made. . . .
> ("On the Marginal Way")

There may be those, viewing the whole enterprise of formal poetry with suspicion or derision, who will suppose that this richness of inflections, this abundance of verbs, has been forced upon the poet by the ruthless exigencies of stanzaic form: the necessity, one way or another, of digging up a rhyme. For those to whom formal poetry is itself unnatural, or archaic, an embarrassed or twisted parlance of one who is self-consciously ill-at-ease holding the floor, any unusual feature of poetry, even its most towering graces, can be thought of as no more than the by-products, the industrial waste, entailed by meter and rhyme; and therefore (in the name of directness, of authenticity, of courage, of any number of Rousseauian virtues that belong exclusively to the underbred and ill-educated) to be deplored as a victimization, as no grace at all but rather a crippled response to life and language. This sort of argument is marvelously self-serving to those who use it. But in any case, there are far too many poets who employ strict formal devices (e.g., Housman, Auden, Graves, Ransom) and in whose work verbs play an almost unnoticed part, to make it plausible to explain this distinctive quality of Wilbur's as no more than an inadvertence over which he had neither choice nor control.

The truth is, if anything, just the opposite. Wilbur has been from the first a poet with a gymnastic sense of bodily agility and control, a delight in the fluencies we all admire in a trained athlete, in the vitality and importance of stamina and focused energy. We are not to be surprised that the poet who can praise

> the dining-car waiter's absurd
> Acrobacy—tipfingered tray like a wind-besting bird
> Plumblines his swinging toes, the sole sure thing
> In the shaken train . . .

should also take it into his head to celebrate the skills of a juggler and the leap of Nijinsky, a Degas dancer, the sinuous and angelic floatings of laundry on a line, the scamper and swirl of blown newspaper, the convening in the air "like a drunken fingerprint" of a flock of birds, even, in the realm of the purely mechanical, a fire truck "blurring to sheer verb" as it rounds a corner. Or that he should write poems called "Running" and "Walking to Sleep."

This delight in nimbleness, this lively sense of coordinated and practiced skill is, first of all, a clear extension of the dexterity the verse itself performs. If it were no more than this it might be suspected for an exercise in that self-approval which, like one of the poet's fountains, patters "its own applause." But of course it is more. Time and again in Wilbur's poems this admirable grace or strength of body is a sign of or symbol for the inward motions of the mind or condition of the soul. Most obviously in "Mind," the very executive operations of the mind correspond to the speed, the passage, the radar intelligence of a bat. But think also how the two contrasted fountains (in the Baroque Fountain poem) represent two alternative postures of the spirit: one of relaxed and worldly grace, the other of strenuous, earth-denying effort. Think, too, of these opening lines:

> As a queen sits down, knowing that a chair will be there,
> Or a general raises his hand and is given the field-glasses,
> Step off assuredly into the blank of your mind.
> Something will come to you. . . .

This poet's recurrent subject is not only the motion of change and transition but how that motion ("In the Elegy Season," "Marginalia," "On the Marginal Way," " 'A World Without Objects Is a Sensible Emptiness,' " "Year's End," "Merlin Enthralled," and "Digging For China" are only random examples) is the very motion of the mind itself.

It is, I think, remarkable that this double fluency, of style and of subject, should be so singularly Wilbur's own, and that his poetry should exhibit so often the most important and best aspects of cinematic film: the observation of things in motion from a viewpoint that can, if it cares to, move with an equal and astonishing grace. But what these poems can do so magnificently that is probably beyond the range of motion pictures is, specifically, a transition, or, rather, a translation, of outward physical action (the bounce of a ball, the heave of a weight, the sprint of a runner) into a condition of the imagination; a dissolving of one realm of reality into another, for which the poem "Merlin Enthralled" might serve as an example. As perhaps these stanzas might also:

> And once my arm was lifted to hew down
>   A cavalier from off his saddle-bow,
> That bore a lady from a leaguer'd town;
>   And then, I know not how,
>
> All those sharp fancies, by down-lapsing thought
>   Stream'd onward, lost their edges, and did creep

Richard Wilbur

Roll'd on each other, rounded, smooth'd and brought
Into the gulfs of sleep.

As it happens, these stanzas are by Tennyson, and I suggest
that they supply a far more likely source for some of Wilbur's
techniques than Hollywood could come up with. The two poets
share an unparalleled musical ear and an enormous sense of
physical vitality. But I think these eight lines worth a little
examination, since I hope to show that they may indicate as
much about Wilbur as about his great Victorian predecessor.
First, the immense variety, ferocity, and activity compressed
within the first three of these eight lines (which, within their
compass of two quatrains contain eleven verbs). The speaker,
armed, in a transitional posture of combat, presumably on
foot, is courageously prepared to challenge a well-seated and,
we may assume, armed horseman—who is either rescuing or,
more likely, abducting a lady from a town under military
siege—as if the whole vast enterprise of war and the fate of
thousands were painted small in the background of a picture
whose main foreground features were the lady and her ab-
ductor on horseback, and the challenging hero. Part of the
huge Delacroix energy of these lines (which could plausibly
remind one of that painter's *The Massacre of Chios*) comes
from the indeterminate antecedent of "That," the first word of
the third line, which can be read as referring to either "saddle-
bow" or "cavalier." But then, after the coiled springs of those
three lines, there follow five of soft, intoxicated swoon. But
they are more than that. As opposed to the compressed action,
alarms and dangers of the first three lines, the swoon here
involves a process of glacial patience and geological refinement, a vast saecular effort of withdrawal, leaving in its wake
a moraine of verbs, like a scatter of heavy boulders come to
rest. It would be easy to believe that these lines and those of
"On the Marginal Way" came out of the same imagination.

Publishers are not always judicious about their dust-jacket

claims, but Wilbur's American publishers have been wise to quote the following from Theodore Roethke's posthumously published notebooks: "Wilbur: can look at a thing, and talk about it beautifully, can turn it over in his mind, and draw truths from a scene, easily and effortlessly (it would seem)—though this kind of writing requires the hardest kind of discipline, it must be remembered. Not a graceful mind—that's a mistake—but a mind of grace, an altogether different and higher thing."

That mind of grace is brilliantly at work in *The Mind-Reader*, and nowhere more than in the title poem, a dramatic monologue of immense poignancy and mastery, which opens with these lines:

> Some things are truly lost. Think of a sun-hat
> Laid for a moment on a parapet
> While three young women—one, perhaps in mourning—
> Talk in the crenellate shade. A slight wind plucks
> And budges it; it scuffs the edge and cartwheels
> Into a giant view of some description:
> Haggard escarpments, if you like, plunge down
> Through mica shimmer to a moss of pines
> Amidst which, here or there, a half-seen river
> Lobs up a blink of light. The sun-hat falls,
> With what free flirts and scoops you can imagine,
> Down through that reeling vista or another,
> Unseen by any, even by you or me.
> It is as when a pipe-wrench, catapulted
> From the jounced back of a pick-up truck, dives headlong
> Into a bushy culvert; or a book
> Whose reader is asleep, garbling the story,
> Glides from beneath a steamer chair and yields
> Its flurried pages to the printless sea.

This deserves to be savored carefully and at length. There is the superb visualization of motion, of diminution into irretrievable distances; but for all the specificity of imagery, the event is all conjectural, hypothetical, the work and motion of the mind itself. The sun-hat is merely proposed as a subject for thought, everything it moves through is contingent ("a giant view of some description:/Haggard escarpments, if you like, . .") as is its own motion ("With what free flirts and scoops you can imagine . . ."). And so, initially, this floating, limpid descent becomes a metaphor for the imagination, the graceful motions of the mind. In this sense, it is part of that important vein of modern poetry, of which Wallace Stevens is one of the grand practitioners, a poetry about poetry. But this is only the beginning. The ease, the smoothness, the very "grace" described in these lines is a grace, a humanity, of their speaker, an old Italian "dipso" who cadges drinks, at a café that is all but his "office," from transient patrons in exchange for his mind-reading act. And he manages with infinite grace and tact to remind us how merciful is that Greek myth which tells us that the dead drink the waters of Lethe, and are immediately blessed with forgetfulness. For, indeed, who could bear, even in life, to say nothing of eternity, to be afflicted with total and perfect recall of all his own failures, his acts of clumsiness and unkindness, his foolish errors and stupidities? Yet it appears that this old man has been singled out for this especial torment. Given the exquisite, interminable anguish of his life, it is not surprising he should seek oblivion in drink, but it is absolutely astonishing that he should be able to address us, his chance patrons, with such affecting civility, such perfect "grace." He is, we recognize quickly, close kin to that tormented insomniac who speaks to himself in Wilbur's earlier poem, "Walking to Sleep."

Splendid as this poem is, it represents only one aspect of a remarkable versatility. One can scarcely hope to do justice to all the skills and excellences here exhibited, so I must resort, weakly, to a sort of list. Few other poets could render so faithfully both the slum-bred, vulgar vitality of a Villon ballade

and the fastidious, well-bred wit of La Fontaine and Voltaire.
And there are the poet's utterly comfortable, colloquial trans-
lations from the modern Russian of Brodsky, Voznesensky,
and Nikolai Morshen. There is a little group of truly funny
poems, of which one in particular, "The Prisoner of Zenda,"
though based on an early version of the film, is fully worthy
of its treatment by Peter Sellers. And there is finally (though
first in the volume) a group of twenty-two lyrics, some of
them as brilliant as anything Wilbur has done. "The Fourth
of July," for example, seems to me to be the best thing by a
native American to have come out of the Bicentennial. But in
this poetic era of arrogant solipsism and limp narcissism—
when great, shaggy herds of poets write only about themselves, or about the casual workings of their rather tedious
minds—it is essential to our sanity, salutary to our humility,
and a minimal obeisance to the truth to acknowledge, with
Wilbur, in poem after poem, but here especially in one called
"The Eye," the vast alterity, the "otherness" of the world, that
huge corrective to our self-sufficiency. The poem is about the
pleasures, the dangers, the temptations merely of "looking,"
and it ends with a prayer addressed to St. Lucy that concludes:

> Forbid my vision
> To take itself for a curious angel.
> Remind me that I am here in body,
> A passenger, and rumpled.
>
> Charge me to see
> In all bodies the beat of spirit,
> Not merely the *tout en l'air*
> Or double pike with layout
>
> But in the strong
> Shouldering gait of the legless man,
> The calm walk of the blind young woman
> Whose cane touches the curbstone.

Richard Wilbur

Correct my view
That the far mountain is much diminished,
That the fovae is prime composer,
That the lid's closure frees me.

Let me be touched
By the alien hands of love forever,
That this eye not be folly's loophole
But giver of due regard.

The Merchant of Venice:
A Venture in Hermeneutics

> *Whoever judges of the Jewish religion by its coarser
> forms will misunderstand it. It is to be seen in the
> Holy Bible, and in the tradition of the prophets,
> who have made it plain enough that they did not
> interpret the law according to the letter. So our re-
> ligion is divine in the Gospel, in the Apostles, and in
> tradition; but it is absurd in those who tamper
> with it.*
>
> *The Messiah, according to the carnal Jews, was to
> be a great temporal prince. Jesus Christ, according
> to carnal Christians, has come to dispense us from
> the love of God, and to give us sacraments which
> shall do everything without our help. Such is not
> the Christian religion, nor the Jewish. True Jews
> and true Christians have always expected a Messiah
> who should make them love God, and by that love
> triumph over their enemies.*
>
> PASCAL, *Pensées*, 606
>
> *A merchant, Stephen said, is one who buys cheap
> and sells dear, jew or gentile, is he not?*
>
> JAMES JOYCE, *Ulysses*

T HIS ESSAY addresses a select set of questions about
The Merchant of Venice. I do not suppose they are the
only questions, nor am I under the impression that I am the
first to consider any of them. But it is my contention that how-

ever discrete and unrelated the questions themselves may appear, the answers I have found constitute an intricate web that is the seamless fabric of the meaning and integrity of the play itself. What I hope to supply is not an "interpretation," which can be set beside other "interpretations," and found more or less satisfactory than they. I am aiming at making an unassailable case in behalf of my answers to the questions I deal with, and these are frankly bold and apodictic.

Here are the questions I want to answer:

1) *The Merchant of Venice* is listed in the First Folio edition among the comedies, but throughout a large part of the eighteenth century and after it was played as a tragedy. Modern productions exhibit a distinct sense of embarrassment and indecisiveness in their confused attempts to arrive at the proper "tone" and "intention" of the play. While it may be claimed that some of the "problem plays" are equally unsettling in their effects, none of them presents quite the same teetering history of interpretation. Why should this be?

2) The "merchant" of the title, Antonio, seems to have been assigned the most passive, ill-defined, and generally uninteresting role in the entire play; Gratiano and Morocco are miracles of characterization in comparison. And when great actors, from Kean to Olivier, elect to appear in the play it is always in Shylock's part, never Antonio's. Macbeth, Hamlet, Coriolanus are indisputably the vigorous and potent central figures of the plays of which they are the titular characters. Why, then, should this play be named for a character who has consistently aroused so little interest?

3) What is the meaning of Antonio's line, which is also the first line in the play: "In sooth I know not why I am so sad"?

4) What is the *real* motive behind Shylock's contract for a pound of Antonio's flesh?

5) What sort of sense are we to make of the last will and testament of Portia's father that could so perilously and ca-

priciously bind his daughter's fate without regard to her own wishes, and according to the rules of a game so apparently frivolous?

6) On what grounds if any can we accept the notion that Portia, a very intelligent but manifestly uninstructed girl, could successfully solve a legal dilemma that appears to have baffled the Duke and his court, and just what *is* the solution she furnishes?

These are my questions, and I believe that the answer to any one of them bears intimately upon the answers to all the others. This, of course, presents expository problems, so that what follows will not take up each question in turn and deal with it till the topic is covered. Yet even though my procedure is less orderly, I hope to be conclusive. But of course it should be clear to the reader that the outline of my aims and purposes as I have just given them means that there are important aspects of the play I shall not be dealing with. There will be no discussion here of such sources of plot materials as *Dolopathos, or the King and the Seven Sages*, the *Cursor Mundi*, Giovanni Fiorentino's *Il Pecorone*, or Gregorio Leti's *Vita di Sisto V*. A brief account of their importance is usefully furnished in *The Jew in the Medieval World* by Jacob R. Marcus (Atheneum, 1969), and relevant portions of a number of these sources appear in the appendices of the Arden edition of the play, edited by John Russell Brown. Too little attention is confessedly paid here to the play's language, to its imagery, to the personal inflections of the speech of individual characters. These matters are important, and the reader should be advised that my neglect of them is a sacrifice I have made in the name of concentrating on what I regard as a search for the play's hidden architecture, its secret skeletal structure.

Let me begin with my third question, regarding Antonio's first line. The play furnishes no distinct explanation for what troubles Antonio, though some odd surmises have been proposed. But before the surmises of the commentators, there are the surmises of Salerio and Solanio, to whom Antonio is speaking. The first suggests that Antonio's melancholy must be connected with money, and the precariousness of his commercial ventures; the second suggests that he must be "in love." Antonio decisively denies both of these conjectures, but in themselves they serve to introduce an insistent binary set of themes that this play dwells upon with remarkable emphasis, so it will not be out of place to take note of them here. Antonio's two friends are pairing love and money as the general, most common causes of unhappiness. Love and money will continue in intimate relationship throughout the play. They are, however, only one set of such pairs that need to be noticed, others being: Venice/Belmont; Old Testament/New Testament; Jew/Gentile; Justice/Mercy; appearance/reality; the letter of the law/the spirit of the law; and, finally, comedy/tragedy.

Antonio dismisses both love and money as the cause of his sadness, and the play furnishes no other explicit account for it. So a number of commentators have proposed that Antonio is here covertly referring to a thwarted and unreciprocated homoerotic passion for Bassanio that can never be consummated because Bassanio is so incorrigibly heterosexual. Critics who maintain this thesis, which I flatly reject, have several kinds of "evidence" to bring forward. There is, first of all, the evidence within the play itself: Antonio speaks of his "love" for Bassanio, and others, including Portia, speak of it; it is in several ways exhibited, by risk of life and the loan of money. The two speeches by Salerio and Solanio that conclude Act II, scene viii, seem confirmatory of a very intense and exclusive kind of passion; Antonio's letter (Act III, scene ii) that concludes, "If your love do not persuade you to come, let not my letter," and the extraordinary comment of Antonio's when the trial is over, urging Bassanio to reward the lawyer who settled the case with the gift of Portia's ring ("My Lord Bassanio, let him have the ring./Let his deservings, and my love withal,/ Be valued 'gainst your wife's commandèment"), seem virtually to set up heterosexual and homosexual passions as rivals, and to require Bassanio to choose between them. To these internal factors, along with some others, such critics add that this theme of unrequited homosexual passion is clearly present in the sonnets, and can be shown to be an obsession to which Shakespeare reverts in various ways as different as Hamlet's relation to Horatio, and Iago's to both Cassio and Othello, as well as in all the "transvestite comedies," like *As You Like It*, in which Rosalind, a girl played by a boy actor, disguises herself, and then, in the garb of a boy, invites Orlando to pretend that he is a girl, and to proceed to woo him as if he were Rosalind: "Come, woo me, woo me; for I am in a holiday humor and like enough to consent."

As I said, I reject such arguments, but for the moment I can only present my case contingently; by which I mean, my answer to this question will in the end have to rely not only on the evidence for or against itself, but on how well this answer supports and confirms the answers to the other questions I have asked. For the present, I want to propose that Antonio's sadness relates to an intuition, obscure and unformulated at the start, about life itself and his own life in particular: about what may be called Fate or Fortune as it presides in the world of this play. The goddess Fortuna is in a way the regnant pagan deity of the play (though I hasten to add that this, along with *Lear* and *Measure For Measure*, is one of the most explicitly scriptural of Shakespeare's plays). The economic fate of all merchants like Antonio rests upon such chance and caprice as is represented by the goddess; and her gold-encrusted figure, mounted above a golden globe, was affixed in the seventeenth century as a weathervane, capriciously turned by whatever wind prevailed, upon the top of the Customs House, that mansion of commercial authority, at the very entrance to the Grand Canal.

After rejecting both love and money as the causes of his sadness, Antonio declares,

The Merchant of Venice: *A Venture in Hermeneutics*

> I hold the world but as the world, Gratiano—
> A stage where every man must play a part,
> And mine a sad one.

And Gratiano replies,

> Let me play the fool!

The whole topic of tragedy/comedy is brought before us in this brief exchange, with the implication that, as the playwright designs his play as tragedy or comedy, or assigns a tragic fate or a comic one to a particular character in his work, so too does some unspecified reigning fate determine who is to be happy and successful and who is not. Here in this early part of the play that presiding fate is as yet unknown. But Antonio is not wrong in intuiting that he is destined to play a dreadful role in life: it will be as a human sacrifice. He does not yet "know" this; but he knows that in some terrible way he is "chosen":

> I am a tainted wether of the flock,
> Meetest for death. The weakest kind of fruit
> Drops earliest to the ground, and so let me.

His role as sacrificial victim is, of course, related to Shylock's designs upon him, as well as to some very specific and inescapable scriptural allusions, particularly to John 11:49–50, as well as 18:14, along with Isaiah 53:2–5. So at this point I must revert to the question of Shylock's *real* motive in bargaining for the pound of flesh.

At two points in the play he is asked why he should stipulate so barbarous, grotesque, and inhuman a demand, and at both points he answers evasively. To Salerio's

> Why, I am sure if he forfeit thou wilt not take his flesh.
> What's that good for?

he replies,

The Merchant of Venice: *A Venture in Hermeneutics*

To bait fish withal. If it will feed nothing else, it will feed my revenge.

Then follows the famous speech of self-justification ("Hath not a Jew eyes?") and the justification of revenge itself. This has been accepted in a vague and general way as Shylock's motive, when the subject is addressed at all; no one seems to think it a great puzzle. The other point at which Shylock is asked to explain himself is the scene of the trial (IV, i) where he gives what amounts to two different answers—different from one another and different from his earlier answer of revenge. In this speech (lines 35–62) he declares that he requires the pound of flesh because he has an oath in heaven that cannot be broken ("by our holy Sabbath I have sworn") but also because of sheer caprice, as though he were himself the agent of the pagan goddess Fortuna.

> You'll ask me why I rather choose to have
> A weight of carrion flesh than to receive
> Three thousand ducats: I'll not answer that,
> But say it is my humor. Is it answered?

This evasiveness deliberately undermines and invalidates the earlier answer of revenge, which Shylock could just as easily have produced here if he had cared to. That he did not is of importance in that it invites us to give thought to his real motives, and further, to suggest that Shakespeare's original audiences might have guessed, without instructive glosses, at what that motive was. It was an ancient and familiar one from medieval times well into Shakespeare's age, and deserves, indeed calls for, extended comment.

As soon as that pound of flesh is first mentioned (I, iii, 139–147), Shakespeare's earliest audiences would instantly have known what Shylock was up to. They would have known from familiar literary sources as well as legendary and religious ones. I think it necessary and useful to offer extensive documentation regarding this problem. The following quotation is taken from the chapters on the Middle Ages, in *The History of the Jewish People*, by Haim Hillel Ben-Sasson, who edited the entire volume (Harvard University Press, 1976).

> During this period a new phenomenon emerged in the relations between Christianity and Judaism—the levelling of false charges. . . . There were two main libels, whose effects were to increase the number of Jewish victims and to give free rein to the debased instincts of the populace. These were the *blood libel* and the *libel of desecrating the host*. The blood libel was the older of the two, having been levelled in a slightly different form against the Christians of the second century.[1] In 1144 the Jews of Norwich in England were accused of having murdered a Christian child. From that time on charges of this kind were levelled against Jews all over Europe. The explanation and logic of those who believed the accusation were that, once the Jews had crucified Jesus, they thirsted for pure and innocent blood. Since the formerly incarnate God was now in heaven, the Jews aspired to the blood of the most innocent of the believers, *i.e.*, the children, the tender Christians. As a result of this reasoning, the season of the most blood libels or charges of ritual murder was that of the Passover festival, which was close to the time of the Passion of Jesus.
>
> Various elaborations were added in the course of time. In Norwich it was claimed that the Jews had tortured their victim and crucified him. In 1255 the Jews of Lincoln were accused of having crucified a Christian boy and, after having taken him down from the cross, of having removed his intestines, apparently for purposes of witchcraft. In 1286 in Munich it was charged that the Jews, in the words of a Jewish lament, 'slay diverse Chris-

[1] Text of footnotes starts on page 220.

tian children, injuring them in all their limbs . . . cruelly drinking their blood.' Jewish acts of sadism and drinking the blood of corpses were added here to the general horror. . . .

Throughout the centuries dealt with here and in those that followed, many Jews were cruelly slain as a result of the libels. Entire communities were wiped out or were compelled to move elsewhere. Even when the Jews were spared destruction and torture, the social and psychological damage remained and left its mark. The result was that within the Western European cultural *milieu* of the Middle Ages the Jew came to be viewed as a menacing demon.[2]

This image can be found in *The Canterbury Tales*, written by the great English poet Geoffrey Chaucer, who was born in 1340, fifty years after the expulsion of the Jews from England. Chaucer completed the work about 1387, almost a century after the Jews had been expelled. The "Prioress' Tale" tells of an innocent Christian child, the son of a widow, who was walking through the street of the Jews singing songs in praise of Mary, mother of Jesus. The Jews seized and murdered him. The crime was miraculously revealed, and the whole community of Jews was put to death. The story indicates that the absence of Jews did not affect the outlook of the poet or of the average English pilgrims whom he described. The cultural heritage had survived; what is repeated here is the blood libel of Lincoln, which had occurred well over a century earlier.

Bernardino da Feltre and the Trent Blood Libel (1475)

An admirer and disciple of Capistrano [a Franciscan saint (1386–1456) known as "The Scourge of the Jews"] Bernardino da Feltre represented a third generation of

Jew-baiting Franciscan preachers. Toward the end of the fifteenth century, he preached against the Jews in many places in Italy. In 1475 he preached in Trent, on the German frontier. His sermons produced a strained atmosphere, falling on fertile ground that had already been saturated with anti-Jewish feeling due to German influence. A rumour spread in Trent about the disappearance of a two-year-old infant named Simon, whereupon the usual charge was levelled against the Jews. The entire community was arrested and subjected to torture, which led to conflicting confessions. Those sentenced were promptly executed, while the remaining Jews were expelled. The impact of the libel was felt far and wide, as we have learnt from the case of Regensburg. The pope at first refused to authorize the adoration of this "victim of the Jews," but in due course he withdrew his opposition. In 1582 the infant Simon was officially proclaimed a saint of the Catholic Church. (In 1965 the Church withdrew its canonization and acknowledged that a judicial error had been committed against the Jews of Trent in this trial.)

Two years before the expulsion [of the Jews from Andalusia, in 1483] a blood libel was brought against the New Christians [converted Jews]—the case of "the Holy Child of La Guardia." In the confused trial, several Marranos were accused of having crucified a Christian boy. According to the charges, they had endeavored to obtain the Christian Host for the purpose of performing witchcraft with it and with the heart of the crucified boy in order to cause all the Christians to perish of rabies. All the accused were burnt in 1491. From the historical point of view, the important aspect here was the Inquisition's exploitation of a charge that had no factual foundation. Whether the inquisitors intended it or not, this charge helped prepare the ground for the expulsion of the professed Jews and to increase the animosity toward the Marranos. The preaching and debating that commenced with Vincente Ferrer and the Tortosa Disputation continued in various forms and degrees of intensity until the expulsion.

In addition to this account it may be worth citing a brief one of the life of William of Norwich, taken from *A Dictionary of Saints* by Donald Attwater.

> William of Norwich, D. at Norwich, 1144; f.d. 26 March. The mutilated body of this twelve-year-old boy was found in a wood outside Norwich; five years later it was alleged that he was the victim of ritual murder by Jews. The authorities seem not to have credited the story; but the common people did, and William was venerated locally as a martyr. This is the first recorded accusation of the kind against the Jews; belief in their killing of Christian children for ritual purposes was rife in the later middle ages, fed by a fanatical antisemitism. No instance of the charge has been substantiated, and it has rightly been called "one of the most notable and disastrous lies of history." Another case was that of the nine-year-old *Little St Hugh*, whose body was found in a well at Lincoln in 1255; a score of Jews were tortured and hanged on a charge of complicity in crucifying him. . . . A prominent continental case was *St Simon*, a child of two-and-a-half, said to have been done to death by a Jewish physician at Trento in northern Italy in 1475. No doubt these and other children were murdered; why and by whom is not known. In 1965 the cultus of Simon was officially abolished.

Francis James Child's collection of English and Scottish Popular Ballads contains a number of versions of a famous song about *Little St Hugh* [III (1890), pp. 233–254; IV (1892), pp.

497–498; V (1898), p. 241] some of which were collected and sung in the United States.

So these traditions of both popular and learned literature, as well as religious tradition, legend and liturgical practice as regards the veneration of the saints of the church, would have served to remind any early audience of the real nature, despite his evasive answers, of Shylock's motives and desires. This is important in its own right for any clear sense of how the play operates; but also because even so thoughtful and sensitive a commentator as C. L. Barber has characterized Shylock as a "miser." But it is emphatically the point that he is not: all preliminary efforts to buy him off with enormous multiplications of his original loan are to no avail, and he perversely holds out for what has no monetary value whatever. Doubtless, he talks a good deal about ducats, and bewails the loss of them as well as of her when his daughter robs him and flees. But this is not cupidity, nor in itself enough to label him "miser," and it bears upon two other themes in the play, one of them impiety and the other thrift and thriving and usurious practice, that I must come to later.

Quite a remarkable number of readers, commentators, actors and directors have made things easy for themselves by taking Salerio and Solanio as sound authorities upon the nature and character of Shylock, and as reliable guides who can tell us what we are entitled or supposed to feel. Such readers embrace especially the eighth scene of Act II, where one of the duo reports what seems like a slapstick, ludicrous oscillation of emotions on the part of Shylock with regard to love and money:

> My daughter!—O my ducats!—O my daughter!
> Fled with a Christian!—O my Christian ducats!
> Justice, the law, my ducats, and my daughter!
> And jewels, two stones, two rich and precious stones,
> Stol'n by my daughter!—Justice!—find the girl,
> She hath the stones upon her, and the ducats!

—a report that brands Shylock as one unable to tell the difference in value between money and love, as one to whom his daughter is merely another possession, and finally as an hysteric with no manly fortitude or stoical reserve. The passage is always "good for a laugh," but it is also taken as grotesquely and comically revealing; and thus constitutes a virtual license to condemn Shylock's values and character by the agreeable means of laughter and ridicule. But the grossness of this report, indeed its very reliability, is called directly into question only two scenes later. There, in agonizing discourse with Tubal, Shylock declares,

> I would my daughter were dead at my foot, and the jewels in her ear: would she were hears'd at my foot, and the ducats in her coffin!

Since he is addressing a fellow Jew, since there is no one here he is trying to mislead, there is no reason for us to doubt that he means what he says. And what he is saying is that he would have the jewels and the ducats buried with his daughter; he would not retrieve or repossess them. His wish to see his daughter dead is to be explained by the fact, as shall appear later, that she has committed a capital offense. But there is no confusion here about Shylock's priorities, and the jest of Solanio now appears to be hollow, if not plainly dishonest, or, simply, abusive.

If Shylock can be accepted dramatically as playing the role of the Jew who yearns to perform ritual sacrifice upon a Christian, Antonio must clearly fulfil the victim's part; he is what Ben-Sasson described as "the most innocent of believers," and, while not a "child" like Hugh of Lincoln or Simon of Trent, is nevertheless meant to be the very personification of loving and submissive Christianity. His willingness to sacrifice himself utterly, both in substance and in person, his identification with the sacrificial lamb ("a tainted wether of the flock" *who takest away the sins of the world*) decisively recall the scriptural passage in John 15:13, "Greater love hath no man than this, that a man lay down his life for his friends." That famous assertion not only applies to Antonio's utter selflessness in behalf of Bassanio, but clarifies a passage alluded to earlier, which some commentators had proposed as redolent of homo-erotic meaning and the defiant requirement that Bassanio make a flat and exclusive choice between the love of his wife and of his friend: ("Let his deserving, and my love withal,/Be valued 'gainst your wife's commandèment"). There is no question that scripture tells us which is the "greater" love, and Bassanio responds accordingly.

If Antonio is not the traditional child-victim, neither is he a Christ figure if, in employing that term, there is any suggestion that this play presents an episode, however stylized or symbolically rendered, from the life of Jesus of Nazareth. He is, rather, a representative of Christian magnanimity and self-lessness, a man so good as to provoke the overpowering and perverse appetite of a Jew whose thirst for innocent blood was insatiably whetted by the shedding of the blood of Jesus. This will also explain and, within the sanctions and assumptions of the play, justify (though not by twentieth-century standards) the outright and undisguised hostility that Antonio exhibits towards Shylock. The two are fated, natural antagonists, and I would claim that Antonio had in effect foreknown this.

> Signior Antonio, many a time and oft
> In the Rialto you have rated me
> About my moneys and my usances.
> Still have I borne it with a patient shrug,
> For suff'rance is the badge of all our tribe.
> You call me misbeliever, cutthroat dog,
> And spit upon my Jewish gaberdine,
> And all for use of that which is mine own.

(This last line of Shylock's is a witty allusion to a New Testament text—by no means the only one to which Shylock alludes in his fencings with others in the play—in this case to Matthew 20:15, "Is it not lawful for me to do what I will with mine own?" Apt as the citation might appear to be, Shylock neglects to mention that the speaker of these words in the parable Christ is telling is supposed to be God Himself, and it is not smoothly to be assumed that mankind is entitled to adopt the same moral postures as divinity.) To this Antonio responds without any apparent shame or disclaimer,

> I am as like to call thee so again,
> To spit on thee again, to spurn thee too.
> If thou wilt lend this money, lend it not
> As to thy friends—for when did friendship take
> A breed for barren metal of his friend?—
> But lend it rather to thine enemy,
> Who if he break, thou mayst with better face
> Exact the penalty.

Antonio's reply, contemptuous as it is, involves a complex of what were once perfectly acceptable conventions. His behavior toward Shylock would have been held to be a witty reversal of, and retaliation for, the mockery of Christ by the Jews as recorded in Matthew 27:29–30, "And when they platted a crown of thorns, they put it on his head, and a reed in his right hand: and they bowed the knee before him, and mocked him, saying, Hail, King of the Jews! And they spit upon him, and took the reed, and smote him on the head." Antonio's actions are a conventional, symbolic and, as it was thought, justified rebuke to the incorrigible Jews, whom it was right to repudiate. It was not considered in the least un-Christian to behave thus toward a Jew, who had inherited the guilt of the murder of Christ, according to Matthew 27:25, "Then answered all the people, and said, His blood be on us, and on our children." Indeed, as a sort of confirmation of Antonio's rightness here, Shylock says virtually the same thing in the trial scene: "My deeds upon my head! I crave the law. . . ." Also, Antonio appears to know that scripture (Exodus 22:25; Psalms 15:5; Proverbs 28:8) expressly forbids Jews to employ usury among themselves. Finally, he resorts to the popular and conventional "wisdom" which holds that Shylock, like all Jews, is bound by an outdated, brutal dispensation and retaliatory morality, so that he cannot be asked or expected to behave generously, and can only rejoice in the primitive law of "Eye for eye, tooth for tooth, . . ." and is beyond comprehending any other kind of behavior.

So Antonio's own brutality here is not in any way meant to impugn what we are to understand as his unambiguous virtue. Nor is there anything incompatible with what we are to take as his virtuous posture and the fact that he is a wealthy merchant. Throughout the Middle Ages and beyond it was fairly common for such a man as Antonio to join in a devout confraternity, a merchants' guild of an explicitly religious cast, called *ecclesia mercatorum*. George Herbert plainly characterizes Christ as a "rich Lord" in his sonnet, "Redemption," the very title of which is both spiritual and commercial. And Matthew (13:45) reports Jesus declaring, "Again, the kingdom of heaven is like unto a merchant man. . . ."

Antonio's hatred and defiance of Shylock are ultimately connected with and justified by his identification of Shylock with the devil; and he does this on grounds quite other than that Shylock has murderous designs upon him personally. At several crucial junctures in the play Shylock is so identified. The first time occurs in this very scene, just after Shylock has alluded to the scriptural story of Jacob and Laban. That story and Shylock's employment of it is absolutely central to the main action of the play, its riddle and epitome—but I must delay dealing with it until later on. For the present, let me also recall the fact that Jessica refers to her home as "hell," and that Bassanio, in the trial scene, declares,

The Merchant of Venice: *A Venture in Hermeneutics*

> Antonio, I am married to a wife
> Which is as dear to me as life itself;
> But life itself, my wife, and all the world
> Are not with me esteemed above thy life.
> I would lose all, ay, sacrifice them all
> Here to this devil, to deliver you.

This identification of the Jew with the devil also has scriptural provenance. The locus is chiefly John, 8:33–44, 13:1–2, and 21–27, but also Luke 22:3. In John's extraordinary account Jesus declares (6:70–71), "Have I not chosen you twelve, and one of you is a devil?" When Jesus later, at the Last Supper, prophesies that he shall be betrayed, Peter asks who shall be the traitor, and Jesus replies, "He it is to whom I shall give a sop, when I have dipped it." The gospel continues, "And when he had dipped the sop, he gave it to Judas Iscariot, the son of Simon. And after the sop Satan entered into him." Judas Iscariot, therefore, becomes possessed by Satan, and thus betrays Jesus. In doing so he becomes the representative figure, in Christian eyes, for all Jews, who, in rejecting Christ and Christian doctrine, are in effect betraying the Messiah who came for their express salvation, and consigning him to sacrificial death. Judas is the murderer-traitor *par excellence*, and as such Dante fixes him in the last and lowest circle of Hell, reserved for traitors and for Satan himself, as traitor to and rebel against God. Here is the headnote to the last Canto of the *Inferno* in the Temple Classics edition.

> The Judecca [Giudecca] or Last Circle of Cocytus, takes its name from Judas Iscariot, and contains the souls of those who "betrayed their masters and benefactors." The Arch Traitor Satan, "Emperor of the Realm of Sorrow," stands fixed in its center; and he too is punished by his own sin. All the streams of guilt keep flowing back to him, as their source; and from beneath his three Faces (Shadows of his consciousness) issue forth the mighty

wings with which he struggles, as it were, to raise himself; and sends out winds that freeze him only the more firmly in his ever-swelling Marsh.

Judas is doomed forever to be held, half, in, half out, of one of the three mouths of Satan, where, his head and trunk within, his legs kicking helplessly without, he is eternally gnawed upon and chewed. (The other two mouths are crammed with Cassius and Brutus.) Now, one account of the first settlement of the Jews in Venice, by John H. Davis, declares: "They first came to Venice as itinerant merchants, setting up businesses in the Rialto district during stopovers between one journey and another. A few merchants remained and raised families, and by the twelfth century there were some 1,300 Jews living in the lagoon area. Most of them settled on the island of Spinalunga, later called the Giudecca."[3] So Venice itself identified the home of its Jews with the lowest circle of hell, and, by literary and traditional association, all Jews with Judas, and Judas with Satan. This powerful and long-standing sorites of associations would have provided enough justification for Antonio's hostile attitude towards Shylock.

Having asserted so firmly that Shylock is no miser, I hope I will not appear to be equivocating if I also insist, as he does himself, that he is thrifty. The difference between the terms is more than a matter of tone or point of view in this case, though admittedly in other texts one term may be used to imply the other, often sardonically, as William Empson has amusingly shown.[4] It must be clear that the goal of obtaining his pound of flesh is more important to Shylock than any financial considerations, and he makes that goal nothing less than a religious obsession, swearing an oath to heaven in regard to it. The solemnity with which he takes that oath is the more awful in that it respects one of the Ten Commandments.[5] And it is the more devout in its conspicuous contrast to virtually all the other oaths in the play, which are made with ease and broken with impunity. Indeed, Shylock's fealty to his oath has a stark and lonely courage about it, a kind of inverted nobility that would be heroic if it were not perverse, and pious if it were God-inspired instead of engendered by the insatiable appetite for the destruction of innocence that I have indicated. Shylock lusts after a choice pound of Antonio's body. There is nothing in this that is explicitly homoerotic, and I think the note is totally absent from the play, and from Shylock's character. But it is doubtless an ingredient of the entire *mythos*, as Dickens knew or intuited.[6]

As for Shylock's thrift, he boasts of it, and it is connected, both linguistically and metaphorically, with "thriving," which means both prospering financially and flourishing in abounding life. It must be one of the minor ironies of the play that Shylock, who sets such store by thrift as a means of thriving, should, as a widower with one child, and that a daughter (a weak vessel to convey the weight of such a patriarchal and dynastic inheritance, both spiritual and material), find his "line," his genealogy and family tree, effectively cut down, all thriving halted by the conversion of his daughter and himself. "Thrift" in the play is one of an important binary set of terms, the other of which is "prodigality." And "prodigality" is no less fertile a term than "thrift," covering both the notion of the generous man as well as the spendthrift and wastrel. The theme enters immediately upon the first appearance of Bassanio. Antonio asks him about love, and his reply is about money. The exchange is worth quoting.

> Well, tell me now what lady is the same
> To whom you swore a secret pilgrimage,
> That you to-day promised to tell me of.

To this request of Antonio's, Bassanio replies as follows:

> 'Tis not unknown to you, Antonio,
> How much I have disabled mine estate

> By something showing a more swelling port
> Than my faint means would grant continuance.
> Nor do I now make moan to be abridged
> From such a noble rate; but my chief care
> Is to come fairly off from the great debts
> Wherein my time, something too prodigal,
> Hath left me gaged. To you, Antonio,
> I owe the most in money and in love;
> And from your love I have a warranty
> To unburthen all my plots and purposes
> How to get clear of all the debts I owe.

It is in many ways a remarkable speech, and were it not couched in an idiom that is distinctly remote from more conventional and transparent discourse (compare it, for example, to the plain lucidity of Bassanio's later offer, quoted above, to give his life, his wife, his world, to save Antonio from Shylock: IV, i, 280–285) it might be easily noticed without gloss with what unashamed and almost brazen effrontery Bassanio seems to speak. There is first the terse admission that he has been living beyond his means, a fact that does not seem to recommend him as a "mature and responsible" young man. Then his confession that he's worried about his debts, engendered during his "prodigal" youth; and the acknowledgment that he is now in fact addressing his chief creditor. Given a praeludium of this kind, we are likely to be astonished, and have reason to expect Antonio, too, to be astonished, when Bassanio coolly follows this with what amounts to his main theme: the request for a further loan!

> In my schooldays, when I had lost one shaft
> I shot his fellow in the selfsame flight
> The selfsame way, with more advisèd watch,
> To find the other forth; and by adventuring both
> I oft found both. I urge this childhood proof

> Because what follows is pure innocence.
> I owe you much, and like a willful youth
> That which I owe is lost; but if you please
> To shoot another arrow that self way
> Which you did shoot the first, I do not doubt,
> As I will watch the aim, or to find both
> Or bring your latter hazard back again
> And thankfully rest debtor for the first.

If we are struck by both the brashness and the candor of this speech, we shall be no less struck by Antonio's openhearted and generous response to it.

> You know me well, and herein spend but time
> To wind about my love with circumstance;
> And out of doubt you do me now more wrong
> In making question of my uttermost
> Than if you had made waste of all I have.

In view of Bassanio's own reference to his prodigal youth, Antonio's response cannot fail to recall the parable of the Prodigal Son in Luke 15:11–32, and recall the kindness, patience and generosity with which his heedlessness was overlooked, and the joy with which he was reclaimed. If, as I think, we are truly reminded of that text, then what follows from Bassanio is more shocking still.

> In Belmont is a lady richly left;
> And she is fair, and fairer than that word,
> Of wondrous virtues. Sometimes from her eyes
> I did receive fair speechless messages.
> Her name is Portia; nothing undervalued
> To Cato's daughter, Brutus' Portia;
> Nor is the wide world ignorant of her worth.
> . . . .
> And many Jasons come in quest of her.
> O my Antonio, had I but the means
> To hold a rival place with one of them,

The Merchant of Venice: *A Venture in Hermeneutics*

I have a mind presages me such thrift
That I should questionless be fortunate.

Though an "advantageous marriage" was a respectable and admired way for a penurious but otherwise eligible young man of breeding, especially a younger son, to advance himself in the world, still a number of things should amaze us. Bassanio has moved from rhetorical obscurity in the discussion of his faults and debts to the undisguised crassness of his scheme to redeem his indebtedness by latching onto a wealthy heiress. The gradual clarification of Bassanio's diction seems strangely to add to the shocking effect. Especially in speaking of Portia, he manages to allude to her "worth" in such a way as to allow us, and Antonio, to measure it simultaneously in terms of virtue and hard cash, and thereby to keep love and money neatly intertwined. He even speaks, as Shylock does, of "thrift," and means by it here just what Shylock means: to thrive, to succeed. His confidence, of course, is based on those "speechless messages"; she has already let him know that he's favored.

But "thrift" is the counterpart of "prodigality," and it is to Bassanio's word "prodigal," and Antonio's allusion to the parable of prodigality in Luke that I wish to return. The word will again be used by Shylock, when, in parting from his daughter to dine with Bassanio, he says,

But yet I'll go in hate to feed upon
The prodigal Christian.

I have gone out of my way to emphasize the bad impression that I think Bassanio initially makes—as a sponger, spendthrift, a crass and almost tasteless exploiter of his best friend, and would-be exploiter of Portia—because I think the text has invited this, and because I believe Shakespeare has done so in order to entrap us. I mean that the playwright has deliberately invited us to misread Bassanio's nature, to reprehend his character, to suspect him of crudeness if not of baseness; and all in

161

order to oblige us to reorient and reorder our own impressions upon further thought. This "reconsideration" is demanded by the text; and it is nothing more nor less than a prelude to the whole action of reordering values which the play itself enacts. In correcting ourselves we do what Portia does in solving the riddle of the trial.

Curiously, paradoxically, the very faults that must initially strike us with force about Bassanio can, by further thought, be understood in a "new light" as nothing less than virtue. His heedlessness about money is precisely a reflection of his innocence; his recklessness is a recklessness enjoined upon us all by Christian doctrine and scripture. Despite the fact that these verses are well known, I think it pertinent to furnish them here at sufficient length.

And he said unto his disciples, Therefore I say unto you, Take no thought for your life, what ye shall eat; neither for the body, what ye shall put on.
The life is more than meat, and the body is more than raiment.
Consider the ravens: for they neither sow nor reap; which neither have storehouse nor barn; and God feedeth them: how much more are ye better than the fowls?
And which of you with taking thought can add to his stature one cubit?
If ye then be not able to do that thing which is least, why take ye thought for the rest?
Consider the lilies how they grow: they toil not, they spin not; and yet I say unto you, that Solomon in all his glory was not arrayed like one of these.
If then God so clothe the grass, which is to-day in the field, and to-morrow is cast in the oven; how much more will he clothe you, O ye of little faith?
And seek not ye what ye shall eat, or what ye shall drink, neither be ye of doubtful mind.

The Merchant of Venice: *A Venture in Hermeneutics*

For all these things do the nations of the world seek after:
and your Father knoweth that ye have need of these
things.

>(Luke 12:22–31; there is a comparable
>passage in Matthew 6:21–31)

Now when Jesus heard these things, he said unto him,
[a rich young man], Yet lackest thou one thing: sell all
that thou hast, and distribute unto the poor, and thou
shalt have treasure in heaven: and come, follow me.
And when he heard this, he was very sorrowful: for he was
very rich.
And when Jesus saw that he was very sorrowful, he said,
How hardly shall they that have riches enter into the
kingdom of God!
For it is easier for a camel to go through a needle's eye,
than for a rich man to enter into the kingdom of God.

>(Luke 18:22–25; there is a comparable
>passage in Mark 10:21–25)

What Bassanio exhibits from the first, and throughout the
play, is that innocence and trusting heedlessness about money
which satisfies the biblical injunction to take no thought of to-
morrow, and to trust in providence. It is precisely this careless
aspect of "prodigality," which is the very opposite and counterpart of "thrift" that is careful and prudential, and that
characterizes the caution and care of Shylock, in which Bassanio's virtue inheres. Shylock is everywhere meticulous and
detailed, a legalist; Bassanio is improvident to the point, it
almost seems, of foolishness. But it is the foolishness of the
trusting child and innocent Christian. The demand that Jesus
makes upon the rich young man to give away everything and
follow him is a call to take the most total and complete of all
risks: in Mark's text it reads, "and come, *take up the cross*, and
follow me." What is important is precisely the total risk involved; the risk and its completeness. Risk, of course, is the

163

very stuff of the life of commerce, as everyone in the play comes to know. But most importantly it is the motto of the right casket, the leaden casket that contains Portia's picture and hand in marriage: "Who chooseth me must give and hazard all he hath." That injunction is the same one Jesus makes; it is also commercial in its language (Jesus was addressing it to a *rich* young man) and so it is suitable that when Bassanio solves the casket riddle he should claim his reward in commercial terms: "I come by note, to give and to receive."

I hope to show that I'm not being merely tricky or clever in reclaiming Bassanio to the camp of virtue, or in declaring that Shakespeare obliges us to revise our own reactions to him as the play proceeds. We are, I maintain, invited to misread and misinterpret him, and required to correct ourselves. This invitation and requirement is a duplication of the main action of the play, and results in an illumination, a genuine revelation, such as we are especially likely to recognize when we discover the truth after having been blindly and unregenerately wrong. It is like, with pointed, dramatic relevance, the experience of conversion. Our discovery is made the more emphatic for our having dwelt at first in the realms of error; just as the play gives us Morocco and Arragon before it allows us to reach the gospel truth with Bassanio. What I am describing here is a *peripeteia*, a reversal which is also a reappraisal the reader or member of the audience is forced to go through, and which imitates the reversal upon which the dramatic crux of the whole play turns. It is a play of revelations, rich with secret and hidden meanings, of which the caskets themselves are very eminent symbols.

I turn now to Shylock's biblical citation of the story of Jacob and Laban in Genesis 30: 25–43. It is worth noting that within the first eighty-odd lines of his appearance Shylock adverts three times to scriptural reference: in addition to the Jacob-Laban story, he alludes to the story of the Gadarene swine in

The Merchant of Venice: *A Venture in Hermeneutics*

Luke 8:26–33, as well as to the "fawning publican" of Matthew 5:44–46.[7] Shylock's paraphrase of the Jacob-Laban story seems to function on three levels, of which Shylock is aware of two. On the second level, which Antonio is not meant to grasp, the story serves as a justification for trickery, for legalistic ingenuity of the sort that very soon will entrap Antonio. Shylock intends to play a legal game involving a contract, just as Jacob did with Laban; and by meticulous observation of the letter of the law Shylock intends to triumph. I will reserve the third level of meaning for a moment and direct my attention to the biblical story itself. It is a story curious enough, and curiously enough embedded in ancient dictions, both Shakespearean and biblical, to justify quoting some modern glosses.

The J[1] narrative told of the proposal of Jacob, who had hitherto been working for Laban, to set up an establishment for himself. . . . Laban, unwilling to lose his services, thereupon offered to allow him to fix his own wages. Jacob replied that he wanted nothing at the moment, but proposed that Laban should remove from his flocks all the *speckled* and *spotted* animals. . . . These were to be set apart by themselves. . . . Jacob would then care for the rest of the flock and would receive as his wages any speckled and spotted that might be born to these normally colored animals in the future. To this Laban promptly agreed . . . —indeed, why should he not accept a proposal so favorable to himself? [And, indeed, why should not Antonio accept the proposal of Shylock's contract that looks so favorable and easy to fulfil?] If Jacob was such a fool as to suggest it, let him take the consequences!

But Jacob, though he may have been a knave, was no fool. He placed rods upon which he had peeled white streaks before the eyes of the stronger animals in the flock at rutting time, with the result that [by homeopathic influence] the young born to them were *striped, speckled and spotted,* and so belonged to him. . . . Thus his substance increased rapidly, . . . and Laban was left with the feebler animals.

> (Cuthbert A. Simpson, "Exegesis of
> Genesis," *Interpreter's Bible.*)

The chronicler must have set down this account with a very human and perhaps unregenerate pleasure. Here was Jacob, the progenitor of Israel, outsmarting the uncovenanted Laban. [Another covert parallel of Shylock's.] From a natural point of view that seemed eminently appropriate. More than once Laban had deliberately cheated Jacob. He had promised him Rachel to wife, and after Jacob had served seven years for her he withheld Rachel and gave him Leah instead. According to Jacob, Laban had also changed his wages ten times. . . . Jacob had good reason therefore to be suspicious when Laban tried to persuade him to stay and work further, . . . and all the more so when Laban added unctuously, *for I have learned by experience that the Lord hath blessed me for thy sake.* Anybody would have said that if Laban could be cheated in his turn, it would be what he thoroughly deserved.

As a matter of fact, Jacob does not cheat him. He carries through exactly the terms of the agreement which he had proposed to Laban, and which Laban explicitly accepted. He was not false to Laban; he was simply more inventive and adroit. When he had proposed to Laban that all he asked in the way of wages was that little fraction of the flock which might be odd in color, that seemed to Laban a highly desirable bargain, especially since he, Laban, took the opportunity then and there to remove from the flock all the sheep and goats that might breed the type that would belong to Jacob. The trouble was that he did not foresee the extraordinary device by which Jacob would be able to make the flock breed according to his interest—a device not ruled out by the bargain.

So by every secular standard Jacob was entitled to his triumph. But the interest of the Old Testament story lies in the fact that the narrator was not judging by secular standards. He believed that Jacob's triumph was directly linked to his religion. He describes Jacob as saying to Rachel and Leah, "God hath taken away the cattle of your father, and given them to me" (31:9). Moreover, an angel appears to Jacob and gives him God's message thus: "I have seen all that Laban doeth unto thee. I am the God of Bethel, . . . where thou vowedst a vow unto me" (31:12–13). In other words, Jacob's clever stratagem and the success it brought him are the result of the commitment he believed God had given him at Bethel to make him prosperous.

> (Walter Russell Bowie, "Exposition
> of Genesis," *Interpreter's Bible.*)

As these commentaries indicate, the narrative of Laban and Jacob offers Shylock a covert means of telling us that he intends, for his own private purposes, to work some legalistic ruse upon the uncovenanted enemy, Antonio; that he hopes to thrive by cunning and ingenuity, as Jacob did; and that as Jacob triumphed and was awarded prosperity, a thriving by thrift, in consequence of the partisanship of God, just so shall he succeed. There is here a mixture of trickery and piety, both in Shylock and in his exemplary text. But Shylock is one of the benighted, who does not know the *real*, or at least the *whole*, meaning of his tale. However, before I take up the third level of meaning, I must return to the ostensible reason the story was told in the first place: its bearing upon the practice of usury.

This is a touchy subject, and has been so from the first. As I have already indicated, the ancient Jews seem to have had a double standard of behavior with regard to usury: while there are explicit prohibitions in the scriptures against its use between Jews themselves, it is clear that these very scriptural texts allow that the prohibition does not apply to the practice of usury when conducted between a Jew and a Gentile. The prohibitory texts have been used by Gentiles to stigmatize both the practice and the Jews (as if they were the solitary practitioners) from the earliest times right down to so late and vehement an anti-Semite as Ezra Pound, whose fulminations upon usury constitute some of the most interesting and musical parts of the *Cantos*.[8] It is indisputable that the economic systems of virtually all modern nations are frankly based on the process of usury; that it is fundamental to the workings of all banks, insurance companies, merchants who sell on credit, and governments that issue bonds. As a practice, it obviously has some practical features to recommend it, and it was precisely such practical considerations that medieval Jews pointed to in their debates with Christians and in defense of their practices.

In a disputation with Christians held in 1500 at Ferrara in Italy by Rabbi Abraham Farissol of Avignon, the Jewish position on interest, as it was crystalized vis-à-vis that of the Catholic Church, was clearly expressed. Rabbi Abraham's main argument was that the structure of human society as well as the incentives for economic activity, on the one hand, and the patterns of mutual aid, on the other, had changed since the times of the ancient legislators who had discredited interest as being unnatural. The world known to him and to the clerics with whom he was debating was one of distinct nationalities, each concerned for its own interests, and of individuals, each working for himself.

"This has brought into being a new situation and

168

new obligations, a new order of things differing in-
trinsically from the previous; namely [the neces-
sity] to assist one's fellow man in return for payment
due from the one in need, and not to give something
for nothing to one, unless he is a pauper, when he be
aided for pity's sake. . . . In other cases when a man
needs something of which his comrade has plenty . . .
he purchases it at a price. Hence . . . the established
practice of paying for the hire of houses and work-
ers . . . all of whom have their price. . . . For if Nature
and Wisdom were to demand that aid be given to
everyone who needs it so as to satisfy his wants, and
that money be loaned without interest to those who
need money, then Nature would also require that if
anyone needs a house or a horse or work to be provided for him, they should all be supplied without
payment." [Abraham Farrisol, *Magen Avraham*,
manuscript]

Rabbi Abraham maintained that if the practice were different "it would cause envy, quarrels, trouble and en-
mity . . . such as who should provide and who deserves to
be helped. That is why the practice and the rule have
spread of helping and working for a fair price and an
agreed wage; and on these all customs and laws are based"
(ibid.). Thus, although theoretically he could envisage a
different "order of Nature," he could accept only a social
nature in which aid is paid for in every field and charity
is reserved for the absolutely poor.

The Black Death marked the end of an epoch and a turning point for the Jewish communities of central Europe,
as old anti-Jewish tendencies again began to emerge at
an increasing rate. Hatred and fear of the Jews were universal during the period of the plague, which began in
1348. . . . At first sight it might appear that this hatred

was promptly compensated for, as various districts began
to allow Jews to return to their cities, even while they
were being slaughtered elsewhere. From 1349 we hear of
the admission of Jews at an increasingly rapid pace into
cities from which they had been expelled "forever" or
into cities that had sworn not to admit them for at least
another 200 years. However, readmission was motivated
by and based on social assumptions and carried out in
legal terms that, taken together, indicate a definite wors-
ening in the settlement situation and the economic, social
and legal status of the Jews, particularly in northwestern
and central Europe.

An analysis of the reasons that induced the bishops and
the cities to readmit the Jews indicates that the latter were
urgently required for various purposes, chiefly economic
ones. In the first stage, the Jews had been massacred or
driven away; their residential districts had been burnt
down, either by the Jews themselves or by the Christian
masses, or had remained standing while their real estate
and debts owed to them were left behind. Various groups
began to compete for possession of the spoils, the remaining buildings and plots of land. The townsmen who had
murdered and pillaged promptly came to an agreement
with the rulers whereby they were forgiven the massacre
and the property of the Jews was handed over to them. As
a rule the emperor and princes agreed to this arrangement in return for high fees. Thus the cities undertook
large financial burdens in order to enjoy the spoils of their
deeds against the Jews. However, the emperor, the princes
and the bishops soon felt the lack of the very considerable
taxes that the Jews had been paying them annually. The
townsfolk quickly discovered that there was no substitute
for the Jewish loans on interest, which were required for
consumer purposes, both major and minor. They turned

The Merchant of Venice: *A Venture in Hermeneutics*

to Christian money-lenders, but the latter raised their interest rates in the absence of Jewish competitors.

Thus the cities found themselves burdened with debts due to the departure of an economic and social element whose presence was valued only after it had vanished, whereupon they sought the return of the Jews. The cities, sometimes together with a more central authority—such as a bishop or a prince—granted the Jews protection in return for a considerable sum of money, payable upon admission, and the payment thereafter of a heavy annual tax. However, Jews were no longer admitted permanently but only for a fixed period of time—three, five or ten years. This arrangement left the experienced rulers of the cities with the option of cancelling the Jewish right of domicile and withdrawing their protection whenever they saw that the masses were again rising against these aliens.

(H. H. Ben-Sasson, *A History of the Jewish People*)

So we find ourselves presented with a puzzling set of facts. Jews were forbidden to practice usury among themselves, though apparently they were unclear about or completely ignorant of the reasons for the prohibition. As Ben-Sasson says, "In fact, during the Middle Ages the prohibition of interest was for most Jews an obligatory 'decree' for which no reason was given, and it was therefore binding only on what was explicitly forbidden. In fact, in the entire range of Jewish commentators, scarcely an argument is offered to account for the prohibition of interest. . . ." At the same time, they undertook to justify the practice in their debates and dealings with Christians, as I have indicated, and to suggest that the practice was both sensible and moral, as well as socially useful. The Christians were no less double-minded about the matter, finding it convenient to have Jews who would lend money at interest, and at the same time condemning them as immoral for doing so. In any case, Antonio's position, like Christ's in whipping the moneylenders from the temple, seems unequivocal—though it is nowhere suggested, of course, that Shylock has profaned a temple with his usury.

I am now creeping up to the third level of meaning of the Jacob-Laban story, and I will approach it circuitously by way of Launcelot Gobbo. A word, to begin with, about his name. There is a Venetian landmark of interest and relevance identified in the guidebooks. In front of the Church of San Giacomo di Rialto, surrounded by an iron railing, can be seen the block of granite which was used as a platform to proclaim the laws and decrees of the Republic. At the foot of the block there is carved the figure of a kneeling man, supporting a flight of steps, by which the town crier mounted to the summit of the pillar and proclaimed from there the edicts to the people. This monument was popularly called the *Gobbo di Rialto,* The Hunchback of the Rialto, and was made by Pietro da Salo in 1500 and thoroughly repaired in 1836.[9] Since the proclamations delivered here were often "bad news" in the way of taxes, the jest of the name implied that the burdens of government rested so heavily upon the back of the public as to give it a hump, and that officialdom stood high and haughtily upon the economic deformity of the people. But the Hunchback was a traditional Venetian hero for another reason as well, and one that has special bearing upon this play. He was, in fact, one of the popular figures of the commedia dell'arte, known as Pulcinella (Pulliciniella, Polliciniello, Punchinello) and in his English and American incarnations as Punch.[10] He was a figure of license and fun, and clearly associated with the spirit and festival of Carnival, a spirit and a holiday that certainly inhabits important parts of this play, as Professor Barber has persuasively shown.[11] As a figure of license and fun, Gobbo-Punchinello stands for a boisterousness and freedom meant to be the very opposite and counterpart of the severity and essentially saturnine character of Shylock, his employer at the beginning of the play. Shylock is opposed to the whole spirit of Carnival.

> What, are there masques? Hear you me, Jessica:
> Lock up my doors; and when you hear the drum
> And the vile squealing of the wry-necked fife,
> Clamber not you up to the casements then,
> Nor thrust your head into the public street
> To gaze on Christian fools with varnished faces;
> But stop my house's ears—I mean my casements;
> Let not the sound of shallow fopp'ry enter
> My sober house.

In explicit and direct contrast to this, Jessica says to Launcelot Gobbo:

> I am sorry thou wilt leave my father so;
> Our house is hell, and thou a merry devil
> Didst rob it of some taste of tediousness.

Shylock, by this contrast, belongs to that camp of Puritan spoilsports who range all the way from Malvolio in *Twelfth Night* to Angelo in *Measure For Measure*. His house is "sober," and sobriety cannot allow him to regard the Carnival aspect of life with anything but contempt and hatred.

We first encounter Launcelot Gobbo and his father, Old Gobbo, in the second scene of the second act, when, in a comic burlesque of Genesis 27:1–45 (in which Jacob steals Esau's blessing from their father, Isaac) Launcelot begs for and receives the blessing of his own father, who is blind, as Isaac was. And since Old Gobbo does not even know whether his son is alive or dead, the "recognition scene" that is presented here is a *rebirth* as a consequence of the blessing. Launcelot identifies himself to his father by saying, "I am Launcelot—your boy that was, your son that is, your child that shall be" (with its evident comic echo of the "Gloria Patri": "As it was in the beginning, is now, and ever shall be, . . ."). Now, Jacob's "theft" of his brother's blessing from Isaac fulfils a promise and a prophecy made to Rebekah, mother of the twin boys (of whom Esau was nevertheless the older, and the one therefore traditionally designated to inherit the blessing) by God Himself. But in order to secure that blessing along the lines of inheritance God had ordained, Jacob and Rebekah had to resort to guile. The situation, therefore, is sufficiently like that of Jacob and Laban to demand attention. Why should two such curious Old Testament texts, both involving ingenuity and cunning on the part of a young man trying to secure a sort of inheritance or legal claim from an older man—Laban was Jacob's uncle and adoptive father, even as Isaac was his father—be offered to us, one in direct narration, the other in parodic charade, very early in the course of this play? Is there any significance to the fact that Jacob has two fathers, and that Punchinello does too? (cf. note 10)

The answer seems to me inescapable. Launcelot is "reborn" by being discovered by his father, but his rebirth also entails his moving from a Jewish home to a Christian one. And the first thing that Bassanio, the master of Launcelot's new home, does is "prodigally" to order that liveries for him be put into making. Such generosity he was not used to. Bassanio, then, becomes his adoptive father, while it remains true that he tricks his real, blind old father into blessing him, just as Jacob had done. That blessing was "stolen" in both cases. And so is Jessica's inheritance; and she, too, moves, just as Launcelot Gobbo does, from a Jewish home (which is "hell") to a Christian one when she elopes with and marries Lorenzo. And, lo and behold, the very sign of that movement from Judaism to Christianity is a blazed trail of ostentatious "prodigality," reported to Shylock at heart-breaking length by Tubal. What so profoundly offends Shylock in this scene is the excruciating complex of religious *and* filial infidelity, compounded by the reckless flouting of all prudence and "thrift" that is the very staple of the moral code by which he lives. The profligacy of the young couple appalls him, and all his lamentations about ducats refer rather to these violations than to the mere loss of money, which is what most critics have declared to be his sole concern. Jessica resorts to trickery to secure her rights and needs no less than Launcelot; in her case the trickery is disguise, appropriate to the season of Carnival and of masques, a specifically Christian celebration and repudiation of the sobriety Shylock so prizes. Jacob, too, is reborn to prosperity after seven years of servitude to Laban, just as Jessica and Launcelot advance to new worlds of affluence.

So the two Genesis tales are archetypal narratives that describe a pattern of change from bad fortune to good through the working of ingenuity and guile, and the securing of a valuable patrimony against difficult odds by ingenious maneuvering within the strict limits of the letter of the law; and the narratives apply to the behavior and the fortunes of Jessica and Launcelot Gobbo. But they apply to the fate and fortunes of Portia as well. Portia is caught in the toils of the unalterable strictures of her father's will. It is her business to abide by them, and at the same time to secure the good fortune she desires, which is to have Bassanio for husband. Like Jacob, Launcelot, and Jessica, she, too, will prove herself equal to the task, which is dauntingly difficult; difficult enough, indeed, to account for the note of melancholy in her first words in the play:

> By my troth, Nerissa, my little body is aweary of this
> great world.

These are the opening lines of the second scene in the play, and they bear a striking resemblance to the opening lines of the first scene, in which Antonio spoke of his obscure sadness. I have attempted to hint at what I think lay at the root of Antonio's vague foreboding. The situation with Portia is somewhat different. The constricting terms of her father's will, the apparent irrationality of that will, the ludicrous situation in which she is placed vis-à-vis all her suitors, her total and hopeless lack of freedom—all these I believe are symbolic of the "law" of the Old Dispensation, from which the young generation must somehow contrive to free itself. Portia is challenged to get the better of her father's will, to free herself from the legalities of the Old Testament without violating the *letter* of its law, and to secure for herself what she desires: the freedom and love represented by the *spirit* of the law (which includes charity, forgiveness, and mercy) as it is expressed in the New Testament. Therefore, paradoxically, it is a sign of the greatness of the New Dispensation that Bassanio errs, that he should break his vow by giving away his ring, in order that mercy and forgiveness, the characteristic signs and virtues of the New Dispensation, may be exhibited.[12] But Portia's dilemma at the start is manifest in the lines in which she and Nerissa discuss a particularly unattractive, drunken German suitor. Portia remarks,

> An the worst fall that ever fell, I hope I shall make shift
> to go without him.

This is splendid. That "make shift" can innocently mean "endure," so that the sentence bears the sardonic, amused burden of, if worse comes to worst I guess I can stand doing without him. The point, the irony, is clear. However, that phrase, "make shift," more nearly means "contrive," which carries a double burden. It bears both the ironic meaning already indicated, and it also means "take ingenious measures" to do without him. This, in other words, is the first indication that Portia may have something up her sleeve. So evident is this to Nerissa that she says,

> If he should offer to choose, and choose the right casket,
> you should refuse to perform your father's will if you
> should refuse to accept him.

Portia responds,

> Therefore, for fear of the worst, I pray thee set a deep
> glass of Rhenish wine on the contrary casket, for if the
> devil be within and that temptation without, I know he
> will choose it. I will do anything, Nerissa, ere I will be
> married to a sponge.

Doubtless this is largely light-hearted banter, as light-hearted
as it can be in these precarious circumstances; but the conclusion of the speech—"I will do anything, Nerissa, . . ."—
ought to give us an index of Portia's desperation and determi-
nation. Nevertheless, and in virtually the same breath, she
punctiliously acknowledges that she will abide by the rules of
the game, the laws of the Old Dispensation:

> If I live to be as old as Sibylla, I will die as chaste as Diana
> unless I be obtained by the manner of my father's will.

And while the terms of the deceased Lord of Belmont's will are
admittedly peculiar, they are not altogether mad. They constitute in fact a kind of Rorschach or depth psychology test, in
which the aspirant, under the impression that he is reacting to
something external, something objective and neutral, is actually reacting to himself, and led to exhibit his true nature.
Morocco, self-consciously concerned with appearances (his
first lines, "Mislike me not for my complexion,/The shadowed
livery of the burnished sun,/To whom I am a neighbor and
near bred," should recall the Song of Songs 1:5–6, "I am black
but comely, O ye daughters of Jerusalem, . . . Look not upon
me because I am black, because the sun hath looked upon
me . . ."), fittingly judges by appearances, and chooses gold.
Arragon is equally deluded, and being an arrogant man, allows pride to govern his choice. As we can see, the meaning of
the test is that it can be won only by someone who is selfless
enough to have overcome all self-regard. And the real, incontrovertible evidence of Bassanio's selflessness will only finally

appear in the trial scene, where, in response to Antonio's willingness to sacrifice himself, Basanio makes the same reciprocal offer.

So the trial by casket is not without its own logic and even sound moral sense.[13] It represents that apparently heartless and rigid law of the Old Testament which is to be tempered, interpreted, altered into loving terms by the New Testament. And we are clearly called upon to remember two scriptural passages: "Think not that I am come to destroy the law, or the prophets: I am not come to destroy, but to fulfil. For verily I say unto you, Till heaven and earth pass, one jot or one tittle shall in no wise pass from the law, till all be fulfilled" (Matthew 5:17–18) and ". . . the letter killeth, but the spirit giveth life" (II Corinthians 3:6).

The relationship between the Old Testament and the New, as it is here conceived, and the relationship between Portia, Jessica, Launcelot Gobbo, and their elders from whom they seek to secure their rights and inheritances are not only described in the paradigmatic stories in Genesis of Jacob and Isaac, and Jacob and Laban. There is a further text that may serve as a gloss upon these three careers in the play.

Now I say, That the heir, as long as he is a child, differeth
nothing from a servant, though he be lord of all;
But is under tutors and governors until the time appointed
of the father.
Even so we, when we were children, were in bondage
under the elements of the world:
But when the fulness of the time was come, God sent forth
his Son, made of a woman, made under the law,
To redeem them that were under the law, that we might
receive the adoption of sons.
And because ye are sons, God hath sent forth the Spirit
of his Son into your hearts, crying, Abba, Father.

The Merchant of Venice: *A Venture in Hermeneutics*

Wherefore thou art no more a servant, but a son; and if
a son, then an heir of God through Christ.

(Galatians 4: 1–7)

I have said that in the trial scene Bassanio exhibits that
"selflessness" required both by the commandment of Jesus to
give up everything and follow him, and by the challenge of
the leaden casket, "Who chooseth me must give and hazard all
he hath." But when Bassanio presents himself at Belmont as a
suitor, Portia has little if any ground upon which she can con-
fidently predict that he will indeed prove to be such a man. So
to secure her prize, and to prize it out of the legal entanglements of her father's will, and in fitting parallel to the show
of wit and ingenuity exhibited by Jacob, she takes a delicate
but telling and decisive hand in the proceedings. Her liking
for Bassanio was announced in the play's first scene; the her-
alding of his coming, and all the happy auguries of grace have
been made the more clear by contrast with the impossibility
of all the other suitors we hear of or see. And now that Bassanio has come to Belmont, Portia does not conceal either from
him or from us her absolute and candid bias in his favor. The
treatment he receives at her hands is altogether different from
that of any of the other suitors, and she virtually declares her
love. But, loving though she may be, she observes the law of her
father.

Obviously, I am one who firmly agrees with those critics who
maintain that the song Portia arranges to be sung and played
while Bassanio deliberates is a signal, a tip-off, an ingenious
and not-expressly-forbidden way around the binding letter of
the law of her father's will. Not only do the first three lines of
the song end in words that rhyme with "lead," a sound that
could be made the more prominent by a judicious musical setting, isolating and prolonging those signal syllables by suitable
fermatas; but the entire burden of the song's text invites dis-

179

trust of the superficially visible, of the deceptions of the eye. By inference and contrast, of course, it commends the world of the spirit. But even if Bassanio should be too dense to grasp this, he could not but be aware that the song tells him how short-lived is that passion which is predicated on mere appearances; and if you have gold, silver, and lead to choose among, the inference could scarcely be clearer. Bassanio proves to be not altogether dense; and the telling effect of the song is evident in his first lines when the song has concluded:

> So may the outward shows be least themselves;
> The world is still deceived with ornament.

Indeed, he continues in this vein in what amounts to a speech very sermonlike in character; and then, in a richly ambiguous gesture, indicating either that he has picked up Portia's tip or else that he is indeed the selfless and risk-taking prodigal who would be spiritually summoned by the motto on the leaden casket, he proceeds, to the delight and satisfaction of Portia and the audience, to pick the right casket. I am convinced that the collusion and trickery of Portia is there in the play's text, not only because the text suggests as much locally, but because such trickery is consistent with all the occasions on which it has importantly appeared in other, seemingly unrelated, parts of the play. Portia actively takes part in winning her freedom, just as Jessica, Launcelot Gobbo, and Jacob do, and it would be a grave misreading of the play to suppose that she did not.

No sooner have the young lovers triumphed than shocking news arrives, dramatically reversing the temper and mood of the proceedings and altering, or at least somewhat muting, that triumph. The main action of the play takes place during the lenten season, just before Easter. In Act II, scene v, there is talk of masques, such as would be suitable in the pre-lenten Carnival festivities. Now at the very moment Bassanio wins Portia as his bride comes news of the sacrifice of his life that

Antonio is about to make; whereupon all nuptial and connubial rites are set aside, chastity is firmly observed in spite of the pledges of love, Portia and Nerissa declare that they intend "To live in prayer and contemplation," and "as maids and widows" to lead a "monastic" life, and all attention is focused upon sacrifice and salvation. Since, in Act I, scene iii, it is stipulated that Shylock's bond is to fall due in "three months," it is plausible to conjecture that the due date would fall some time near Easter. As a matter of fact, the "three months" is a term Bassanio seems himself innocently to have proposed, but it is dwelt upon and repeated insistently—once, as if he had forgotten this feature of the agreement—by Shylock. That insistent repetition should alert the audience, and I think we are meant to realize that Shylock's calculations here are not monetary but calendrical: with mounting but concealed excitement he is quietly coming to realize that the due date proposed would present itself right at the Easter season—the traditional season of the blood sacrifice.

With an ambiguity that seems to me calculated to match Bassanio's when he makes his choice of caskets, Portia chooses the name of Balthazar as her disguise and mask for her courtroom appearance. It is possible the name was suggested to her by the character with the smallest part in this play, and perhaps in any play of Shakespeare's. A servant and messenger of Portia is instructed to go to Portia's cousin, Dr. Bellario, in Padua, and there to obtain the necessary documents and articles of clothing by which the two women, Portia and Nerissa, will be able convincingly to pass themselves off as a distinguished lawyer and his clerk. The servant, who has one line in the whole play, "Madam, I go with all convenient speed," is named Balthazar. Portia addresses him by name. And I think we are allowed to suppose that the name suggests itself to her because she has just used it: it is handy and convenient. But surely another reason for the choice presents itself. Balthazar

The Merchant of Venice: *A Venture in Hermeneutics*

was a traditional name for one of the Wise Men, the Magi, those who were among the first to see and know and acknowledge the revelation of a new truth, which was the Incarnate Word. And it is in this role of gifted and enlightened sage, of the wise man to whom the truth has been especially vouchsafed that Portia is to make her courtroom appearance. Needless to say, her disguise is at the same time consistent with the general Carnival spirit and custom of license, mask, and buffoonery that presides in the festive comedies, and that has its parallel in the disguise of Jessica, as well as Jacob's passing himself off as Esau, and Bassanio's pose as a rich young man when he first appears at Belmont. So the true nature of Portia's adopted role is complex.

And now we come to the courtroom scene, the trial at which Shylock is so decisively defeated. Just how that defeat is effected may not instantly be clear. But, to begin with, we are not allowed to doubt the completeness of that defeat, because Shylock openly declares himself bested. What has happened that leads to his utter and unquestioned collapse? And how did Portia bring it about when the Duke himself and all the legal forces at his command, so clearly partial to Antonio, could not, at the beginning of the scene, discover any legal protection against Shylock's murderous designs?

We find ourselves in a court of law, and it is to the law that Shylock insistently appeals.

> If you deny me, fie upon your law!
> There is no force in the decrees of Venice.—
> I stand for judgment. Answer; shall I have it?

> I stand here for law.

> My deeds upon my head! I crave the law, . . .

> I charge you by the law,
> Whereof you are a well-deserving pillar,
> Proceed to judgment.

The Merchant of Venice: *A Venture in Hermeneutics*

So before everything else, the question that needs first to be considered is, what is "the law"? And we would be ill-advised to come to hasty decisions on this topic, or to rely upon easy assumptions, for this is just what Shylock himself does, and because he does so he is lost.

In considering the question, we might do well to remember the story from Genesis about Jacob and Laban that Shylock himself volunteers so early in the play, and recall Walter Russell Bowie's valuable exposition of it quoted above. It is a story centering on a legal-contractual arrangement; it is a story about "the law," or at least about some aspect of it. And I remarked in my discussion of the passage that Shylock himself, though he was the one to introduce the citation from Genesis, did not fully comprehend its meaning. As Bowie indicates, there is a secular sense, a plain and ethical interpretation of the meaning of Jacob's triumph over the niggardliness of his adoptive father; but there is a far more transcendent meaning to the text as well by which we know that a divine purpose is expressing itself. Shylock, fancying he knows the Genesis text and its meaning better than Antonio could possibly know it, is nevertheless one of the benighted, denied understanding of the "spiritual" as contrasted to the "carnal" senses of the text. Fittingly, Shylock is entirely absorbed by the "carnal" sense when citing the Jacob-Laban story, which is considerably more subtle and complex than he realizes.

Now if, as I have suggested above, the story of Jacob and Laban is a story in which an adopted son strives by craft and guile to win his true inheritance from a grudging and legalistic surrogate father; and if that story in turn represents the difficulty presented by winning from the legal entanglements of the Old Testament ("the law" Jesus speaks of in the passage from Matthew 5:17–18 cited above) the New Dispensation of love, freedom, and mercy, which at the same time acknowledges and derives from the Old Dispensation, then that story has a supremely important meaning of which Shylock is

183

manifestly unaware. For the story explains and justifies *before the fact* Jessica's conversion, as well as her disguise and theft—matters that Shylock could only find shocking and intolerable.[14]

Moreover, when Jesus says, "one jot or one tittle shall in no wise pass from the law, till all be fulfilled," there is some debate about the meaning of the last four of those words. One interpretation has it that the *consummatum est* on the cross is itself that fulfilment. Thus Morton Smith has written,

> We turn now to the fifth of the traits of Pauline baptism which were listed as probably derived from Jesus. This is the fact that it results in liberty from the Mosaic Law. Paul expresses this as a consequence of the death of Jesus: By his death Jesus satisfied the demands of the Law, so that it had no further claim on him; the baptised, being united with him, are also beyond its claims (e.g., Rom. 7.4). There has been much speculation as to how Paul— reportedly a Pharisee—came to hold such a theory, so alien to his training and his moralizing temperament and therefore probably not his own invention.[15]

But even if we prefer to believe that "all" is not yet "fulfilled," and assign that "fulfilment" to some eschatologically appointed time or some apocalyptic event, the claim of Jesus that he shall not abrogate the law but instead fulfil it must mean not only that there is an intimate connection between "the law" of the Old Testament and the "spirit" of the New one,[16] but that the earlier text can only be properly and completely understood in terms of the later one because the second is precisely the fulfilment and completion of, as well as the ultimate gloss upon, the first. Which is to say, the Old Testament cannot be completely understood as a discrete and autonomous work; its meaning arises out of, takes shape from, is colored and augmented and clarified by its necessary relationship to the New Testament. And this has been for a very long time a widely accepted Christian commonplace, and an unthinking assumption.

It was Shylock who cited the Jacob-Laban story as a sort of justification for usury, and without apparent awareness that the story carried any further burden of religious, or even legal, meaning. It is Shylock who in this crucial scene appeals to "the law," in the firm conviction that the law is purely a secular matter that pertains to and governs the Republic of Venice. He is wrong in both cases. The contract he has made with Antonio is an analogue, its heartlessness grotesquely magnified, of the uncharitable and niggardly contract offered by the uncovenanted Laban to the young Jacob. And the relationship between the two parties is not merely secular but religious in both cases. So the solution to the problem must be a religious one.

When Portia, in her guise as Balthazar, asks Antonio if he acknowledges the bond, and Antonio confesses that he does, Portia judicially remarks, "Then must the Jew be merciful." To this brilliantly pregnánt and ambiguous injunction, Shylock replies, "On what compulsion must I? Tell me that." In answer to Shylock, Portia offers her celebrated speech on mercy, and how it cannot be compelled; how, like love and grace, it is gratuitously offered. The speech clearly echoes Matthew 5:44–46, already cited, with its reference to God's gift of rain that falls alike upon the just and the unjust; and it also echoes these no less ringing words:

> Be ye therefore merciful, as your Father also is merciful.
> Judge not, and ye shall not be judged; condemn not, and
> ye shall not be condemned: forgive, and ye shall be for-
> given: Give and it shall be given unto you; good measure,
> pressed down, and shaken together, and running over,
> shall men give into your bosom.
> For with the same measure that ye mete withal it shall be
> measured to you again.
>
> (Luke 6:36–38)

The Merchant of Venice: *A Venture in Hermeneutics*

But let us return to the word *must* in Portia's declaration, "Then must the Jew be merciful." Shylock construes it simply as legal compulsion, and mocks it implicitly by his question, which points to the absurdity of trying to legislate human feelings. Mercy cannot be compelled any more than love can, and Portia's great speech is not simply instructive, since it agrees in positive terms with what Shylock's question has implied. Since Portia knows and beautifully declares that mercy cannot be compelled, there must be another sense than that of legal compulsion to her observation, "Then must the Jew be merciful." And indeed, the meaning of "must" here, as the rest of the trial will make clear, is not the requirement of law, or even of threat, but of logic. The Jew must be merciful because there is no alternative. And this will prove to be the case. And how is it proven? By what amounts to a symbolic exercise in hermeneutics, in a skilful reading and interpretation of "the law," in the ability to present an apodixis, an incontrovertible demonstration of the "right" meaning of "the law."

Shylock has staked his case on the law, legalist that he is, and makes his claim in the name of justice. The trial scene is in fact a head-on confrontation of Justice and Mercy, as Nevill Coghill noted in his essay "The Governing Idea," in *Shakespeare Quarterly*, I (London, 1948). They not only confront one another in Portia's famous speech about the quality of mercy, but in the very persons of the opposing parties in the trial, Shylock and Antonio. Shylock, refusing to show mercy at the start and throughout most of the scene, is then treated by Portia according to the terms that he has himself elected: according to the strict letter of the law. He is told that he may have his due according to the bond, but neither more nor less than what the bond expressly stipulates. If Shylock wishes to be a literalist, a punctilious observer of legal detail, then the bond must be interpreted with greater literalness than even he himself had thought of at the moment when he had it drawn up. Since no blood was specified in the bond, he is not

The Merchant of Venice: *A Venture in Hermeneutics*

entitled to shed blood; since a precise pound was specified in the bond, he must, on pain of death, be precise in his surgery and extract (without bloodshed) neither more nor less than a pound. This judgment of Balthazar's is nothing more nor less than a ludicrously literalist rendition of the text of the bond, which proves it both absurd and impossible. And in so doing a demonstration is made to Shylock that is beyond his capacity to refute: *the law, the letter of the law, literally construed, without the aid of mercy or the agency of the New Dispensation, is both nonsense and inoperable.* And this is why the Jew "must" be merciful. From the moment Portia-Balthazar says, "Tarry a little; there is something else" up to Shylock's complete capitulation, he is presented with the useless and empty consequences of a literalist and legalistic solution, till he is forced to acknowledge that it will not serve. The demonstration involves two stages. If blood, not stipulated in the bond, is shed, the penalty ("thy lands and goods/Are by the laws of Venice confiscate/Unto the state of Venice") is that "thriving" is cut off. This is Portia's answer to the earlier exchange between Antonio, who asks, "Or is your gold and silver ewes and rams?" and Shylock's rejoinder, "I cannot tell; I make it breed as fast." The second stage has to do with the exact measuring of the pound to be cut, and the penalty imposed is death. *The letter killeth.* The alternative solution is then proposed by the titular figure of the play, and its most selfless and generous figure, Antonio. And Antonio's solution exacts prodigality and life in the place of thriftiness and death.

The "proof" that Portia offers is in fact demonstrated theologically by the "penalties" imposed upon Shylock when judgment is found against him. This is an issue that has invariably been misunderstood. Shylock is made to become a Christian, not to oblige Antonio, nor as a punishment, since mercy cannot be compelled; he becomes a Christian because, in the world of this play, there is no logical alternative, once "the law" in all its new richness of meaning has been made clear to him.

The Merchant of Venice: *A Venture in Hermeneutics*

Just as what appeared to be Bassanio's defects of profligacy, once seen in a new light, became his virtues of prodigality; just as the most intimidating of the mottoes, the one on the most unattractive casket, concealed the true and only wealth; just so "the law" is either unseen or gravely misinterpreted (as Laban failed completely to understand the nature of his contract with Jacob) until it is revealed by someone wise and pure, passing under the name of a Wise Man, a Magus, but secret and innocent as Portia. And the logical demonstration of the ultimate fulfilment of the law in the dispensation of the New Testament not only leaves no doctrinal alternative to Christianity for Shylock, but requires by logical inexorability that he must now behave like a Christian and give away his substance to his daughter and son-in-law, thereby devoting himself completely to the only true faith. And where does all this appear in the play? In the following terse exchange:

SHYLOCK: Is that the law?

PORTIA: Thyself shalt see the act; . . .

Portia did not invent the law; it was always there on the books. Yet it was there without being understood, even by those in authority, like the Duke, who might be expected to be the first to understand it. It was there, yet unseen, or misunderstood, like Bassanio's virtue or the motto of the leaden casket. And since all the legal authorities of Venice were nonplussed by the contractual dilemma that Antonio found himself entangled in, it seems clear from both the dilemma itself and from its parallel to the paradigmatic story of the Jacob-Laban contract that the law here, too, must be more than the secular law of the city of Venice, about which Portia would be very unlikely to possess any expertise, or be able to bone up on enough to solve the problem in the short time she has at her disposal. But if the legal problem is instead really a spiritual one, then we may explain her success—her success in the face of the obtuseness of "legal authority"—by her purity, by those virtues Bas-

188

The Merchant of Venice: *A Venture in Hermeneutics*

sanio boasts of to Antonio, and by her Jacobean, favored, and native wit. And indeed, just as Launcelot Gobbo enacted the very scene of Jacob's theft of patrimonial blessing from his blind father, Isaac; and just as Shylock, spiritually blind, has his patrimonial blessing wrested from him here; just so is another major biblical text enacted on the stage, right before our eyes, though it has gone as undetected as the law by which Portia wins her case. The text is this one.

And the child grew, and waxed strong in spirit, filled with wisdom: and the grace of God was upon him.
Now his parents went to Jerusalem every year at the feast of the passover.
And when he was twelve years old, they went up to Jerusalem after the custom of the feast.
And when they had fulfilled the days, as they returned, the child Jesus tarried behind in Jerusalem; and Joseph and his mother knew not of it.
But they, supposing him to have been in the company, went a day's journey; and they sought him among their kinfolk and acquaintance. And when they found him not, they turned back again to Jerusalem, seeking him.
And it came to pass, that after three days they found him in the temple, sitting in the midst of the doctors, both hearing them, and asking them questions.
And all that heard him were astonished at his understanding and answers.
And when they saw him they were amazed: and his mother said unto him, Son, why hast thou thus dealt with us? behold, thy father and I have sought thee sorrowing.
And he said unto them, How is it that ye sought me? wist ye not that I must be about my Father's business?
And they understood not the saying which he spake unto them.[17]

(Luke 2:40–50)

The Merchant of Venice: *A Venture in Hermeneutics*

Just as the twelve-year-old prodigy amazes and confounds the doctors in the temple, where "the law" is pondered and discussed, so here in this courtroom Portia, a "mere slip of a girl," astonishes the Duke and his courtiers, and outwits her opponent in a manner that must be meant to resemble those many historical debates between Christians and Jews to which I have alluded. And how does she do this? The text presents us only with a symbolic answer, which we must undertake to interpret, just as all the suitors were required to interpret the texts of the caskets, and as we have already been required to interpret and reinterpret the initially enigmatic character of Bassanio.

Here is a court of law (the palace of the Doge of Venice is precisely where the most important trials took place, and it is connected to the state prison by the celebrated Bridge of Sighs) in which a man's life is at stake. According to the law as it dispersedly appears in Exodus, Leviticus, and Deuteronomy, there are some thirty-six crimes punishable by a death sentence, eighteen of them by a sentence of stoning. The other prescribed methods of execution are burning, beheading, and strangulation. (It may also be added that Talmudic law in effect rescinded the death penalty altogether by making the kinds and quantities of evidential materials required for conviction, by their multiplicity and specificities, virtually impossible to procure.) These capital offenses include murder, blasphemy, incest, adultery, the practice of magic, sorcery, and filial disobedience or disrespect. With regard to the last of these, the prohibition is an emphatic gloss upon the one of the Ten Commandments that reads, "Honor thy father and thy mother: that thy days may be long upon the land which the Lord thy God giveth thee." J. Coert Rylaarsdam's comment upon this Commandment declares (in part), "The honoring of parents is a form of piety," and in regard to the prohibition in the next chapter of Exodus he remarks, "The death sentence . . . bespeaks the respect for parents inculcated in Israelite society. The central point of the law is that children must obey their parents, as the Deuteronomic expansion of the law makes clear (Deut. 21:18–21)." Now, by that established and ancient dispensation, what Jessica has done is decidedly an act of filial impiety, and by that law she would be condemned to death. This is no small part of the grief Shylock suffers in discovering her elopement, theft, and conversion. But Jessica, as I have tried to show, is a representative figure for all those young people in the play who are trying to win a prize or inheritance they feel entitled to, and wrest it from the tyrannous grasp of an elder generation. And this generational opposition, requiring wit, guile, and cunning, is like the opposed yet familial relationship between the Old Testament and the New.

The crime that Jessica committed, along with other capital offenses enumerated in the Torah, was punishable by stoning, a traditional method of execution. It is the one used for Stephen, to which the man who would become Paul was witness. And as the canonical punishment for adultery, it is referred to by Jesus:

> They say unto him, Master, this woman was taken in adultery, in the very act . . .
> So when they continued asking him, he lifted up himself, and said unto them, He that is without sin among you, let him first cast a stone at her.
>
> (John 8:4–7)

In these words there is, by clear inference, a remission of the death penalty insofar as it would apply to this woman taken in adultery; and by further inference, this constitutes a remission of the death penalty per se. For if no one is blameless enough, even among the disciples, to cast the first stone, who among us shall declare himself fit for the task? This not only has the effect and force of clearing Jessica, it frees Antonio.

The Merchant of Venice: *A Venture in Hermeneutics*

What has happened here is that the old "law" has been revised and amended by a new interpretation of it, as Jesus has come to "fulfil" the law of the Old Testament. And what Portia accomplishes symbolically in this scene is a demonstration to Shylock that the New Testament is the necessary, the logical, the prophesied fulfilment of the Old; and by this demonstration— a matter that Christians often quite simply take for granted— she proves the contract between Shylock and Antonio null and void, and shows that Christianity is nothing more nor less than the very destiny of Judaism, and that consequently Shylock, by his own law, has no option but to become a Christian. It is simply a version of the ancient Jewish-Christian debates, in which the Christians win. This, then, is Portia's legal case, and she wins it.

If it be objected that Shylock seems to exhibit no joy whatever in being converted to the doctrines of love and joy, I think there are two plausible answers. He is, after all, a personification of the devil, who cannot be expected very much to delight in defeat at the hands of his spiritual adversary. But in his person as a mortal man, Shylock has undergone a terrible shock that has undermined everything he has ever believed or stood for, and the obvious dejection and sickness that he feels must be of the order of that other astonished and disturbed convert to Christianity, who appears to be far from overjoyed: the speaker of Eliot's "Journey of the Magi."

So Portia, having freed herself from the "Old Dispensation" of her own father's will, now, in the guise of a Wise Man and witness to the Truth in an epiphany, releases Antonio from the toils of misapprehended law, and the homicidal perversities of the devil in the guise of an "infidel" Jew. It is another of the small but telling ironies of the play that Shylock, the "infidel," is the only one in the play who resolutely refuses to break his oath, while all the rest do so with abandon—even the Duke himself, that awesome figure who seems to represent the very "law" itself, since he presides at the trial and is the chief officer of the state. Impetuously he orders Shylock to obey all Antonio's demands:

> He shall do this, or else I do recant
> The pardon that I late pronouncèd here.

The controversy between Portia and Shylock over "the law," confined though it is to a single line, to a brief question and a terse answer, is the very controversy—the on-going Disputation between Christians and Jews, continuing over centuries— of which the example of the debate between Rabbi Abraham Farissol of Avignon and his Christian opponents at Ferrara in the year 1500 has already been cited. Haim Hillel Ben-Sasson furnishes many other examples. Religious disputation was a common and public event, often undertaken by the orthodox in contention with those they regarded as heretics. And while this play presents the debate only in symbolic form, there is no doubt that Portia's legal triumph is in fact a moral triumph, a triumph of life over death, and a generous religious dispensation over one conventionally thought to be strict, stingy, and ungenerous. Portia's triumph is hermeneutical: a revelatory and inarguable reading of the text of "the law," a reading made possible by her virtue, understanding, and faith.

It may fairly be objected that the brief debate I have cited, confined as it is to a single line of iambic pentameter, is a rather feeble instance of forensics; and I may be accused of extrapolating an enormous and complex controversy, of immense range and challenging subtlety, on which mortal and spiritual life depend, out of a few noncommital syllables. And I would have to admit that the words in question carry little resonance. My argument is by analogy. All the liberations of the play enact something of the kind. And it may be added, not irrelevantly, that religious disputation, if actually written into the script, would run the risk of boring the audience, taking up too much time, diverting interest from other aspects of the play, and generally unbalancing the design of the whole. So we are once again, as with the initial mystery of Bassanio's character, left to infer, by careful thought, or by a painstaking "reading" of the text, how Portia astonishes the court and saves the day.

The final act of *The Merchant of Venice* is nothing more nor less than a melodic and thematic recapitulation of the rich materials that have appeared before. It begins in darkness, and moves steadily toward a growing dawn. The darkness is in part the darkness of ignorance, and it is represented in the charming and bantering antiphon of exchanges between Jessica and Lorenzo at the beginning of the act. All the people they speak of, themselves excepted, are pagans, for whom love is a doomed matter. But the love of this couple before us is clarified and symbolized by a celestial glory, and Lorenzo offers his gorgeous aria of poetry in tribute to the beauty of the night, the music of the spheres, and, by inference, of course, their holy and angelic attendance.[18] This is a world redeemed from the pagan one, and love itself is thereby perfected. In the very next moment, when Portia enters, she remarks on the wonder and strength of light in darkness, recalling not only the Star of Bethlehem that guided the Wise Men (one of whom she recently portrayed) but also the text that reads:

> Let your light so shine before men, that they may see your good works, and glorify your Father which is in heaven.
>
> (Matthew 5:16)

But, magnificently, and within the brief space of some thirty-four lines, the first clear signs of a coming dawn make a distinct, if ambiguous, appearance.

> This night methinks is but the daylight sick;—
> It looks a little paler. 'Tis a day
> Such as the day is when the sun is hid.

The imagery here is doubly ambiguous. In addition to the manifest uncertainty about whether it's night or day, there is the question of whether this is due purely to the transitional phase of slowly increasing light at the beginning of dawn (a straightforward, naturalistic interpretation) or whether something far more revelatory is being suggested. The lines themselves are brief, and the topic quickly dismissed, yet so strange does this imagery seem that we may suspect it as possibly intended to recall an extraordinary prophetic utterance from the last chapter of Zechariah that is usually taken to describe the advent of the New Dispensation:

> Behold, the day of the Lord cometh, . . .
> And it shall come to pass in that day, that the light
> shall not be clear, nor dark:
> But it shall be one day which shall be known to the Lord,
> not day, nor night: but it shall come to pass, that at
> evening time it shall be light.
>
> (Zechariah 14:1–7)

And now there follows the light-hearted banter about oaths, and the mock-horror at the discovery of the gift of the rings, and the mock-threats of retaliation in kind. But all this is preliminary to forgiveness; and the two women know that the oaths were broken in behalf of a "greater love" that is sanctioned by religion. Once the forgiveness is offered, once the law of loving mercy is exhibited, it remains only to distribute the rewards of virtue. And the rewards come in the form of *words*. This is good news, the good news of the gospels, and of the Word that gives life. To Jessica and Lorenzo the text of a deed, making them heirs of Shylock's estate. To Gratiano and Nerissa a letter, and another to Antonio, each text conferring good fortune, revelation and clarification. Lorenzo's apt response is,

> Fair ladies, you drop manna in the way
> Of starved people.

The Merchant of Venice: *A Venture in Hermeneutics*

The word, in other words, becomes edible and nourishing, and the Old Testament (manna) prefigures the New (the Eucharist). Portia's next words are, "It is almost morning." The manna that is spiritual as well as carnal nourishment, the arriving morning that is illumination of every hopeful and insightful kind, join in manifesting a new and gospel truth, quietly and clearly triumphant at the end of the play.[19]

Before proceeding to the last two of my questions, a word, however perfunctory, needs to be said about the play's language. In contrast, on the one hand, to the almost purely verbal world of *Love's Labour's Lost*, with its relentless Euphuistic wit, or, on the other, to the stainless and magical world of *A Midsummer Night's Dream*, where everyone, from Bottom, through the human and fairy lovers, to Theseus and Hippolyta, is "translated" by and into poetry that renders each immune to grief, the *Merchant* is down-to-earth, written in a language of energy and with the cunning of reserve. Energy, indeed, marks the speech of nearly everyone in the play, with the possible exception of Antonio. As for reserve, I mean that the play is full of careful omissions, detours and deceptions, guiles and disguises, which both we and the play's characters are challenged to figure out.

The play employs the word *fortune*, sometimes capitalized to signify a deity or supernal force, sometimes in lower-case plural, some twenty-three times, along with two mentions of *misfortune*, and one use of *fortunate*. Less conspicuously, the word *suit* is employed at crucial junctures, in regard both to law and the process of litigation, and to the pursuit of courtship. It is in fact the word that links these two aspects of the play, and fuses them into a single action. It bears, moreover, not only its legal and romantic burden but a theological one as well. It can be no accident that within the small compass of thirty-two lines Bassanio, who is about to advance his own suit in Belmont, first hires Launcelot Gobbo, accepting his petition for employment with these words, "I know thee well, thou hast obtain'd thy suit," and then, in response to Gratiano's importunate, "I have a suit to you," replies, without waiting to hear particulars, "You have obtain'd it." Surely we are expected to read some Christ-like compliance and magnanimity into these verbal gestures, and encouraged to hope that when it comes Bassanio's turn to present his suit he will be answered with no less generosity. (Just why Gratiano is so importunate here is smoothly glossed over by the playwright, who is no less high-handed about how Portia comes to possess the letter she gives to Antonio in the final scene, assuring him of the safety of some of his mercantile ventures.)

There is a generous use of classical allusions, most of them explicit, some of them buried, by virtually all persons in the play, irrespective of social class, with the conspicuous exceptions of Shylock and Antonio. Even Launcelot Gobbo, an innocent Malaprop and simple clown, who ludicrously mangles language throughout, nevertheless makes an apt and correct reference to Scylla and Charybdis. Most of the classical allusions, however, are used in contexts at once heroic and romantic, as in Bassanio's description, in the first scene, of Portia, and of her suitors as so many Jasons. Portia herself is likened not only, by virtue of her tresses and her wealth, to the Golden Fleece, but also to Portia, the daughter of Cato and wife of Marcus Brutus, one of the conspirators against Caesar. After Brutus committed suicide, his wife did so too (by the hideous method of stuffing her mouth with burning coals), thus becoming a severe example of marital loyalty, a topic that is much considered in this drama. The other suitors, Morocco and Arragon, continue the grand heroic style, and when it comes Bassanio's turn, Portia does it for him, sparing him the dangerous vanity of using such language about himself. These classical images that so often recall heroic exploit serve brilliantly to dramatize what amounts to the play's ingenious contrast of two sorts of heroism: the secular, pagan, swaggering, and unredeemed kind, and the Christian, sacrificial, and redemptive kind. The drama furnishes generous room for both.

It may be worth attending to a few local passages in some detail, and we may begin with Solanio's observation, after Antonio has acknowledged that he is sad, but denied that this is due to considerations of either money or love,

> Not in love neither: then let us say you are sad
> Because you are not merry; and 'twere as easy
> For you to laugh and leap, and say you are merry
> Because you are not sad. Now by two-headed Janus,
> Nature hath fram'd strange fellows in her time:
> Some that will evermore peep through their eyes,
> And laugh like parrots at a bagpiper:
> And other of such vinegar aspect,
> That they'll not show their teeth in way of smile
> Though Nestor swear the jest be laughable.

We have here not merely the classical allusions to Janus and Nestor but the implied masks of the classical theater that represented Comedy and Tragedy, here linked in two-headed Janus. The word *merry*, which Shylock will twice use to characterize the supposed frivolity of the bond he proposes, will surface again near the end of the play in a serious comment of Jessica's. But here the two masklike characteristics, Tragic and Comic, taken mockingly and unseriously by Solanio, will find their personal spokesmen in real characters in the play. If the tragic has already been personified by Antonio, Gratiano is about to appear to make an extended claim for the comic, with his speech that begins, "Let me play the fool," and which implies that anyone who contrives to be otherwise than heedless, easy-going, and devil-may-care (including his interlocutor, Antonio) is merely putting on airs. Yet however much of a free-wheeling joker Gratiano may be, the cheerfulness he advocates has its Christian and doctrinal sanctions, though he is not likely to be aware of them. (Cf. Matthew 6:16–17;

The Merchant of Venice: *A Venture in Hermeneutics*

9:14–17; II Cor. 9:7; Rom. 12:8.) The two modes of drama and feelings are presented to us in person and capsulized as masks within the first hundred lines of the play.

Launcelot Gobbo's first speech is a splendid comic set-piece in prose, of a sort that will come to assume different shapes in later plays, but always with wonderful effect. It is a speech the playwright must have enjoyed writing, and one that an actor cannot help rejoice in delivering: a solo, a brilliant divertimento or cadenza of virtuosity. It's a little temptation scene, meant probably to parody such scenes as they appeared here and there throughout Marlowe's *Doctor Faustus*, where the tempters are Good and Bad Angels, as well as in earlier dramas and morality plays. Not the least of the wit here lies in the fact that "conscience" bids Launcelot abide by conventional morality, and remain faithful to his infidel employer, while "the fiend" counsels disobedience to convention, and fidelity to the higher morality of fleeing, that is, to *infidelity*. The fiend even urges his cause in pious terms: " 'Fia!' says the fiend, 'away!' says the fiend, 'for the heavens rouse up a brave mind,' says the fiend, 'and run.' " There is more wit to this than a mere confirmation of Antonio's bromide that "the devil can cite Scripture for his purpose." Launcelot allows us to see quite early in the play how equivocal is the whole nature of morality, and to confirm in advance Portia's disconcerting admission near the end of the play: "Nothing is good (I see) without respect"—a confession of the relativity and instability of all judgment.

I turn now to a speech which I confess I am unsure how to read or in what spirit to comprehend. It seems to me the sort of speech that cautions us against the dangers of unsupported personal reaction. It is Salerio's speech, II, viii, in praise of Antonio.

A kinder gentleman treads not the earth,—
I saw Bassanio and Antonio part,

The Merchant of Venice: *A Venture in Hermeneutics*

> Bassanio told him he would make some speed
> Of his return: he answered, "Do not so,
> Slubber not business for my sake Bassanio,
> But stay the very riping of the time,
> And for the Jew's bond which he hath of me—
> Let it not enter in your mind of love:
> Be merry, and employ your chiefest thoughts
> To courtship, and such fair ostents of love
> As shall conveniently become you there."
> And even there (his eye being big with tears),
> Turning his face, he put his hand behind him,
> And with affection wondrous sensible
> He wrung Bassanio's hand, and so they parted.

To which Solanio responds, "I think he only loves the world for him." Solanio's rejoinder will not allow us to miss the Christian and devotional aspects of this relationship. Nevertheless, the play is ostensibly secular, and is surely intended to be read and played on that level throughout, whatever more serious theological burden it may bear. And in purely secular terms, Antonio's behavior is as peculiar as Hamlet's dumb show, reported to her father by Ophelia. It is nearly ludicrous in its melodramatic posturings. And the more ludicrous in that Antonio has already attempted to allay Bassanio's scruples and anxieties with these words in the first act:

> Why fear not man, I will not forfeit it,—
> Within these two months, that's a month before
> This bond expires, I do expect return
> Of thrice three times the value of this bond.

And since between that assurance and the parting of the two friends no news of calamity to Antonio's ships has been delivered to him or even hinted at, the averted face, the backward handclasp, the tears, are, as it seems, excessive. It is not easy to believe that after such a send-off Bassanio will be able to enjoy an altogether carefree voyage. There are also Antonio's equivocal references to the purpose of Bassanio's journey as both "business" and "courtship," which at the very least may serve once again to fuse and confuse love and money. In II, vi, Gratiano and Salerio are puzzled to find Lorenzo late for his tryst and elopement with Jessica, Gratiano remarking that "lovers ever run before the clock," in confirmation of which Salerio declares,

> O ten times faster Venus' pigeons fly
> To seal love's bonds new-made, than they are wont
> To keep obliged faith unforfeited!

And Gratiano continues,

> That ever holds: who riseth from a feast
> With that keen appetite that he sits down?
> Where is the horse that doth untread again
> His tedious measures with the unbated fire
> That he did pace them first?—all things that are,
> Are with more spirit chased than enjoy'd.
> How like a younger or a prodigal
> The scarfed bark puts from her native bay—
> Hugg'd and embraced by the strumpet wind!
> How like the prodigal doth she return
> With over-weather'd ribs and ragged sails—
> Lean, rent, and beggar'd by the strumpet wind!

At this crucial juncture in Lorenzo's career such comment, which appears to be prompted by his situation, is cynical and unpropitious. It is the more ominous and resonant if, by extension, we think of applying it to the persons of Bassanio and Portia. And since Gratiano's instances conclude with nautical imagery, we are surely invited to apply them to Antonio's commercial ventures as well. In all these regards, the speaker's cheerful cynicism is unnerving. We have here, in miniature, a Rake's Progress, the young gallant beginning in fashionable attire that attracts the avaricious whore, and concluding with his raiment in tatters, having been taken for all he's worth. "The strumpet wind" is simply the goddess Fortuna, fickleness personified. Curiously, Shakespeare's metaphor is vaguely compromised by his obligation to keep the ship, which represents the Rake, female in gender to comply with nautical tradition, which always refers to ships in this manner. But this odd confusion is to be dramatically echoed a moment later when Jessica appears disguised, and says, "Cupid himself would blush/ To see me thus transformed to a boy," and Lorenzo remarks that Jessica is "obscur'd" "even in the lovely garnish of a boy." But the essential point is that we have been introduced to the chilling note of decayed marital passion, to illicit sexuality and tainted virtue, themes that are to be continually repeated, e.g., in the banter between Jessica and Lorenzo that begins the last act, in the tauntings by Portia and Nerissa of their husbands at the end, in almost all the instances of infidelity, enacted or proposed in the course of the play. All stories that end, "and they lived happily ever after," are not only romances, but for children; and adults are entitled to a silent smile of superior, if sullied, knowledge. *They* know that such an ending is not likely to be true, and is in any case not an ending. And the purity of romantic attachments, the incontaminate domain of love, is constantly being called into question from the beginning to the end of this play by jests and jibes at the expense of marriage and fidelity. And this may explain why the play ends not just with a bawdy joke, but with a monitory one. It is not the only play of Shakespeare's with such an ending.

In profoundly moving contrast to this recurrent motif stands a brief speech of Shylock's, who does not lose the occasion, in the courtroom scene, to make light of the devotion of Christian husbands. But earlier he is allowed to exhibit, in the midst of ludicrous, comic equivocation, a moving devotion to the memory of his dead wife. The scene with Tubal near the beginning of Act III is comic in the manner of a set piece, its jest residing in Shylock's alternate emotions of self-pity and malicious glee being played upon as on an instrument by the perfectly adept Tubal. We are surely not invited to inquire into Tubal's motives for eliciting this display, motives which could only be characterized as cruel, and would contradict our clear sense of Shylock's manifest confidence in and affection for the man. There is even further ground to bind the two in sympathy: Shylock has not enough money of his own to make the three-thousand-ducat loan to Bassanio and has to apply to Tubal ("a wealthy Hebrew of my tribe") for supplementary funds. Shylock proposed the terms of the bond, and we know that he never intended to receive or accept a financial settlement if the terms were not met; which means either that he intended to cheat Tubal out of the return of money that was properly his, or that Tubal was a sympathetic supporter of the barbarity Shylock is planning. But I don't believe these matters are meant to be considered. We have here instead a scene of emotional oscillation in which the jest consists of Shylock's limitless sympathy and pity for his own predicament, a self-centeredness so pronounced (at the moment) that Tubal cannot refrain from reminding him that "other men have ill luck too," to Shylock's no less limitless ruthlessness and lack of sympathy for Antonio. It seems ludicrous that anyone could feel so victimized by Fate, and at the same time feel no sympathy for another victim; it quite obviously relieves us of the burden of extending our own sympathy to him. The scene is a little charade or masque based on the joke about "the good news" and "the bad news." But into the midst of this buffoonery, prompted by Tubal's news that a sailor produced a ring "he had of your daughter for a monkey," there appears this, as I think, touching outbreak from Shylock:

The Merchant of Venice: *A Venture in Hermeneutics*

> Out upon her!—thou torturest me Tubal,—it was my
> turquoise, I had it of Leah when I was a bachelor: I would
> not have given it for a wilderness of monkeys.

William Empson is surely right in remarking on the sexual
symbolism of the monkey; and to Jessica the purchase of one
at the expense of her father's ring was emblematic of many
kinds of emancipation and defiance. But to Shylock the ring
represents affection and fidelity even beyond the grave, and
devotion of a personal sort that many other parts of the play
call cynically into question.

Indeed, just before this comic turn of equivocating emotions,
Shylock is offered what many regard as his chief scene in the
play: his great prose aria of self-justification—"Hath not a
Jew eyes? . . ." This speech exhibits so much energy and
rhetorical force, so sound an appeal (so it seems to us in our
hasty sympathy) to the qualities of our common humanity,
that readers and commentators have reacted to it almost in
isolation, and in odd and fallacious ways. There is current, in
fact, what may perhaps be called the Compositional Fallacy,
which can be stated roughly as follows: Shakespeare gathered
his materials from various sources, laid them out according to
a scheme of action and the necessities of dramaturgy, and
found that he had bought himself a vengeful and malicious
villain. But since his genius lay (as Matthew Arnold said) not
in his gift for language but in his capacity to imagine an infinite variety of humanity, and to endow each with convincing
life (as though all this were somehow done *without* language)
his own deep humanity could not refrain from making Shylock
more sympathetic than he was originally intended to be, and
providing him with justifications that all but win our consent.

There are a number of things wrong with such arguments,
which presume to test the nature of Shakespeare's dramatic
devices upon the litmus paper of the soul of the one who holds
such views, one who entertains an admiring if sentimentalized,

and necessarily imperfect, sense of Shakespeare's broad *humanity*. It may first be objected that the spokesman for this argument has nothing but conjecture to show what Shylock was to have been before Shakespeare, overcome by irrepressible generosity and humanity, complicated and came near compromising his own drama by lending to poor Shylock a depth of feeling and dimension of character that the playwright was virtually powerless to withhold. And it may be added that Shakespeare had no trouble withholding sympathy from Iago and Claudius and Goneril and Regan. This positing of an author of uncontrollable loving-kindness does little to advance our real sense of the play, nor even of the persuasiveness of the scene.

Instead, I will venture a few observations that I hope will prove pertinent. Shylock's appeal in this scene to the sensations of common humanity, running as they do through a wide gamut of involuntary responses, concludes, shockingly, with one of the most debatable of human motives, revenge, which is, by inference, also meant to be an involuntary response, like laughing when being tickled, or dying when poisoned. That such rhetorical force should be marshalled in behalf of so brutal an argument is merely consistent with the views of other Shakespearean cynics. In addition, Shylock's argument rests ultimately upon the same sort of moral relativism that haunts the play from beginning to the end, and which Portia somewhat disconcertingly epitomizes near the end with her comment, "Nothing is good (I see) without respect." This calling into question of the motives and character of nearly everyone, while it does nothing to redeem the character of Shylock, and is not, as he seems to think, a justification for his actions, nevertheless invites us as readers or audience to withhold a too swift and easy judgment of what has been set before us. Finally, I am convinced that the raw power of the speech and its essential cynicism, coming as it does in the first scene of the third act, serves dramatically to contrast the cutthroat antagonisms that constitute the commercial world of Venice with the comparatively innocent and amorous world of Belmont that shall appear in the next scene. Admittedly, the play has shifted back and forth between Venice and Belmont before. But here they are brought into their most dramatic contrast. The commerce of which Shylock speaks, the diseases, the weapons, the enemies, the bleeding, poison and revenge, these, which are parts of a world Shylock reckons as familiar, are utterly absent in Belmont, which we now see unblemished by Portia's anxiety about the outcome of the casket trial, or by the presence of unsuitable suitors. Shylock's speech, for all its force, is a dissonance which is to be contrasted to the manifest music of the next scene, in which actual music makes its first appearance in the play.

And so it is right to turn to that scene and to Portia's speech that immediately precedes the music, and Bassanio's more than merely fortunate choice.

> Nerissa and the rest, stand all aloof.—
> Let music sound while he doth make his choice,
> Then if he lose he makes a swan-like end,
> Fading in music. That the comparison
> May stand more proper, my eye shall be the stream
> And wat'ry death-bed for him:—he may win,
> And what is music then? Then music is
> Even as the flourish, when true subjects bow
> To a new-crowned monarch: such it is
> As are those dulcet sounds at break of day,
> That creep into the dreaming bridegroom's ear,
> And summon him to marriage. Now he goes
> With no less presence, but with much more love
> Than young Alcides, when he did redeem
> The virgin tribute, paid by howling Troy
> To the sea-monster: I stand for sacrifice,

The Merchant of Venice: *A Venture in Hermeneutics*

> The rest aloof are the Dardanian wives,
> With bleared visages come forth to view
> The issue of th'exploit: Go Hercules!
> Thou live, I live—with much much more dismay,
> I view the fight, than thou that mak'st the fray.

This is an extraordinary speech, and in an idiom that I think it is not wrong to call operatic: it is self-conscious, stylized, and contrived. This does not mean it is false or devoid of feeling, but that it stands in brilliant contrast in its grand gestures to the sort of raw and undigested feelings of Shylock's recent outburst in prose. It is, rather, a Veronese or Tiepolo fresco, filled with gorgeous pomp and classical personages; and it fulfils a number of lovely functions virtually simultaneously. It introduces the theme of music, which not only will exhibit itself in literal performance at the close of Portia's speech, but in the richly embroidered verse of the last scene will present us with harmonies both worldly and heavenly. Moreover, Portia suggests two contrasting modes of music. The first, if Bassanio fails, becomes his swan song, and suggests (without exhibiting any alarm on Portia's part, nor inviting any on our own) that if he fails he will die. This is part of the convention of rejected lovers, and Shakespeare is by no means alone in taking it light-heartedly. In Marlowe's *Hero and Leander*, Hero is described as wearing

> Her kirtle blue, whereon was many a stain,
> Made with the blood of wretched lovers slain.

Note that the music, whatever may be played, will consort with whatever the issue of his choice may be, a relativity or pathetic fallacy that will recur in the last scene. The metaphors, starting with Bassanio's swanlike end, are exaggerated enough for us to withhold a literal reading of them, and they continue their mode of hyperbole with the image of the eye that will supply the watery deathbed for the hero-swan. If, on

the other hand, he chooses right, the music is itself transformed into a flourish, a trumpet-sound of triumph; or else to
"those dulcet sounds at break of day,/That creep into the
dreaming bridegroom's ear,/And summon him to marriage."
It is certainly suitable to conjure up a bridegroom in the happy
event that Bassanio should make the right choice, but surely
these lines are meant to be echoed in altered form when we
later hear this:

> Here will we sit, and let the sounds of music
> Creep in our ears—

Moreover, these contrasted modes of music, one of them suitable to be the accompaniment of death, the other of triumph,
are restatements of the matching and twinned themes of tragedy and comedy, here represented by their respective modal
styles.

And now heroic hyperbole, likening Bassanio, faced with a
choice of caskets, to Hercules subduing a sea monster and rescuing a sacrificial virgin, would invite at least a smile had not
both the previous suitors we have met, Morocco and Arragon,
seen themselves and the test of the caskets under the figure of
heroic exploit. Nerissa and the rest have been told to stand
"aloof," like the Trojan wives, beyond the arena of "the fray,"
but able to witness what shall take place. And the passage concludes with what amounts to an emblematic tableau, such as
we know from paintings by Raphael and Titian, and which
are part of a conventional iconography. Hercules's rescue of
Hesione, daughter of Laomedon, from the sea monster to
which she was to be sacrificed, is another version of Perseus
and Andromeda, and even of Saint George and the dragon,
which usually represents the saint overcoming a monster while
a helpless young woman stands by. But the iconography here
has a special burden of meaning. Portia's "I stand for sacrifice," is later to be countered and opposed by Shylock's "I
stand for judgment," in the trial scene. And this present scene

The Merchant of Venice: *A Venture in Hermeneutics*

in Belmont is of course a trial scene of a different sort. If Portia is cast as sacrificial virgin to be rescued by the hero, Bassanio-Hercules-Perseus-Saint George, then the sea monster from which she is to be rescued is the enchaining Old Dispensation of her father's will and testament, from which the bridegroom she desires will release her. In point of fact, in the *Dictionary of Subjects and Symbols in Art* by James Hall, the entry on Saint George declares, "To the early Christians a dragon symbolized evil, in particular paganism. The conversion of a heathen country to Christianity by a saint would thus be depicted in symbolic form as the slaying of a dragon with a spear. [Cf. Saint Patrick driving the snakes out of Ireland.] Saint George was shown in this manner to signify the winning of Cappadocia for the faith, the place itself being personified by a maiden (a normal convention . . .)." Moreover, by identifying herself with the sacrificial victim, Portia identifies herself with the salvationist role of Antonio. And indeed, once Bassanio's choice is made and the task accomplished, once triumph has been achieved, Portia responds to deliverance from the bonds of the law in which she was confined with

> *Myself* and what is mine, to you and yours
> *Is now converted.*

I think there is reason to suppose that Bassanio and Antonio may have been intended to resemble one another physically as well as spiritually. We have already noticed the telling reciprocity of Bassanio's offer of his life for Antonio's. But there are hints that the two are also look-alikes. The early comedies feature a number of pairs of twins, and their usefulness to Shakespeare might have been abetted by the actual presence of twins among his acting company. At the very least, Portia offers grounds to suppose such a resemblance (III, iv).

> I never did repent for doing good,
> Nor shall not now: for in companions
> That do converse and waste the time together,

209

The Merchant of Venice: *A Venture in Hermeneutics*

> Whose souls do bear an egall yoke of love,
> There must be needs a like proportion
> Of lineaments, of manners, and of spirit;
> Which makes me think that this Antonio
> Being the bosom lover of my lord,
> Must needs be like my lord. If it be so,
> How little is the cost I have bestowed
> In purchasing the semblance of my soul,
> From out the state of hellish cruelty!

Note that in saving Antonio, who is the semblance of Bassanio, who is her soul, she is saving her soul from perdition. These sentiments may be read as deriving partly from Aristotle's description of friendship in the *Nicomachean Ethics*. But I suspect there is something more to the matter, and that the spiritual identity, manifest at the moment of crisis, takes a back seat to the physical one in the distinctly bawdy context of the last scene. After Bassanio has been obliged to confess to giving away the ring he promised never to part with; after begging forgiveness and swearing he will never break his oath again; and after Portia's legitimate jests about trusting the word of one who has already perjured himself, Antonio volunteers a small echo of his major sacrifice.

> I once did lend my body for his wealth,
> Which but for him that had your husband's ring
> Had quite miscarried. I dare be bound again,
> My soul upon the forfeit, that your lord
> Will never more break faith advisedly.

To which Portia responds, "Then you shall be his surety." The nature of this transaction is not entirely clear. In fact it is very difficult to see what Portia's recompense is to be if only Antonio's soul is being offered here. But certainly one way to read Antonio's "bond" is something like this: I once offered my body for him, and, upon my soul, I'm prepared to do so again. It may at least be argued that Portia seizes upon this reading, and instantly accepts. There would be a good deal of comic point to this if the two men actually looked like one another.

As for the song, and Bassanio's speech that follows it, I have already indicated my sense of their relationship. I would here add in confirmation of what I have proposed that Bassanio's first word after the song concludes, "So," can refer grammatically only to the text of the song itself, having no other antecedent. And that in striking contrast to the other suitors we have met, Bassanio takes no notice whatever of the texts on the caskets, but addresses himself, as he was clearly meant to do, to the text of the song; and his speech before choosing is no more nor less than an elaborate extrapolation of the song's text.

The most beautiful and sustained passage of poetry in the play seems to me, as well as to many others, the opulent tribute to music in the last act that runs from Lorenzo's command to Stephano to "bring your music forth into the air," up to the very cessation of the music itself. This passage, which runs to a little more than fifty lines, employs the word "sweet" or one of its cognates nine times. Once it is used by Jessica, when she says, "I am never merry when I hear sweet music." This does not mean the music depresses her, or that she has no ear for it. Her use of "merry" here is like Shylock's earlier in regard to his bond, and intends something like "frivolous," or "careless." Lorenzo, comparing her reaction to those of wild colts, with some want of gallantry, remarks that as instinctively as they she recognizes the angelic solemnity that music represents, but without comprehending the doctrinal reasons for this, being new as she is to Christianity. This is allowed to pass unnoticed.

But I must now return to the two questions I posed at the beginning of this essay, and which still remain unanswered. So I address first the question of the passivity, the characterlessness, of Antonio, who is, after all, the titular merchant and as such the chief figure of play. As I have indicated, he is a blameless and unblemished Christian, and for that very reason the ideal victim for satanic designs such as Shylock entertains. He is, moreover, the legitimate son and heir of the innocent pilgrims who were the protagonists of the early morality plays. John Dover Wilson[20] has pointed out that "before its final secularization in the first half of the sixteenth century, our drama was concern with one topic, and only one: human salvation. It was a topic that could be represented in either of two ways: (i) historically, by means of miracle plays, which in the Corpus Christi cycles unrolled before the spectators' eyes the whole scheme of salvation from Creation to the Last Judgment; or (ii) allegorically, by means of morality plays, which exhibited the process of salvation in the individual soul on its road between birth and death, beset with the snares of the World or the wiles of the Evil One. . . . But Youth at the door of opportunity, with Age or Experience, Charity or Good Counsel, offering him the yoke of responsibility, while the World, the Flesh and the Devil beckon him to follow them on the primrose path to the everlasting bonfire, is older than even the medieval religious play. It is a theme to which every generation gives fresh form, while retaining its essential substance." Dover Wilson goes on to illustrate the presence of the theme in the plays of Plautus and Terence as well as in the parable of the Prodigal Son. From a purely dramatic point of view it became increasingly clear with time that while salvation and its attainment may have been a major theme of the plays, and was certainly a desirable end, all the excitement, suspense, and crude "human interest" resided precisely in that part of the story devoted to frivolity, temptation, and sin. And in due course, the salvationist theme was reserved for a final and nearly perfunctory coda to a text that dwelt with evident relish upon all the worldly and agreeable aspects of vice and debauchery. *The Second Shepherds' Play* is a handsome and beautiful instance of such deliberate unbalance. For the fact is that virtue very often consists in resisting temptation or wickedness, and while resistance may require enormous strength, it is in itself not an active or initiatory form of behavior. It is provoked by something active and other than itself; in its finest manifestation it expresses itself in martyrdom, which is an exquisitely measured form of acceptance that is not resignation, and hope that is unworldly. It is, in any case, an inward condition that, because of its inwardness, presents to the dramatist almost insuperable problems as regards dramatic presentation, as I think is evident in both *Murder in the Cathedral* and *The Cocktail Party* by T. S. Eliot. Antonio's assigned role in this play is that of innocent victim and Christian hero such as Hugh of Lincoln or William of Norwich or Simon of Trent—or Christ himself in his role of mute sufferer. His inwardness keeps his mystery to himself, that obscure sadness that knows there always will be a people who will need a sacrifice, and always a Caiaphas to advise that it would be expedient "that one man should die for the people." And that while Christ died for this very purpose, the need for the sacrifice has turned out to be unappeasable: a ravenous, destructive and eternal appetite. Antonio, therefore, seems the least vivid character in the play because he is the most secret one, and, despite his mercantile concerns, the most unworldly.[21]

Finally, I will venture an answer to my first question, regarding the distinct uncertainty of most interpreters of the play as to its "tone," and its ambiguous character as potentially either a comedy or a tragedy. Doubtless, some of the ambiguity derives from a plain misunderstanding of the play itself, documentation for which abounds upon the shelves of criticism. Such misunderstanding is much abetted by the apparent paleness of Antonio's character in distinct and dramatic contrast with Shylock's. It is the understandable instinct of a theatrical director to seize upon such events and persons as will prove most arresting to an audience. And the fact is that

The Merchant of Venice: *A Venture in Hermeneutics*

Shylock, if he be the devil, is the devil in a very human guise, full of plausible self-justification, and able to see himself rather as the victim than as the aggressor. Since Shylock's motives can be deduced (as Antonio's still more inward secret cannot be) deduction is invited and required of us. But if we indolently decline the invitation, we are subject to error: for Shylock never comes forward to us, as Iago does, to admit shamelessly to his villainy. Throughout he presents (except perhaps with regard to his "contract," about which he is less than candid) a convincing aspect of righteousness and aggrieved persecution. And many actors and producers have been completely persuaded by him. This sympathy has been strengthened by a conviction that the penalties imposed upon Shylock at the end of the trial are ruthless and Inquisitorial and that his conversion is imposed upon him with all the barbarity that was once actually employed in Spain and elsewhere.

There is some justification for this feeling of sympathy in behalf of Shylock, as critics have been quick and numerous to point out almost from the first. And there is no denying that at the end of the trial the ultimate coercion is frankly brandished before him in the form of a threat of execution. It is, of course, essential to my conception of the play that this threat is decidedly not the cause of Shylock's ultimate capitulation, though that is not a matter to be demonstrated with an unassailable show of proof. But I can offer in evidence Shylock's own acid comment, which is itself a pointed echo of Ecclesiasticus, or the Wisdom of Jeshua, the son of Sirach, 34:22, "The man who takes away his neighbor's living murders him."

> Nay, take my life and all, pardon not that,—
> You take my house, when you do take the prop
> That doth sustain my house: you take my life
> When you do take the means whereby I live.

While it may be argued that this is merely a rhetorical and sardonic plea for mercy, an attempt to shame his oppressors, I would claim that Shylock is indeed prepared to die for what he regards as his principles, and in order to mock and defy what he has found to be the customary and traditional inhumanity of the Gentiles. The threat of execution offered him is the more hideous in that it comes from the Duke, who had first ostentatiously offered a gratuitous pardon from that extremity; and the pardon, ironically, is granted by way of demonstrating how far superior morally is the Christian ethic to the Jewish one.

> That thou shalt see the difference of our spirit,
> I pardon thee thy life before thou ask it.

Amazingly, within the space of little more than a score of lines, we find the Duke withdrawing his vaunted magnanimity.

> He shall do this, or else I do recant
> The pardon that I late pronouncèd here.

This outright and unabashed betrayal of his own oath, of legal principles, and of the very spirit of mercy on the Duke's part nevertheless does not invalidate the case against Shylock presented by Portia, whose interpretive skills imposed no death penalty, leaving that to the Duke. If the Duke's behavior is plainly cruel, the reason may lie, ironically, in the difference between the civil, the secular, law, with all its imperfections— but the very law to which Shylock thought he was appealing at the beginning of the trial—and the divine law that Portia represents.

Those who have taken the play as a tragedy have, of course, seen Shylock as its hero. But quite apart from this, it must be admitted that the play frankly alludes to the equivocalness of man's fate, and the caprices of Fortuna (the only pagan goddess to persist into Christian times and Christian iconography) who could award good or bad fortune, and thereby turn comedy to tragedy or the reverse. Something of that sort is clearly being hinted at in the early exchange already cited between

Antonio and Gratiano, employing explicitly theatrical meta-phors.[22] But this complexity is expressed in other ways, in ways that relate to very edgy and potentially tragic elements in biblical texts. If it is virtually inarguable that Launcelot Gobbo and his father enact the theft by Jacob of Isaac's blessing, it is only slightly less evident that another biblical "parody," of Job and his comforters, is enacted by Shylock and Tubal in the second half of Act III, scene i. More ominously, Launcelot says, comically, to Jessica,

> Yes truly; for look you, the sins of the father are to be laid upon the children. Therefore, I promise you I fear you. I was always plain with you, and so now I speak my agitation of the matter. Therefore be o' good cheer, for truly I think you are damned.

For all the comedy, a serious text is being cited.

> The Lord is longsuffering, and of great mercy, forgiving iniquity and transgression, and by no means clearing the guilty, visiting the iniquity of the fathers upon the children unto the third and fourth generation.
>
> (Numbers 14:18)

The meaning of that passage cannot but be harrowing, to the "innocent" as well as to the "guilty." More seriously, and more comically still, Launcelot goes on to complain at the too great conversion of Jews to Christians, saying that there won't be enough pork and bacon to go around if things go on this way. But his jest has its serious, even sinister, undertone: it implies that not everyone can be or ought to be saved. Cassio says as much outright in *Othello*, and he is following no less an authority than Saint Mark.

> And he said unto [his disciples], Unto you is given to know the mystery of the kingdom of God: but unto them that are without, all these things are done in parables:

The Merchant of Venice: *A Venture in Hermeneutics*

> That seeing they may see and not perceive; and hearing
> they may hear, and not understand; lest at any time they
> should be converted, and their sins should be forgiven
> them.
>
> (Mark 4: 11–12)

There seems to be ample evidence in this play that its author
was richly aware of all the spiritual perils he and his characters were toying with.

Still and all, the play is really and finally a comedy in the
very sense that Dante employed the word about his own great
work, and which word he explained as follows to his patron
and protector, Can Grande della Scala of Verona:

> The title of the work is, "Here beginneth the *Comedy*
> of Dante Alighieri, a Florentine by birth, not by char-
> acter." To understand which, be it known that *comedy*
> is derived from *comus*, "a village," and *oda*, which is,
> "song"; whence comedy is, as it were, "rustic song." So
> comedy is a certain kind of poetic narration differing from
> all others. It differs, then, from tragedy in its content,
> in that tragedy begins admirably and tranquilly, whereas
> its end or exit is foul and terrible; and it derives its name
> from *tragus*, which is a "goat," and *oda*, as though to say,
> "goat-song," that is fetid like a goat, as appears from
> Seneca in his tragedies; whereas comedy introduces harsh
> complication, but brings its matter to a prosperous end, as
> appears from Terence, in his comedies. And hence, cer-
> tain writers, on introducing themselves, have made it
> their practice to give the salutation: "I wish you a tragic
> beginning and a comic end."
>
> (Epistola X)

To this may be added one final point regarding the scriptures
themselves. They may be said to contain both the elements of
comedy and tragedy, and the illustration of this could entail a

big book in itself. I will confine myself to two representative
citations, which may stand for all those many biblical narratives that have served poets and dramatists as the tragic or
comic core of their scenarios. And I suggest that the amplitude
of the bible in this regard is clearly exhibited in this play,
which is so intimately based upon and colored by scriptural
texts. The last words of what has come to be known as the Old
Testament, though containing a hopeful call for future amity,
conclude with an ominous and terrific threat:

> And he shall turn the heart of the fathers to the children,
> and the heart of the children to their fathers, lest I come
> and smite the earth with a curse.
>
> (Malachi 4:6)

The last words of the New Testament, speaking here only with
benign assurance, are these:

> He which testifieth these things saith, Surely I come
> quickly. Amen. Even so, come, Lord Jesus.
> The grace of our Lord Jesus Christ be with you all. Amen.
>
> (Revelations 22:20–21)

It is perhaps worth adding that this so striking contrast is set
before us only by the Christian reordering of the books of the
so-called Old Testament. The Hebrew scriptures end with II
Chronicles, and with this verse:

> Thus saith Cyrus king of Persia: All the kingdoms of the
> earth hath the Lord, the God of heaven, given me; and He
> hath charged me to build Him a house in Jerusalem,
> which is in Judah. Whosoever there is among you of all
> His people—the Lord his God be with him—let him go up.

I beg leave to offer some personal comment by way of conclusion. I hope not to be taxed with supposing that I have done
justice to the play, that I have said everything that needs saying, that I have even attempted completeness. And I hope,

moreover, that I will not be accused of reducing the rich and complicated characters of the play to the sort of ciphers that normally occur in allegory. In claiming, for example, that Shylock represents the devil, I do not wish to deny him all the complexities of thought and motive and feeling and human vulnerability that make him the irresistibly interesting figure that he is. If I have scanted these matters it has not been for want of respect for them, but because they have been dwelt upon to great effect by a number of eminent critics.

Also, I wish to say that while presenting the conventional, widespread and vulgar view of the Bible that regards the Old Testament as hidebound, impotent, blind as the people that walked in darkness in Isaiah, and the New Testament as uncomplicated light, revelation, and love (as if the injunction to love God and our neighbors as ourselves, which Jesus recognizes as the most important commandments, were not enjoined upon us in those benighted and forbidding books, Leviticus and Deuteronomy), it is a view which, along with other matters expressed in the play, I confess to finding anywhere from distasteful to abhorrent. Nevertheless, I should make it clear that I am not claiming that Shakespeare wrote this play in order to express private biases and bigotries of his own. The ideas in this drama were popular, current, much in the air of the times, as G. K. Hunter has clearly shown in his book *Dramatic Identities and Cultural Tradition*, in which he anticipates and confirms much of what I have written here. The prevailing ideas about Jews, for instance, were bound to be based largely upon ignorance.[23] I am claiming no more than that the playwright made use of ideas that he could count on his audience instantly recognizing and accepting; that he made a brilliant and exciting play out of them, which is at the same time something of a tour de force of covert meanings stunningly unveiled, a miraculous amalgam of buried and revealed truths of which the caskets and the scriptures are both examples. My purpose throughout has merely been to discover and to display such design as integrates and unifies the play, and this has involved me in a sort of hermeneutics of my own which perhaps resembles Portia's. But in my own behalf I would like to plead that at least I have found in this Shakespearean text more plausibility and coherence than has Harley Granville-Barker, who opens his remarkable discussion of it with these words: *"The Merchant of Venice* is a fairy tale. There is no more reality in Shylock's bond and the Lord of Belmont's will than in Jack and the Beanstalk."[24]

NOTES

1. "Jesus broke the bread ('Mazzoth,' the unleavened bread, 'the bread of affliction') and gave it to the disciples and said to them that they should take and eat it, for 'this is my body;' he also gave them to drink from his cup, saying, 'this is my blood, the blood of the new covenant, which is shed for many'; and he may have added: 'for the forgiveness of sins,' and also: 'Do this in remembrance of me,' though this last occurs in neither Mark nor Matthew.

"This was the origin of the rite of the 'Lord's Supper' and the mystical theory of 'Transubstantiation' (the conversion of the bread into the body of the Messiah, and the conversion of the wine into his blood), which induced the heathen of those days to believe that the Christians used blood for their Passover. And when, in their turn, the heathen became Christians they accused the Jews, on the basis of this Christian belief, of kneading their unleavened bread in Christian blood. But the rite arose much later than the time of Jesus."

Joseph Klausner, *Jesus of Nazareth*, translated from the Hebrew by the Rev. Herbert Danby, pp. 327–8.

The *blood libel* has an even earlier origin than the one cited by Ben-Sasson and alluded to by Klausner as having been levelled against the early Christians. Jeremiah three times adverts to the topic of human sacrifice (7:31; 19:5–9; 32–35), of which the following is the first instance: "And they have built the high places of Tophet, which is in the valley of the sons of Hinnom, to burn their sons and their daughters in the fire; which I commanded them not, neither came it into my heart." The temptation of Abraham and sacrifice of Isaac, related in Genesis 22, is not unconnected to the topic.

2. The libel of the *desecration* or *profanation of the host*, while intimately related to the libel of *ritual murder*, plays no explicit part in this play, and is in consequence relegated to the indignity of a note. It was based on the premise that the mystical event of *transubstantiation*, the translation, in the course of the Mass, of the bread and wine into the body and blood of

The Merchant of Venice: *A Venture in Hermeneutics*

the Savior, was quite literally a resurrection of the body of Jesus, restoring his flesh to life and to sentience. There were pious legends of Christians whose doubts were overcome, and whose faith was confirmed, by the pricking of the host with a pin, and seeing it bleed. But these pious legends brought with them virtually as a corollary a no less powerful consequence for the Jews. It was assumed not only that the original murder of Jesus had whetted an insatiable and inherited appetite, but that the host itself should continue always to be something that Jews were determined to violate as a repetition of their original murder. "The first recorded charge of this kind," reports Ben-Sasson (op. cit. p. 483), "dates from 1243, from a place near Berlin. The charge usually ran as follows: a Jew was supposed to have bribed or persuaded a Christian man or woman to provide him with a piece of the host. This was then taken to the home of the Jew or to the synagogue. There it (i.e., Jesus) was tortured, either by an individual or by the community. It was stabbed and trampled upon. The Jews would run a risk in order to fulfil their desire 'to torture Jesus again.' When a Jew was suspected of such an action, he would be subjected to grievous torment. Whether or not he 'confessed', he was usually burnt, and his family and community punished. Entire areas of Jewish communities were devastated as a result of this libel." So widely was it accepted as proven fact that it made its way into a painting by Paolo Uccello that is to be seen in the Galleria Nazionale della Marche in Urbino. In the predella to a painting by Justus van Ghent of the *Consecration of the Host* Uccello presents a series of scenes, showing first a woman redeeming her cloak from a Jewish moneylender at the price of the consecrated host, and the attempted destruction of the host; and then showing the execution of the repentant woman and the Jew and his family being burnt. (James Beck, *Italian Renaissance Painting*, p. 75)

3. John H. Davis, "Venice: Art and Life in the Lagoon City," pp. 75–76.

4. "Probably indeed most people would say that there is a real difference of meaning, which they could expound [between "thrifty" and "miserly"], and so they could; the puzzle for the linguist is that different people would expound quite differently, and yet they can realize this without feeling that the words themselves are made useless by it. The *use* of the words, in fact, is to sum up your own attitude to the practical questions they raise, and it is their business to be fluid in meaning so that a variety of people can use them. This is widely recognized, I think. ' 'E's what I call thrifty,' the charlady will say, with a rich recognition of the possibilities of using the other word."
William Empson, *The Structure of Complex Words*, p. 30.

5. In the trial scene Shylock declares, "I have an oath in heaven;/Shall I lay perjury upon my soul?" This, along with his other assertions of having made a vow, relates to Exodus 20:7, "Thou shalt not take the name of the Lord thy God in vain: for the Lord will not hold him guiltless that takes his name in vain." The modern notion of the meaning of this prohibition is the common one that it is anything from bad taste to blasphemy to refer to God when cursing. This is, if present at all, but a small part of the burden of the commandment. J. Coert Rylaarsdam, offering exegetical

The Merchant of Venice: *A Venture in Hermeneutics*

comment on the text in *The Interpreter's Bible*, writes thus: "The Third Commandment . . . deals with the use of God's name *in vain*, i.e., for that which lacks reality or truth. The name of God expresses his character and power. To call upon unreality, i.e., that which is not an expression of the divine character, by means of the divine name is to use the name *in vain*. Not only perjury but also the practice of magic, which constitutes the invocation of ultimate powers with whom God stands in conflict, and the invocation of the dead, were in all probability among the specific prohibitions implied by this commandment at its inception." Shylock's pious concern here is with the element of *perjury*: one does not make an oath to God and then break it with impunity, as, he witheringly remarks, the Christians do.

A modern Jewish commentary declares, regarding this Commandment, that an oath "means taking the name of God upon oneself, i.e., placing oneself under the name of God; submitting oneself to the power and might of the God who intervenes in earthly affairs, as His Name (the 4-lettered one) expresses it; calling it down upon oneself in the event of one's spoken word not being true, or of not carrying it out. It is clear that, in an oath, the two phases of the acknowledgement of God are jointly expressed— His watching over all our deeds (and our words essentially belong to our deeds) and His power of ordering our fate. An oath in the name of God implies both, and by the actual submission of our whole future under God's power of deciding our fate, wishes to prove the truth of our statements and honesty of our actions. Hence, conversely, a false oath is the most direct denial of God in the most contemptuous manner. . . . The Law reckons four kinds of such oaths. (1) . . . an oath that denies a self-evident fact, [and thereby asserts] that black is white, stone is gold, etc. (2) . . . that affirms a self-evident fact, 'I swear by the Name of God that two is two.' (3) . . . [an oath of one] who swears to do something that is physically impossible for him to do, e.g., to fast for a week, to jump over the moon, etc. (4) . . . [an oath of one] who swears to do something that is morally impossible for him to do, e.g., not to lay [i.e., don] Tephillin [i.e., phylacteries], to take revenge on somebody, etc. In all these cases the oath is either useless, superfluous or without object or effect. Here the sin occurs even in the promissory oaths at the moment the oath is taken, the swearer is immediately punishable, but the vow has no effect. Swearing (in God's Name, of course) useless, superfluous oaths, or oaths without object or effect, is simply playing with the most solemn of all solemn acts of man, with the submission of his words and deeds to the judgment of God Who decides and fixes his future and his fate."

The Pentateuch, translated and explained
by Samson Raphael Hirsch, pp. 265–266.

6. The ancient libel of ritual murder uniformly involved victims who were young males and murderers who were mature males. The idea of sexual molestation and abuse is an easy one to project upon such a set of characters, and the idea consorted well with the further notion that, given the Jews' unappeasable appetite for the flesh and blood of innocence, it would have been part of their purpose to degrade and deprave that innocence before murdering it. By the same token, the Roman way around their own law that virgins could not be put to death was for their execu-

The Merchant of Venice: *A Venture in Hermeneutics*

tioner to rape them first. Charles Perrault's tale of *"Barbe Bleue"* touches, *mutatis mutandis*, upon this same theme of innocence depraved and destroyed by vile maturity, though here the victims are tastefully altered to wives. But it has been plausibly conjectured that Perrault's ultimate sources were the lives of Commore the Cursed, a sixth-century Breton chief, and still more explicitly, Gilles de Rais (1404–1440), that celebrated precursor of de Sade and whoever was responsible for the recent deaths of more than twenty black boys in Atlanta, Georgia. Gilles is credited with the torture and death of at least 140 young victims, almost all of them boys, whom he kidnaped and upon whom he had sexual as well as homicidal designs. He fought, incidentally, at the side of Joan of Arc at Orléans. Doubtless it was from a slightly milder brew of the same ingredients that Dickens concocted Fagin, whose young apprentices are chiefly male, who are degraded and depraved into criminal careers, and each of whom Fagin, with terrible and pointed iteration, addresses as "my dear." Not a few actors have chosen to play him with a pronounced and effeminate lisp.

7. But I say unto you, Love your enemies, bless them that curse
   you, do good to them that hate you, and pray for them which
   despitefully use you, and persecute you;
   That ye may be the children of your Father which is in heaven:
   for he maketh his sun to rise on the evil and on the good,
   and sendeth rain on the just and the unjust.
   For if ye love them which love you, what reward have ye?
   do not even the publicans the same?

   (Matthew 5:44–46)

"In the Gospels 'publicans and sinners' form a usual pair (Mt. 9:9–13; 11:19; 21:31f; Mk. 2:13–17; Lk. 5:27–32; 7:34; 15:1). Publicans are also paired with Gentiles (Mt. 18:17). The morality of the publicans is presumed to be at the lowest level (Mt. 5:46; the parallel in Lk. 6:32 reads 'sinners')."

John L. McKenzie, S.J., *Dictionary of the Bible*, p. 707.

8. Here is a segment of Canto XLV.
   With *Usura*
   With usura hath no man a house of good stone
   each block cut smooth and well fitting
   that design might cover their face,
   with usura
   hath no man a painted paradise on his church wall
   harpes et luthes
   or where virgin receiveth message
   . . . .
   WITH USURA
   wool comes not to market
   sheep bringeth no gain with usura
   Usura is a murrain, usura
   blunteth the needle in the maid's hand
   and stoppeth the spinner's cunning. Pietro Lombardo
   came not by usura
   Duccio came not by usura

nor Pier della Francesca; Zuan Bellin' not by usura
nor was 'La Calunnia' painted.
Came not by usura Angelico; came not Ambrogio Praedis,
Came no church of cut stone signed: *Adamo me fecit.*
Not by usura St Trophime
Not by usura Saint Hilaire,
Usura rusteth the chisel
It rusteth the craft and the craftsman
It gnaweth the thread of the loom
None learneth to weave gold in her pattern;
Azure hath canker by usura; cramoisi is unbroidered
Emerald findeth no Memling
Usura slayeth the child in the womb
It stayeth the young man's courting
It hath brought palsey to bed, lyeth
between the young bride and her bridegroom
CONTRA NATURAM
They have brought whores from Eleusis
Corpses are set to banquet
at behest of usura.

There is undoubted power here, and a certain manifest beauty of incantation, along with what we are doubtless supposed to regard as high and moral indignation. But it is not entirely clear just what the poet means. Apart from the traditional, Thomistic condemnation of usury as "contra naturam," against nature in that money is made to beget money without the essential participation of *labor*—an unnaturalness to which Shakespeare is apparently referring when he has Shylock declare that he can make gold and silver "breed as fast" as ewes and lambs, and for which Dante coupled usurers with sodomites in the same circle of *Inferno*—there is in Pound's Canto the puzzle about the specific artists and works of art mentioned. If he is declaring that certain particular artists were not usurers, this is not very wonderful. But some of the works, like the churches, for example, are by unknown artists, and the Canto as a whole suggests strongly that the greatest, the loveliest and the most pious works of art of the Middle Ages and the Renaissance *could not have been produced* "with usura." But this is flatly wrong, and the chances are good that Pound knew it, which a good deal undermines his lofty stance and condemnatory tone. Witness the following:

"In 1300 the wealthy Enrico Scrovegni of Padua purchased a piece of land from the Dalesmanini family, . . . a property which included an oval area that had once been a Roman arena. On the perimeter of the arena Enrico built the family palace, a sprawling edifice that was remodeled during the Renaissance and torn down in the nineteenth century. . . .

Next to the palace Enrico built a chapel dedicated to the Virgin of the Annunciation, Santa Maria Annunziata. The family wealth had been amassed by Enrico's father, Reginaldo, whom Dante singled out as the arch usurer of his *Inferno*, . . and there is a good deal of evidence to suggest that the Arena Chapel [which contains what some believe to be Giotto's greatest frescoes, though admittedly Pound does not include them in his Canto] was erected as a means of expiating the father's sin of usury which hung over the family."

James Stubblebine, *Giotto: The Arena Chapel Frescoes*, p. 72.

9. Attilio Scrocchi, editor and publisher, *Venice and Neighborhood*, p. 72.

10. "The doom of duality was pronounced against Pulcinella even before he was born, for he had, it appears, the special privilege of having two fathers, Maccus and Bucco. Inasmuch as Maccus and Bucco were not in the least alike, Pulcinella was always drawn toward opposite poles by his dual heredity. . . .

Pulcinella belongs to so ancient a house that the noblest of the noble barely keep their heads above the common crowd in comparison with him. In order to prove his lineage we have only to compare the little antique bronze figure which was unearthed at Rome in 1727 with the portraits of the seventeenth-century Pulcinella in the Museum of the Comédie-Francaise. Never was a case of direct descent more clearly established.

After his appearance in Rome in 540 there is no trace of Pulcinella until the sixteenth century. . . .

The son of two fathers and doubly hump-backed, Pulcinella was born twice at the same time in different quarters of the town of Benevento, formerly the capital of the Samnites. Like Bergamo, Benevento is built on the side of a mountain, and the people of the upper town are entirely unlike those of the lower. The 'upper' Pulcinella is intelligent, sensual, sly, keen; in him the blood of Bucco predominates. The 'lower' Pulcinella is a dull and coarse bumpkin. Yet both of them have as much the same nature as twin brothers. . . .

Pulcinella was never one to be bowed down by the cares and responsibilities of a profession. He was by turns a magistrate, a poet, a master, and a valet, but rarely a husband or father of a family. As a general rule he appeared as an old bachelor, an eccentric and selfish old curmudgeon strongly inclined to sensual and epicurean gluttony. As he possessed a great deal of wit, and his hump was chock full of a sense of humor, his chief weapon of defense was to feign stupidity. Being self-centered and bestial, Pulcinella had no scruples whatever, and because moral suffering from his physical deformity reacted upon his brain at the expense of his heart, he was exceedingly cruel.

But Pulcinella grew mellower with age, and lapsed into a sort of second childhood which softened his cruelty into mere teasing and his sensuality into coarseness. He became an honest citizen and waxed dull, though fortunately he never lost his wit entirely. He was always good for an occasional flare of repartee, which would start off well, only to die away abruptly. He could still manage a sharp quip or two now and then, but he eventually preferred to amuse himself by eating macaroni out of an enormous chamber-pot. Pulcinella was not endowed with the gay and lively imagination for vulgarity which saved Harlequin from obscenity. For all his cleverness Pulcinella was sadly lacking in delicacy, and he was epicurean only in the most popular sense of the word. . . .

The Neapolitan Pulcinella found his way into England at the end of the seventeenth century, and there he proceeded to give rein to all the cold-blooded ferocity which he had stored up in his nature. His irony then took

225

The Merchant of Venice: *A Venture in Hermeneutics*

on an English tone, and he developed into a great seducer of the young girls of the people. A ballad of the eighteenth century affirms that his ardour became so intense that he required at least twenty-two women to keep him satisfied.

In *The Adventures of Punch and Judy*, Punch, in spite of his hump, seduces a young girl, and has a child by her. Later he 'keeps a woman.' He tosses the baby out of the window, kills his mother- and father-in-law, flees, seducing women as he goes, and finally knocks down the devil (Old Nick) with his cudgel after having hanged the executioner sent to hang him."

> Pierre Louis Ducharte: *Italian Comedy: The Improvisations, Lives, Scenarios, Attributes, Portraits and Masks of the Illustrious Characters of the Commedia dell' Arte*, trans. by Randolph T. Weaver, pp. 208–224.

11. C. L. Barber, *Shakespeare's Festive Comedies*, pp. 163–186.

12. Moreover the law entered, that the offence might abound.
     But where sin abounded, grace did much more abound. . . .
                                            (Romans 5:20)

13. At I, ii, 26–33 Nerissa remarks, in a seemingly chilling response to Portia's plea for sympathy about the imprisoning terms of her late father's will, "Your father was ever virtuous, and holy men at their death have good inspirations,—therefore the lott'ry that he hath devised in these three chests of gold, silver, and lead, whereof who chooses his meaning chooses you, will no doubt never be chosen by any rightly, but one who you shall rightly love. . . ." At this early part in the play, such assurances sound like the implausible assertions of blind faith. Only later do we discover their astuteness.

14. Early in his "History" (I:53) Herodotus tells how Croesus sent to the oracular shrines to learn whether it was propitious for him to go to war with the Persians. ". . . the oracles agreed in the tenor of their reply, which was in each case a prophecy that if Croesus attacked the Persians, he would destroy a mighty empire, and a recommendation to him to look and see who were the most powerful of the Greeks, and to make alliance with them." The irony of Croesus's celebrated misconstruction of those oracles is tersely dealt with later (I:86) when Herodotus declares: "Thus was Sardis taken by the Persians, and Croesus himself fell into their hands, after having reigned fourteen years, and been besieged in his capital fourteen days; thus too did Croesus fulfil the oracle, which said he should destroy a mighty empire,—by destroying his own." Shakespeare has Shylock make precisely the same self-serving and self-aggrandizing mistake of interpretation of a text no less riddling and richly ambiguous than were the Grecian oracles. In citing the Jacob-Laban story, Shylock obviously identifies himself (his thrift, his cunning, his God-ordained good fortune and success) with Jacob, and finds in the text a sacred precedent, justification, and promise. Ironically, the biblical text proves to be profoundly pertinent to the action and the characters of this play, but only when Shylock is properly identified—as the uncovenanted and misguided, the would-be deceiver and self-deceived Laban.

15. Morton Smith, *Clement of Alexandria and a Secret Gospel of Mark*, p. 248.

16. Woe to you, scribes and Pharisees, hypocrites! for ye
pay tithe of mint and anise and cummin, and have omitted
the weightier matters of the law, judgment, mercy and
faith: these ought ye to have done, and not to leave the
other undone.

(Matthew 23:23)

For the law was given by Moses, but grace and truth came
by Jesus Christ.

(John 1:17)

For what the law could not do, in that it was weak through
the flesh, God sending his own Son in the likeness of
sinful flesh, and for sin, condemned sin in the flesh:
That the righteousness of the law might be fulfilled in
us, who walk not after the flesh, but after the Spirit.

(Romans 8:3–4)

For Christ is the end of the law for righteousness to
everyone that believeth.
For Moses describeth the righteousness which is the law,
That the man which doeth these things shall live by them.
But the righteousness which is of faith speaketh on this
wise, Say not in thine heart, Who shall ascend into
Heaven? (that is, to bring Christ down from above;)
Or, Who shall descend into the deep (that is, to bring
up Christ again from the dead.)

(Romans 10:4–7)

17. It may not be completely irrelevant that in this passage Jesus is explicitly declared to have two fathers (which accounts for the bewilderment of his parents in the final verse cited), just as Jacob had, and just as Punchinello had. Regarding the last of these figures, Marcia E. Vetrocq, in the catalogue of *Domenico Tiepolo's Punchinello Drawings* exhibited at the Frick Museum in New York in early 1980, comments on the first drawing in the series: "A solitary Punchinello contemplates the monument on which Domenico Tiepolo has inscribed the title. . . . Byam Shaw discerns in the drawing Domenico's 'blasphemous parody' of his title page to the *Via Crucis* etchings. . . ." And there are other details of Punchinello's story, garbled though it is, that are parodic of the life of Christ. Punchinello is hatched from an egg (a miraculous birth, engendered by a turkey, the ludicrous equivalent of the Dove of the Holy Spirit); he is interred beneath the city pavement but rises again; he is executed (more than once, and in more ways than one) and is again revived.

18. The beautiful and celebrated panegyric on music and harmony in the final act carries the more force by virtue of its contrast, retrospectively, to metaphors for dissonance that are carefully placed at judicious moments

227

earlier in the play; and that are insistently embodied in the sound of the bagpipe. This instrument is by no means purely Scottish, and as a musette has enjoyed a long and varied continental life in France, Italy, and elsewhere. Everywhere it is characterized by an unvarying and monotonous drone, above and in grating contrast with which the melody is piped as an uncomfortable obbligato. The pipes of the instrument are pliantly connected with a large bladder that is inflated by the player's breath and deflated by the pressure of his arm. References begin as early as I, i, 52–3, with Solanio's "Some that will evermore peep through their eyes,/And laugh like parrots at a bagpiper. . . ." But Shylock carries the principal burden of dissonance. In II, v, 28–31 he commands: "Hear you me Jessica,/ Lock up my doors, and when you hear the drum/And the vile squealing of the wry-neck'd fife/Clamber not you up to the casements then. . . ." The fife here is the instrument, not the player, as the Arden note suggests, and it is wry (awry) necked because of the pliant jointure of pipe with bladder, and the positioning of the pipes at the convenience of the player. The great and scathing aria of dissonance appears, suitably, at the beginning of the trial scene with Shylock's merciless ironies: "Some men there are love not a gaping pig!/Some that are mad if they behold a cat!/And others when the bagpipe sings i'th'nose/Cannot contain their urine—for affection/(Master of passions) sways it to the mood/Of what it likes and loathes,—now for your answer:/As there is no firm reason to be rend'red/ Why he cannot abide a gaping pig,/Why he a harmless necessary cat,/ Why he a woolen bagpipe, but of force/Must yield to such inevitable shame,/As to offend himself being offended:/So I can give no reason. . . ."

19. "It is she [Portia, the mistress of Belmont], disguised as a young man, who finally defeats the villainous schemes of the Jewish usurer—by a verbal quibble which had not occurred to the wisest men in Venice. Surely Shakespeare is at his most irresponsible and it is irrelevant to ask for themes and meanings. Fantasy and wilfulness continue to the end. When the main conflict is over, the scene is set in a garden graced with moonlight and the gentle throb of music, and the talk is of heavenly harmony and ancient loves; into this garden walk the romantic leads and, in a moment, they fall to wrangling and talk of cuckoldry and unfaithfulness. The play ends with a bawdy joke about the chastity of a waiting-woman.

"Shakespeare seems to have been quite unembarrassed about the improbabilities of his story. According to a sonnet prefixed to the first edition of *Il Pecorone*, it was written of fools, for fools, and by a fool, and yet *The Merchant* accentuates some of its improbabilities."

This grotesque account of the play appears in the Introduction to the Arden Edition, edited and introduced by John Russell Brown, p. xlix. I hope my own account has succeeded in making the play appear less foolish and capricious and unintelligible than Mr. Brown suggests, but with one point of his I would like to agree. When he claims, derisively and dismissively, that "the play ends with a bawdy joke about the chastity of a waiting-woman," he is more than simply literally correct. All thoughts of carnal love having been set aside in the serious name of chastity from the very moment the principals learn of Antonio's peril and his sacrificial situation; and that same chastity having been preserved throughout what amounts to the symbolic lenten season—which is to say, until Easter, or until Antonio is delivered from his ordeal—we return again at last to the world of quotidian concern and carnal love, from which we had been absent during the season of sacrifice. Life has been restored, and with it, sex.

20. John Dover Wilson, *The Fortunes of Falstaff*, pp. 17–19.

21. Thomas of Monmouth, a contemporary of the events which he relates, wrote *The Life and Miracles of St. William of Norwich*, a Latin work composed about 1173. Here is an excerpt: "Now, while he was staying in Norwich, the Jews who were settled there and required their cloaks or their robes or other garments (whether pledged to them or their own property) to be repaired, preferred him before all other skinners. For they esteemed him to be especially fit for their work, either because they had learnt that he was guileless and skilful, or, because attracted to him by their avarice, they thought they could bargain with him for a lower price. Or, as I rather believe, because by the ordering of divine providence he had been predestined to martyrdom from the beginning of time, and gradually step by step was drawn on, and chosen to be made a mock of and to be put to death by the Jews, in scorn of the Lord's Passion, as one of little foresight, and so the more fit for them." (Translated by Jacob Marcus in *The Jew in the Medieval World*, p. 122.) The problem of dramatizing, or even expressing and revealing, this inward heroism, like the unworldliness of William of Norwich, is one that Gerard Manley Hopkins struggled with in "The Windhover" and "St. Alphonsus Rodriguez."

22. "The tendency of comedy is to include as many people as possible in its final society: the blocking characters are more often reconciled or converted than simply repudiated. Comedy often includes a scapegoat ritual of expulsion which gets rid of some irreconcilable character, but exposure and disgrace make for pathos, or even tragedy. *The Merchant of Venice* seems almost an experiment in coming as close as possible to upsetting the comic balance. If the dramatic role of Shylock is ever so slightly exaggerated, as it generally is when the leading actor of the company takes the part, it is upset, and the play becomes the tragedy of the Jew of Venice with a comic epilogue."

Northrop Frye, *Anatomy of Criticism*, p. 165.

23. For example, *The Play of the Sacrament*, an anonymous fifteenth-century drama about the desecration of the Host by a Jew named Ser Jonathas, who bribes a wealthy Christian merchant to steal it for him, has the Jew refer a number of times to his God as "almyghty Machomet" (i.e., Mahomet, Mohammed). This peculiar confusion of Jews and Moslems, perhaps a convenient way for the popular Gentile mind to lump all "infidels" together, also occurs in a painting, *The Crowning with Thorns*, by Hieronymus Bosch, in the National Gallery, London, wherein one of the tormentors of Christ wears the unmistakable star and crescent of Islam embroidered on his apparel. This confusion of miscellaneous "infidels" is a topic addressed by G. K. Hunter in *Dramatic Identities and Cultural Tradition*.

24. H. Granville-Barker, *Prefaces to Shakespeare*, Vol. I, p. 335.

Shades of Keats and Marvell

> *"One feels at moments as if one could with a touch convey a vision—that the mystic vision & sexual love use the same means—opposed yet parallel existences."*
>
> W. B. YEATS, in a letter of May 25, 1926, quoted in Richard Ellmann's *Yeats: The Man and The Mask.*

T HIS ESSAY proposes to put Marvell's "The Garden" and Keats's "Ode to a Nightingale" * side by side, and in comparing them to remark some important resemblances that I think have not been noticed before. It seems proper for me to begin by saying that I very greatly admire both of these poems, and I do not think myself in danger of using one of them (or its author, or its period) to humiliate the other. Furthermore, it will be important to me, to make clear not only the correspondences I seem to find, but the differences as well, so that I have every hope of respecting the rich integrity of each poem as a discrete work of art. If I am right in supposing a common theme and design in the poems, and perhaps even (to the degree that these can be articulated) a corresponding set of feelings, then perhaps at the end it would be possible to make some tentative remarks about the shift of sensibility between the two periods involved, and to see this shift as something legible in the poems themselves.

* The full texts of the two poems will be found at the end of the essay.

230

Shades of Keats and Marvell

To generalize at first. Each is a private meditation of the poet, alone and in a natural setting; in both cases, as a consequence of an extraordinary and superior passivity, an exquisite secular and sensuous ecstasy is experienced; in both cases this ecstasy seems like the departure of the soul from the body, and like an inkling of a blissful death; and in both cases the return to the natural setting, the "real world," at the end of the ecstasy is accompanied by an intimation that perhaps only the ecstasy itself was real, and that while ecstasy had been identified with death at the highest moment of its experience, it might rather be the most intense sense of life, whereas the return to the transitory world might be a return to dying and to death. Both poems depend upon a deliberately ambiguous feeling about death: death is a constituent of the physical world of contingency and flux, and to participate in that world is to be at the mercy of death; but death is also the static and passive state of isolation which is the initial condition for the ecstasy, and which the ecstasy envisions. Both poems, by their secular settings and sensuous detail, and by their peculiar insistence upon the poets' isolation, present us with a sort of *Liebestod*, which is self-induced and autoerotic.

"The Garden" opens on a note of contempt for the vanity of human effort, particularly that effort which the world esteems and delights to crown with a symbolic wreath of victory. The most honored worldly pursuits are made to seem no more important than a footrace; at least the athletic and artistic competitions, and even wars, are seen as mere games. And since the crown is spare and symbolic, "some single herb," it cannot afford the ample comfort of cool shade one would want after so much strenuous endeavor. One should not accept the figurative satisfaction for the real thing—at least, so the first stanza suggests. But this is not a cheap and easy cynicism; the joke at the expense of labor is very lightly stated, and if the poet seems to be recommending a kind of sloth, it is sanctified by nature. "Consider the lilies of the field, how they grow; they toil not,

231

neither do they spin." This is not only a Christian sentiment but a conventional part of the pastoral mode of feeling. Nature is innocent because it is unconscious of its virtue, and its perfect existence is therefore effortless. The sweaty endeavors of men are doubly shameful in being, even at their best, conscious attempts at different sorts of virtue, and in appropriating the innocence of the garden to symbolize this vanity. The garden stands opposed to the world, not only in the genuine comfort it offers to the overheated, but also because of its association with the Garden of Eden, and of Paradise, and through both of these as well as independently, with death. The association with death I think is clearest at the end, when the sundial is mentioned: by which both bees and men compute their time, as the mortuary tone of sundial inscriptions solicits us to do. In the first stanza, however, the garden is not merely set off against the world, but it has a wreath of victory superior to the world's crowns.

> While all Flow'rs and all Trees do close
> To weave the Garlands of repose.

I have no doubt that the primary meaning is the obvious one suggested above, but I cannot believe that the idea of a funeral wreath is improper here. When men have run their race they go to their ultimate repose in a sort of garden; and I take this to be merely the first hint of a theme that is insisted upon more strongly later in the poem. It is a part of Marvell's wit to let us discover late in the course of things that the natural world is one vast cemetery. *Et in Arcadia ego*, the mild words of Death, were a familiar enough theme in the pastoral poetry and painting of the Renaissance. And the theme served this particular dramatic purpose: it prevented the image of utopian innocence and bliss, the pure pastoral life, from being too far removed from actual experience.

But the cemetery, which is the proper emblem of repose and solitude, is still a garden, and conveniently maintains its double identification with life and death. Its plants are themselves the innocent emblems of the abstract and Platonic perfections which the ecstasy is moving toward, and while they are part of the perishable, created world, they partake of an ardent and incorporeal greenness, which is irreducible and everlasting. Green is "lovely," being at once amorous and beautiful; more beautiful and amorous than women because it invites us toward a contemplation of its pure and disembodied essence, absolute Beauty and absolute Love, which is to say, Paradise. The slighting remarks about women's beauty are not to be taken, I feel certain, as stern-minded Puritan asceticism, or even as stern-minded Platonism. The human faculties shall receive their peculiar satisfactions, and the body shall not be denied. Love runs its heat, like the athletic competitors, but it is wiser than they in aspiring at last to the garden.

> When we have run our Passion's heat,
> Love hither makes his best retreat.

This seems to suggest not only that when we have exhausted our carnal passions we will be fit initiates for a more sublime Love (which, as novices, we must approach in the manner of a religious retreat; also, properly to advance is to go back— retreat—to the simplicities and elemental truths of nature) but that the garden provides the ideal garland for the victor in Love's race, as the gods themselves have proven. And not only the gods—the women they chased, as well.

> The *Gods*, that mortal Beauty chase,
> Still in a Tree did end their race.
> *Apollo* hunted *Daphne* so,
> Only that She might Laurel grow.
> And *Pan* did after *Syrinx* speed,
> Not as a Nymph, but for a Reed.

On the surface there is the ingenious misreading of the myth to suggest that the gods had metamorphosis in mind as the ultimate aim and ambition of their chase. This has the ironic effect of reversing the whole motive force of the original stories in a sort of comic euphemism, and ascribing to Apollo and Pan a surprising and unlikely chastity. At the same time, it was the women, in the original myths, who elected transformation to escape a fate worse than death. But there are grounds upon which we can accept this as more than a sophisticated joke. Mortal beauty is precisely mortal, and these women have immortalized themselves in myths by becoming sacred emblems of the gods. They are the vivid and present symbols of divine perfection, and are therefore more beautiful than they were as women. So that the conceit of trees being more lovely than women is given its serious ground.

Certainly the gods' pursuit of beauty, and the purifying of that beauty by metamorphosis, leads directly to the altered state of the poet. The fifth, sixth, and seventh stanzas invite the ideal satisfaction of the body, the mind, and the soul. The body has its dignified and respectable place in the scale of being, for the body most simply and directly apprehends the garden. The delicious substantiality of the fifth stanza is not entirely innocent of sexual overtones. The poet is certainly completely passive as Nature forces herself upon him in a quite overpowering way. There is a species of physical rape going on here which is acceptable because it is pleasant, and because Nature cannot be gainsaid, and because this delightful passivity is the first state and condition of the ecstasy which is leading the poet to purer and rarer pleasures. And finally because it is innocent: we are in a version of Eden. The body here is accepting the figurative satisfaction for the real, as we were warned not to do at the beginning. But this is as far as the body can go, and the mind, in any case, is not deceived.

> Meanwhile the Mind, from pleasure less,
> Withdraws into its happiness:
> The Mind, that Ocean where each kind

Shades of Keats and Marvell

> Does streight its own resemblance find;
> Yet it creates, transcending these,
> Far other Worlds, and other Seas;
> Annihilating all that's made
> To a green Thought in a green Shade.

The final couplet of this stanza must always have seemed one of the most striking and puzzling things in the poem, and not least of all because of the odd construction, "annihilating . . . to." If I am right about the poem as a whole, it presents us not merely with a graduated series of raptures, but with graduated states of consciousness, the highest form of which seems almost like unconsciousness, or death. But on the way, several little deaths have been experienced; a process of purification by metamorphosis is going on, and has already been hinted at by the transformations of Daphne and Syrinx. This progress agrees with the language and ritual of the mystery cults, which Plato used to describe the advance toward perfection which the soul must make in its search for knowledge and beauty. The "self" is transformed, and is thereby annihilated. And since perfection can only be glimpsed by the purified spirit, the mind must annihilate all that is worldly in the world, and in itself.

To return to the opening of the stanza. The mind has its pleasures, which the body does not understand. For one thing, it can contemplate itself (lines 3 and 4); and then it can contemplate itself contemplating itself (lines 5 and 6); and why should this process end here? such logic seems to inquire. The mind is the mirrored and microscopic image of the world; it is so even unconsciously; but the "reflective" mind may be aware of itself, and may see itself as a repeated image; in which case it has, in that very act of imagination, created a new reflection or mirrored image of the original. And by this process of infinite refinement and detachment, we arrive at the irreducibles; the world and the mind are still there, "a green thought in a green shade," but it is now a nice question which is which. The green thought may be the idea of the world, all that is left of it, and the green shade the purified condition of the mind. Regarded the other way around, the world and the mind are still no more than phantoms of their former "selves." There is something both intoxicating and ghostly about this process, which I believe is very deliberate, and in which both the mind and the world are sublimed away, leaving only their essential greenness.

The body is now in its swoon upon the grass, and the mind has retired beyond itself into greenness, and the great climax of the poem awaits only the satisfaction of the soul, which instantly departs from the body and addresses itself to greenness by gliding into the boughs. This is a momentary death, a preview and promise of what is to come when the soul is "prepared for longer flight." Our feelings here are directed by the delightfulness and cheerfulness of the language, which transfigures this moment of death into life, as Daphne and Syrinx were transfigured. But this has not been a "real" death; it is only a brief state something like death. And the vision of paradise it entertains is only *like* Paradise—as Eden is *like* Heaven but is not the same. It can therefore only be described by analogy: "Such was that happy garden-state. . . ." Now certainly analogy, metaphor, symbol, and simile are the very stock-in-trade of poetry, and it is hardly surprising to find Marvell using them. But I suspect he is using his analogy here in accordance with the Platonic idea that the soul cannot apprehend perfection directly until it has perfected itself. So that when Glaucon asks, in *The Republic*, what the idea of the good is, Socrates can only tell him that it is *like* sunlight, as opposed to the shadows of the mythical cave. And we may notice not only that Marvell has progressed from the "shade" to the "various light," but that in the course of the poem he has repudiated, by graduated steps, diverse satisfactions that seemed to be real, but were discovered to be mere tokens. This was clear enough in the first stanza, but I think we are meant to feel, at the most intense moment of transport, that the garden itself is the microscopic image of Paradise, to be transcended and repudiated when the soul is actually "prepared for longer flight." In the meantime, in the world of time, it is a splendid metaphor of promise and bliss, stretching between two paradisal states: Eden, which came before, and Heaven, which comes after.

But I anticipate. It is the lightness of tone of the seventh stanza which makes this literal, if momentary, death delightful; and the transitional analogy to Eden continues this lightness, with its banter against women; so that only by the shift of tense—"Such *was* that happy garden-state"—do we even suspect that the ecstasy has come to an end, and that we are being gently returned to the worldly garden by way of a digression through Eden. If the joke against Eve is a little more nakedly ruthless than the earlier remarks about women, it perhaps has its biblical justification. But at the same time it reaffirms the notion that ideal Love is not the love of created things, or is so only incidentally. And Eve was not like Daphne and Syrinx in being willing to annihilate herself in the name of a purer and less corporeal love. It has the effect as well of insisting again on solitude as the condition of bliss. (Helpmeets are no help if no help is needed.) And the final couplet of the stanza suggests the distinction between Eden and Heaven. Without Eve, Eden would have been Heaven (i.e., no fall; consequently, no knowledge or need of a more perfect condition) and since there is no marriage or giving in marriage in Heaven, Heaven will be Eden without Eve.

By the return to the poem of the reflective mind in the seventh stanza, we are brought gracefully and easily back to the garden in which we began, and which we now understand as the earliest stage in a series of perfections, passing through Eden to Heaven. But by returning to the world of Time the poet returns to the world of death, where his only reasonable ambition, as opposed to the vain ambitions of worldly men, is to look forward to death by computing his time. He is in an ideal situation to do this: the formal garden is a cosmos in little, worked out in carefully designed flowerbeds. The "milder sun" may itself be composed of flowers at the center of the circle of the zodiac, or it might be the actual sun, whose heat so much troubled the world of competitors and lovers, beginning now to decline from the intensity which it offered at the opening of the poem, and from which the poet had withdrawn into the shade. In either case, the sun and the zodiac are both images of Time, and man's life, though longer than a bee's from one point of view, is really not longer in the light of eternity. Death is here, even in Arcadia; or, as this poet would have it, especially in Arcadia. Yet the hours spent here must be sweet and wholesome, for these flowerbeds are an anticipation of Heaven, both as something expected and as immediate symbol.

I do not for one moment suppose that this brief commentary has exhausted the poem. I have intended only to outline what I take to be its main design and theme, and I hope one day to be able to correct a little bit the haste and crudeness of this account. But I would like to set down here at least one afterthought in defense of what I have written.

Joseph H. Summers, in his chapter "The Alchemical Ventriloquist" in *The Heirs of Donne and Jonson,* has a good deal of fun at the expense of those who hold what he regards as heretical views of Marvell's 'The Garden.' Of these heresies, the first he points to is the Romantic. "In so far as we know, Charles Lamb, Emerson, and Poe were among the earliest enthusiastic readers of Marvell's poems," he remarks, and points out how such readers like to focus almost exclusively on the ecstatic lushness of stanzas v through vii. He then proceeds to the next heresy of "demonstrating enormous complexity in language and attitude," as well as in "philosophical and theological doctrine," and pointedly refers in this regard to William Empson. "But Empson's subtleties are more than equalled by the readers who have found key 'sources' of, or analogues to, the poem's central 'meaning' or 'doctrine' in an extraordinarily impressive range of figures and writings: Buddha and the Canticles and the Mass, Plato and Plotinus and 'Hermes Trismegistus,' St. Paul and the Kabbala, St. Bonaventura and St. Thomas Aquinas, Hugh of St. Victor and the *Ancrene Riwle*, Ficino and Leone Ebreo, Henry More and John Smith, Spinoza, Blake and Keats, Alfred North Whitehead and John Dewey. No one would deny that most of these contain profundities or that many provide either images of or patterns for the good life—or dreams of perfection. One could even suggest that plausible analogies can be discovered (or constructed) between the profound writings associated with these names and the stanzas v through vii of 'The Garden'—if we take those stanzas in isolation." I have no idea whether Keats entered Professor Summers' amused list of pretentious errors because of my essay, written long before his own, but if so it is an impeachment I reject on several counts: I do not focus exclusively upon those three stanzas which he claims form the basis of all the readings he repudiates, nor am I unaware of the lively and consistent *wit* and even levity that governs the poem throughout, and which Professor Summers points to as a key to its "tone." In fact, I believe that anyone who compares his reading with mine will discover that I have indicated a number of jests and paradoxes of which he takes no notice.

If one agrees that the design of Keats's "Nightingale" Ode is like the design of Marvell's "Garden," one might object at least that Keats's gestures, in comparison, seem somewhat exaggerated. But it's hard to say just what "exaggerated" means here. You cannot be hyperbolic about the extremities of existence, and there is nothing in Keats as extravagant as Marvell's cramming of two paradises into one. If Marvell seems to proceed by paradox and oxymoron, this is also truer of Keats's poem than a casual reading might suppose. The first six lines of the Ode suggests that the extreme of happiness is just like the extreme of despair, and, by implication, to feel either one

is to feel its opposite. I think it is right to notice something surprising in the way this paradox about feeling is stated, for it
obliges us to reverse our own feelings in midcareer from the
direction they seemed to be taking in the opening lines. And
we are being directed to more than a contrast or coincidence of
happiness and despair: life and death, mortality and immortality, consciousness and unconsciousness, become the ambiguous ground of the poem, and work toward a momentary
reconciliation. Moreover, in the first two lines we have the
oxymoron: "a drowsy numbness pains/My sense. . . ." If hemlock is a painless, anesthetizing poison, it is still painful to
know that you are dying; so that the states of unconsciousness
and consciousness are simultaneously brought into play, and
the body is divided from the imagination. The third and fourth
lines insist upon this even more emphatically. An absolute
division occurs at the crisis of the poem. But I had better return
to the beginning.

In the spring of 1819 a nightingale had built her nest
near my house. Keats felt a tranquil and continual joy in
her song; and one morning he took his chair from the
breakfast table to the grass-plot under a plum-tree, where
he sat for two or three hours. When he came into the
house, I perceived he had some scraps of paper in his
hand, and these he was quietly thrusting behind the
books. On inquiry, I found those scraps, four or five in
number, contained his poetic feeling on the song of the
nightingale. The writing was not well legible; and it
was difficult to arrange the stanzas on so many scraps.
With his assistance I succeeded, and this was his *Ode to a
Nightingale.*

This famous and impressive anecdote of Charles Brown's is
delightful, and I think there is no reason to suppose it is not
true. To be sure, the poem itself has a nocturnal setting, or at
least it is night by the time we reach the fourth stanza. But I

see no reason to doubt the powers of Keats's imagination enough to deny that he could have written the poem in the morning. And yet, without wishing to make too much of this, I think it interesting to notice that the poem was written in spring, and that the flowers mentioned in the fifth stanza are all spring flowers. The point here would be that both the bird and the flowers are anticipating summer, in the sense of looking forward to it as the season of richness and fulfillment, just as the poet (i.e., the speaker of the poem) looks forward to a consummation. The bird sings of summer, and the coming musk rose will be the haunt of summer flies, and the richness of death is as yet, at the beginning of the poem, only a token and a promise. The sense of emergence I mean to suggest here is insisted upon more strongly in the second stanza, where the wine that was "cool'd a long age in the deep-delved earth," comes out of darkness and burial richly transfigured into life, "Dance, and Provençal song, and sunburnt mirth!" The paradox that wine that has been cooled should taste of "the warm South," and that the brilliance and substantiality of its evocations should make the poet "fade away into the forest dim," is more, I think, than a mere confusion of the senses, though undoubtedly this is part of Keats's method. The stanza presents us with a sort of resurrection, full of immediate joy and happy augury. But at the same time "fade" is both death and an escape from death, and we are bound to have mixed feelings about it.

I must interrupt myself at this point to acknowledge that I have perhaps taxed the word *paradox* a bit too heavily, and to assure the reader that I am not offering a doctrinal reading of this poem according to the strictures of Mr. Cleanth Brooks. In any case, his sense of the poem, as it appears in *Understanding Poetry*, is different enough from mine. Properly speaking, *paradox* is a term of logic applied to propositions; and I have used it rather freely to apply to feelings. And yet, while it is clear that we would be rash in attempting to construct a square of logical oppositions for the feelings, we are used to finding them in dramatic conflict, both in life and in art, and often enough within the individual soul. Not infrequently they propose themselves in terms of polarities, making complex and diametrically opposed claims upon us. There is a very beautiful and explicit description of this "paradox of feeling" in the Christmas Sermon of T. S. Eliot's *Murder in the Cathedral*. The Archbishop explains to his congregation that in celebrating Mass on Christmas Day, "we celebrate at once the Birth of Our Lord and his Passion and Death upon the Cross. Beloved," he continues, "as the World sees, this is to behave in a very strange fashion. For who in the World will both mourn and rejoice at once and for the same reason? For either joy will be overborne by mourning, or mourning will be cast out by joy; so it is only in these our Christian mysteries that we can rejoice and mourn at once and for the same reason." It has seemed very likely to me, moreover, that something of this "paradox of feeling" lies behind the puzzle of Aristotelian Katharsis. If *pity* is that feeling of generous sympathy which at the same time allows us to remember ourselves as members of the audience and therefore exempt from the hero's catastrophe; and if *terror* is that feeling of utter hypothetical identification with the hero, putting us in his shoes upon the stage, we are caught in an impossible dilemma. We can't be on stage and in the audience at the same time, nor at once both subject to terrible calamity and exempt from it. These feelings cast each other out, giving place, as in the religious mysteries, to a new feeling which has about it the mystery of a paradox resolved. The tragic feeling is precisely this: both joyous and sad. We do not weep at a tragedy, for it presents us with a spectacle of human nobility that is exalting and a cause for joy. But the price that must be paid to instruct us in how deep and powerful are the resources of the human spirit is terrible, inscrutable, and inevitably exacted.

To get back to Keats. It is the third stanza of the poem that has given even the most partial critics a moment of embarrassment. Here is the rather severe judgment of Allen Tate. "Looked at from any point of view, this stanza is bad. . . . It gives us a 'picture' of common reality, in which the life of man is all mutability and frustration. But here if anywhere in the poem the necessity to dramatize time, or the pressure of actuality, is paramount. *Keats had no language of his own for this realm of experience.* That is the capital point." Mr. Tate goes on to equate the evasiveness he finds here with Keats's general reluctance to offer any clear, dramatic delineation of sexual love. But he relates it even more intimately to his conviction that Keats is a pictorial poet, a poet of space, "whose problem was to find a way of conveying what happens in time; for it is time in which dramatic conflict takes place. . . . 'The form of thought in Keats,' says Mr. Kenneth Burke, 'is mystical, in terms of an eternal present'—and, I should add, in terms of the arrested actions of painting."

It is hard to know how to defend Keats against such charges as these. The stanza in question is not one of the high points of the poem, but I cannot bring myself to believe that it is quite the blemish it has been made out to be. It seems to me that Mr. Tate is begging the question when he speaks of "*this realm of experience*" for which Keats had no language of his own. No doubt Mr. Tate would answer, "Come, come, let's not quibble about anything so elementary. Any sensible man knows what kind of reality Keats is evading or unable to render here." My answer would be that it is not my quibble, but Keats's. If we once accept the conviction that "reality is an activity of the most august imagination," that the world operates upon the imagination and the imagination, in turn, upon the world in a lively process that is nowhere discontinuous, then it is impossible to appeal to a certain level of reality as being the premise and center of every imaginative act. And this seems to me one of the important points not only of this, but of many of Keats's poems. On the other hand, it is perfectly clear that Keats had some doubts upon this point himself, which account for the touching and very successful end of the poem; and I don't want to sound as if I must eat my cake and have it too. It does seem to me important to rescue the stanza from a sense that it is no more than an adolescent peevishness at the tribulations of life and its insubstantial joys. If it is true that the stanza offers a very simplistic notion of Time as the Author of Ruin, it is also true that the rest of the poem, both what went before and what comes after, is concerned to confute this, and to give to time a more complex and subtle status of reality. To the degree that the poem is an anticipation of bliss, time is an instrument of its consummation.

I suspect that what Mr. Tate is really boggling at here is what he calls, in another essay, "romantic irony." The poet defies the natural world to break him if it can; and of course it can, and it does. I am sure there is something of this in the third stanza; Keats is telling us about all the obstacles he is going to have to overcome, and they are all familiar and insuperable. But his desire to overcome them is at least as serious as the Platonist's, and if they appear as stylized, transparent allegorical figures (fading Youth and Beauty and Love) I should think it might well signify that he has already made some progress toward his goal. And reasonably enough. He feels doped and drunk and poisoned. Certainly the world of simple time must be beginning to dissolve into phantoms, just as the wine has proposed its phantoms in the sense that the wine "tastes" of dance and sunburnt mirth. Moreover, it seems clear that a contrast of phantoms is intended: the first, "unreal" on its primary level, are the images conjured up to the senses by drink, and not even real drink, just imaginary drink, but the images have a substantival life and solidity to the sense; the other phantom is real on its primary level (time *will* destroy youth and beauty) but the images it conjures up are pale, unrealized and ghostly. The first is real to the imagination: wine, and its burden of song and dance. The second is real to the intellect: the *fact* of mortality and failing powers. The effect is therefore more firmly to divide the mind from the imagination.

There is one more point I should like to make; it is rather slight, but worth making. Keats's stanzas here seem like large blocks of poetry with a lot crammed into them, and there is no doubt an inclination to read them all at the same stately pace. But I should like to suggest that the syntax, beginning with the last line of the second stanza and ending with the first line of the fourth, makes of most of the third stanza a sort of large parenthetical aside. It is the word *away* that ties the parts together, and after wishing that he might fade far away, he says (omitting the parenthesis), "Away! away! for I will fly to thee. . . ." The syntactical logic of the poem moves directly from the second stanza to the fourth; though this doesn't mean that the third is unnecessary, any more than an aside is unnecessary.

The transformations that are going on (pain into pleasure, consciousness into unconsciousness, life into death and death into life) bring us, in the fourth and fifth stanzas, to the height of the ecstasy with a division of the faculties so severely insisted on as to amount almost to bilocation. What has gone before (not least of all the third, or disreputable, stanza) provides us with an explanation and excuse for the slightly contemptuous anti-intellectualism of the line about the "dull brain" that "perplexes and retards." The nightingale has gradually been transformed by this time, not so much by references to itself as by the other actions of the poem. At the beginning it was merely a bird whose lovely song provoked pain that was like joy, or joy that was like pain. The imaginary vintage its song inspires presents us with an image of the richness of life emerging from death, and I should think that a myth is being most gently hinted at. Moreover, if the imagination can get itself looped on imaginary wine, it can do better than that: it can ascend on the viewless wings of Poesy. And the ascension is a kind of death, leaving the body, though

fully sentient, in "embalmed darkness," like the buried wine.
And by this series of delicate equations, the bird and its song
have come to correspond to the poet and this poem he is writing, by virtue of their common ability to make pain into joy
and transform death into life. Philomela is never mentioned,
but is as present as Bacchus and Pegasus. We have been ad-
mirably prepared for that stunning line, "Now more than ever
seems it rich to die." Imagination is content to let the wings be
"viewless" and to leave it a matter of speculation as to whether
indeed the "Queen-Moon is on her throne,/Cluster'd around
by all her starry Fays." It is enough to be there, beyond the
reach of earthbound senses, in the nightingale's company. The
senses are down below (as they were with Marvell) and even
they must speculate, by transforming, in their own imaginative method, smell into sight. The body, buried in its embalmed darkness, looks to its resurrection, not only by this
simple but mysterious transformation of senses, but by its
imaginative anticipation, in mid-May, of the richness of summer, the *coming* musk rose, full of dewy wine; not there yet,
but as real and present as the draught of vintage; so that the
body sings "of summer" even as the bird, and even while sep-
arated from the lofty and transcendent imagination.

It seems appropriate to point out—though not to worry—a
certain morbid sexuality here. The body's hankering after fulfillment, no less than the imagination's, has been invested with
strong feelings, and the preparations for this consummation
are like the preparations for death. It seems as if, with Keats,
the embassies of love can only be admitted when the faculties
are helplessly divided, as in the moments before death,* and I
think it is not at all unlikely to see here a prefiguring of Rim-
baud's "deliberate derangement of the senses." In any case, we

* Cf. the letter, dated 25 July 1819, to Fanny Brawne: "I have two
luxuries to brood over in my walks, your Loveliness and the hour of my
death. O that I could have possession of them both in the same minute. I
hate the world: it batters too much the wings of my self-will, and I would
take a sweet poison from your lips to send me out of it."

have on Keats's part a fascination with sex combined with a curious horror of it—and in this poem its presence may have been nearly unconscious to the poet. But it was a deep part of his ritual sense of love that it be inaugurated by a foretaste of sensual pleasure through the heaping up and accumulation of delicious sensory experience in almost a covetous, and at the same time, puritanical way. Such is the case in the "Eve of St. Agnes" and in "Endymion." And in all these cases, the most convincing part of the sexual feeling is in fact conveyed by the relish for tastes and smells—and not of human beings, but of innocent and symbolic substitutes in the form of fruits and sweetmeats. And the reason for this, here as elsewhere, is that description beyond a certain point is impossible precisely because the sexual experience is a trance like death, passive, unconscious. And in the poem, it should be remembered, the poet is approaching this condition in solitary self-absorption. The psychologists have some rather nasty terms to apply to appetites such as this, but they are only slightly more insulting (by virtue of their slightly greater authority) than the original views of Keats's poems by many of his contemporaries. Indeed, the attitude of objective, superior contempt, and the grounds for this attitude, would be the same in both cases; the grounds being, most temperately, a certain unmanly passivity and emotional waywardness unattractive even in a very young man.

And here in the poem we are in the midst of a superb but figurative death which (buttressed by the promise of resurrection) the poet now desires and imagines to be made real. And it is here that Keats lays the trap for himself in which he is caught in the last stanza, and in which he is obliged to confess that the correspondence he had all along implied between the bird's song and his own song, and between the "Immortal Bird" and himself, was a rhetorical device that must at last be abandoned.

Death, the absolute division of the faculties, that utter passivity which is a process of fading away into a simultaneous consciousness and unconsciousness, has been made inviting and delicious; it is solicited and firmly imagined in the next stanza, in which an even more violent division is made than heretofore: ecstasy and consciousness are identified with the bird, numbness and unconsciousness with the poet. He has become the bird's audience, and therefore, in a sense, his own. And yet we cannot quite credit this, for he is still in the very process of writing a poem, and he is no longer depending upon the bird for support, but on the viewless wings of Poesy. Still, he is only imagining what it would be like to die under these pleasant circumstances, "To cease upon the midnight with no pain." The bird's song is and has always been a requiem; the poet's imagined death does not make it so; it simply makes his passivity and unconsciousness absolute and complete. The immortality of art abides the human death. And does it honor by commemoration. That is to say, all songs are requiems, all poems elegies, making something sweet out of life in the very teeth of death. And so the bird is duly acknowledged as immortal, and even from the earliest times there was always someone who had gone before, and whom the nightingale could appropriately mourn. The song is always the same, indirectly suggesting that the bird is always the same, i.e., literally immortal. And yet the bird is certainly immortal by virtue of the immortality of its song. The difference is important; Keats might hope for one kind of immortality, not the other.

The nightingale was heard long ago by all sorts and conditions of people, reminding them of the generations past, and what could have been more apt than the sound of that song to Ruth, who seems even more remote to us (because of the quasi-real context of the Bible) than the ancient days of emperor and clown. And more remote yet, due to a general dubiety about their reality-status, are those "magic casements, opening on the foam/Of perilous seas, in faery lands forlorn." Indeed, "forlorn" is the key word here, not only because it recalls the poet to his isolated self, but because it has to do with the central

problem of the whole poem: a reliance upon and confidence in
the powers of the imagination. The faery lands are forlorn
precisely because nobody any longer believes in them. And on
what grounds are we to claim that Ruth, or the emperor and
clown, are more real and worthy of belief, since it is only by
an act of the imagination that we can apprehend them? And
most important of all, if the faery lands were "merely" the
perishable creations of imagination, now abandoned for want
of belief in them, what confidence, if any, may we have in the
reality of the imagination, including the experience the poet
has just gone through? The degree of self-consciousness in-
voked by that one word, "forlorn," which tolls the poet back
to his "sole-self" is staggering as well as sudden. And this is by
no means the only poem of Keats's in which this problem is
made central and dramatic; in fact, it is one of his major
themes. In the "Ode to Psyche" he laments that the goddess
has "No shrine, no grove, no heat/Of pale-mouthed prophet
dreaming," and goes on to say, "O brightest! though too late
for antique vows,/Too, too late for the fond believing lyre. . . ."
Nevertheless, he volunteers to be her priest, "and build a fane/
In some untrodden region of my mind,/Where branchèd
thoughts, new grown with pleasant pain,/Instead of pines
shall murmur in the wind. . . ." It should be noticed, however,
that in the Psyche Ode the problem is not fully faced because
the continuity between the exterior and interior world is made
so fragile and tenuous as not really to present a problem at all.
It is, in its own mode, thoroughly successful, and has what
may be the most breathlessly passionate ending of any poem
in English. The Nightingale Ode, on the other hand, is busy
making metaphysical inquiries about itself such as the Psyche
Ode does not contemplate; and in my opinion this gives it a
density and complexity which I must deny the other in spite
of its indubitable beauty. The difference between the odes is
precisely the difference between Psyche (goddess and mind)
and a nightingale (symbol of art through suffering and a

bird); in one case there is no need for the *facts* of the outside world to be acknowledged; but the bird starts off as a bird and must remain one, no matter how much mythical weight it is made to bear. Moreover, the fact that the Nightingale Ode ends irresolutely seems to me both dramatic and honest, and in no way to diminish its force and point. For the fact is that we are entitled to an unresolved doubt at the end. It is true, the claims that were made upon the "fancy" were extravagant; but the experience of the poet, up to a certain point, has undoubtedly been real enough, and it was almost entirely predicated on that "deceiving elf," the fancy. Almost, except for the bird song. And that song, like this poem, is both "an ecstasy" and a "requiem." If the bird song "fades" as the imagination fails, and if the poet is left in doubt about the reality of his present lonely circumstances as well as the reality of the ecstasy (which was a kind of token death), we are left with the paradox that the numbness, bewilderment and confusion which he so much desired at the beginning of the poem he now has in plenty, but finds it only distressing. And yet the paradox is not real, for like Marvell, he did not quite die, but was left only with the symptoms of death. And his despair, if that's what it is, arises from being "tolled back" as by a death knell from the sovereign heights above the perilous seas. It is death to faery land, and a sudden vacant, non-ecstatic death to him. But it is death to the imagination only if the whole poem is called into question. There is no doubt that Keats does so call it, but I should think that he hoped it would offer its own uncompromising answer.

And how shall we describe, in general terms, the differences between these poems? In these two ways, I think. First, the Marvell is a gradual ascent to the emotional summit, with an equally gradual and graceful descent; whereas the Keats is a sudden rising, an attempt to sustain flight, and an equally sudden, unexpected deflation. And this can be attributed to the second difference, which lies in the fact that Marvell's poem is debonair and witty, while Keats's is grand and self-conscious. Let me put it in more particular terms. Marvell is speaking in the language of Platonism cum pastoralism cum feelings and is using, most loosely, the old allegorical mode of speech. No reader is supposed to believe that the poet is a rank Platonist and pagan; it is set down by the poet beforehand as a compliment to the reader's own civility and sophistication that he should know better. "This is a mode, reputable in its own time, of describing my feelings," Marvell seems to say.

The subject of Keats's poem is also the feelings, but for better or worse, he lacks the allegorical mode—by which I mean a steady set of correspondences which work in a one-for-one relationship throughout. For Marvell this means a relationship of the garden to Eden and Eden to Heaven, which corresponds loosely to Plato's Divided Line, which corresponds in turn to a right apprehension, through feelings of transport, of the perfection of love and knowledge. Lacking such parallel re-enforcements, Keats is obliged to question his premises, as the man who says, "this is merely a mode of speech," is not. Everything at any point of Keats's discourse might be attacked for its literal relevance, and he is supremely aware of this, as the end of the poem so poignantly shows. Indeed, what he has done is to cast a spell and then anticipate the reader by puncturing it before the reader has a chance—or even an inclination—to do so himself. And this, I think, explains the suddenness of the descent. The Keats poem hangs on a question of *belief*—first and foremost the poet's own belief—in the literal truth of what is being said. The question never comes up for Marvell, who instead describes his feelings by parallel modes of thought. And these he does not ask you to believe in: they are like heresies, false in themselves, but parallel to the truth.

Furthermore, while in both poems the human faculties, though differently delimited and designated, separate from one another in what seems a deathlike process of disintegration, there is a striking difference between them to be seen in the process. In Marvell's case, he may have the best of both worlds, since the disintegration is death, but at the same time a progress paralleling the mystical progress of love from body to mind to soul, it being properly entertained by each. The faculties may be discrete and discontinuous, but the "progress" is a continuous one by virtue of an accepted hierarchy among these faculties. Also for Marvell there is emphatically no division between the rational intellect (which apprehends the facts of the world) and the imagination: this is stated quite explicitly in stanza six. But it is a central point for Keats so to divide them; and I should think this is exactly what he was arguing for, and declaring to be so conspicuously absent in Coleridge's temperament (that inveterate bloodhound and archivist of his own thoughts) in the famous passage, from the letter to his brothers, about Negative Capability.

> . . . and at once it struck me what quality went to form a Man of Achievement, especially in Literature, and which Shakespeare possessed so enormously—I mean *Negative Capability*, that is, when a man is capable of being in uncertainties, mysteries, doubts, without any irritable reaching after fact and reason—Coleridge, for instance, would let go by a fine isolated verisimilitude caught from the Penetralium of mystery, from being incapable of being content with half-knowledge.

Moreover, Keats accepts no absolute hierarchy among the faculties, and for all his homage, here as elsewhere, to the imagination, he acknowledges that it cannot stand alone and unsupported. Yet this acknowledgment, combined with his suspicion and condemnation of a lusting after fact and reason, leaves him at times very restless and insecure. There are many passages in the letters (most notably the declaration that the Poet has no Identity, and therefore may, and perhaps must, take on the identity of other creatures—real or mythical or

imaginary—and of other things; as well as another passage in
a letter to Woodhouse, in which, after being in the company
of Achilles in the Trenches, and Theocritus in the Vales of
Sicily, he "becomes" Troilus, and in the next moment, "I melt
into the air with a voluptuousness so delicate that I am content
to be alone") testifying to the imagination's *seeming* suprem-
acy, independence, and contempt for fact and reason. But
Keats was not absolutely "content to be alone," or to depend
unconditionally on such visionary transports; and there is another letter which must be brought into evidence here.

> I am sometimes so very sceptical as to think Poetry itself
> a mere Jack a lantern to amuse whoever may chance to
> be struck with its brilliance. As Tradesmen say every-
> thing is worth what it will fetch, so probably every men-
> tal pursuit takes its reality and its worth from the ardour
> of the pursuer—being in itself nothing—Ethereal things
> may at least be thus real, divided under three heads—
> Things real—things semireal—and no things. Things
> real—such as existences of Sun Moon & Stars and pas-
> sages of Shakespeare. Things semireal such as Love, the
> Clouds &c which require a greeting of the Spirit to make
> them wholly exist—and Nothings which are made Great
> and dignified by an ardent pursuit—which by the by
> stamps the burgundy mark on the bottles of our Minds,
> insomuch as they are able to 'consecrate whate'er they
> look upon.'
>
> To Benj. Bailey, 13 March 1818

Without any condescension to Keats whatever (for he seems
to suspect as much) it may be said that both as epistemology
and metaphysics this passage leaves much to be desired. The
three categories of Ethereal things are scarcely very distinct,
and the examples he uses reflect Keats's personal tastes and
emotional character far more than they do anything else. More
troubling still is the problem that if all Ethereal things are

made real only by the ardour of the pursuer, it will be impossible to a sufficiently vigorous mind and enterprising spirit to distinguish between Real things and Nothings. But most important of all, the very reality of the existence of all these things (including the Sun and Moon) are called into question; and the mode by which we might apprehend them (which I take to be the imagination) involves us in the frailest and most inconclusive sort of solipsism. We are at liberty, by these terms, to make anything we desire real by the ardour of our pursuit. Yet the very language he uses—"Things real—things semi-real—and no things"—suggests that Keats does not altogether believe what he is saying. His tone *is* sceptical and worldly, though perhaps not quite sceptical enough to please us. And indeed almost exactly a year later he returned to the problem more passionately and more thoughtfully in the "Ode to a Nightingale."

Let me go back again to Keats's statement about Negative Capability. As I understand this passage, it speaks in behalf of an unquestioning acceptance of an intuition or aperçu, characterized by the ease, the grace, the gift of its arrival. I take the word *verisimilitude* to mean "metaphor" at the very least, but to carry with it the weight and authority of a Truth. Keats's belief in the effortlessness of getting at this metaphoric Truth (for which means we might supply the name of inspiration or imagination) is touched upon in his famous statement to the effect that "if Poetry comes not as naturally as the Leaves to a tree it had better not come at all." In Lionel Trilling's introduction to his selection of Keats's letters, he reflects upon the occasion ("not a dispute but a disquisition" addressed to Dilke as Keats walked home with him and with Charles Brown after a Christmas pantomine) which led to this formulation about Negative Capability. "The disquisition touched on 'various subjects' which are not specified," Trilling reminds us, "and Keats says that as it proceeded 'several things dove-tailed in my mind and at once it struck me. . . .'" In undertaking to

explain the meaning of what follows, Trilling seems confident that Keats had in mind at the time a lively sense of his
own estimate of the character of Dilke. "It is essential to an
understanding of what Keats meant that we have in mind
the kind of person who was Keats's interlocutor in the 'disquisition' during which the idea came to him . . ." says Trilling, and he proceeds to cite several instances, from later
letters, of Keats's repudiation of the "doctrinaire" and "over-
systematic process of thought" which he felt would prevent
Dilke from ever coming "to a truth so long as he lives; because
he is always trying at it." (Not only is rigor objected to, but
effort as well.) It is precarious, of course, to speculate beyond
what the letter tells us on just what Keats did have in mind at
the time; what the "various subjects" were, and what were the
"several things" that "dove-tailed." Trilling's suggestion that
Dilke's character was itself at that moment a part of the
thought seems to me unlikely; or at least I should think it might
have inhibited the disquisition of so kindly a person as Keats.
It seems more likely to me that the observations on Dilke,
while thoroughly fitting, may have come after the fact. But I
take courage from Trilling's willingness to conjecture, and
propose another suggestion, though of course it has no better
claim to the truth of this matter than his own. Let me present
it by way of quotation.

"What then," I objected, "O Diotima, is Love ugly and
evil?"—"Good words, I entreat you," said Diotima; "do
you think that every thing which is not beautiful, must
of necessity be ugly?"—"Certainly."—"And everything
that is not wise, ignorant? Do you not perceive that there
is something between ignorance and wisdom?"—"What
is that?"—"To have a right opinion or conjecture. Observe, that this kind of opinion, for which no reason can
be rendered, cannot be called knowledge; for how can
that be called knowledge, which is without evidence or

reason? Nor ignorance, on the other hand; for how can that be called ignorance which arrives at the persuasion of that which it really is? A right opinion is something between understanding and ignorance." . . . "Observe, then, that you do not consider Love to be a God."—"What then," I said, "is Love a mortal?"—"By no means."—"But what, then?"—"Like those things which I have instanced, he is neither mortal nor immortal, but something intermediate."—"What is that, O Diotima?"—"A great Daemon, Socrates; and everything daemoniacal holds an intermediate place between what is divine and what is mortal."

These celebrated passages from Plato's "Symposium" may perhaps be nothing more than fortuitously close to the subject at hand; and I have no care to claim more for them. But they may be seen as bearing handsomely upon the problem of Negative Capability as well as upon the Nightingale Ode. They present us first of all with a mode of apprehension which arrives at the truth without resort to fact or reason (and by a sophistical use of reason in a passage I have omitted, reason is shown to be inadequate in arriving at the truth). Secondly, they make a correspondence, by analogy, between this kind of apprehension (inspiration, imagination) and Love; a correspondence which becomes more than analogy later in Diotima's discourse; a correspondence to be found in other parts of Keats's letters (particularly the one to Bailey, dated 13 March, 1818) as well as in the Nightingale Ode. Third, and most important of all to the Ode, that daemon is held to be an intermediate between "what is divine and what is mortal," as inspiration or right opinion is an intermediate between ignorance and knowledge: i.e., half-knowledge, with which Coleridge could never be content. And the famous passage that follows, about Love's parentage, and about the qualities and character that are his by inheritance, is a quite thorough-going analogy for the perilous efforts of Keats's imagination to negotiate between the upper and lower regions. It offers some marked parallels to the formulas for desolation in the third stanza; and prefigures, as do Diotima's later remarks about the loneliness and isolation of all mortals, the pitiful and affecting uncertainty of the poem's end.

If the foregoing can tentatively be accepted as a fair description of the case, two possible conclusions may be drawn. One is that Marvell had more confidence in the authenticity and generality of his feelings than Keats, so that they could support his analogies when the analogies could not support them. And I think perhaps this is partly true, but it is only a small part of the truth. On the other hand, the alternative (which concerns the whole question of "belief"—the poet's and the reader's) requires an investigation into the very nature of poetry itself, vastly beyond my present scope and purpose.

THE GARDEN

I

How vainly men themselves amaze
To win the Palm, the Oke, or Bayes;
And their uncessant Labours see
Crown'd from some single Herb or Tree.
Whose short and narrow verged Shade
Does prudently their Toyles upbraid;
While all Flow'rs and all Trees do close
To weave the Garlands of repose.

II

Fair quiet, have I found thee here,
And Innocence thy Sister dear!
Mistaken long, I sought you then
In busie Companies of Men.
Your sacred Plants, if here below,
Only among the Plants will grow.
Society is all but rude,
To this delicious Solitude.

III

No white nor red was ever seen
So am'rous as this lovely green.
Fond Lovers, cruel as their Flame,
Cut in these Trees their Mistress name.
Little, Alas, they know, or heed,
How far these Beauties Hers exceed!
Fair Trees! where s'eer your barkes I wound,
No Name shall but your own be found.

Shades of Keats and Marvell

IV

When we have run our Passion's heat,
Love hither makes his best retreat.
The *Gods*, that mortal Beauty chase,
Still in a Tree did end their race.
Apollo hunted *Daphne* so,
Only that She might Laurel grow.
And *Pan* did after *Syrinx* speed,
Not as a Nymph, but for a Reed.

V

What wond'rous Life in this I lead!
Ripe Apples drop about my head;
The Luscious Clusters of the Vine
Upon my Mouth do crush their Wine;
The Nectaren, and curious Peach,
Into my hands themselves do reach;
Stumbling on Melons, as I pass,
Insnar'd with Flow'rs, I fall on Grass.

VI

Meanwhile the Mind, from pleasure less,
Withdraws into its happiness:
The Mind, that Ocean where each kind
Does streight its own resemblance find;
Yet it creates, transcending these,
Far other Worlds, and other Seas;
Annihilating all that's made
To a green Thought in a green Shade.

VII

Here at the Fountains sliding foot,
Or at some Fruit-trees mossy root,
Casting the Bodies Vest aside,
My Soul into the boughs does glide:
There like a Bird it sits, and sings,
Then whets, and combs its silver Wings;
And, till prepar'd for longer flight,
Waves in its Plumes the various Light.

VIII

Such was that happy Garden-state,
While Man there walk'd without a Mate:
After a Place so pure, and sweet,
What other Help could yet be meet!
But 'twas beyond a Mortal's share
To wander solitary there:
Two Paradises 'twere in one
To live in Paradise alone.

IX

How well the skilful Gardner drew
Of flow'rs and herbes this Dial new;
Where from above the milder Sun
Does through a fragrant Zodiack run;
And, as it works, th' industrious Bee
Computes its time as well as we.
How could such sweet and wholsome Hours
Be reckon'd but with herbs and flow'rs!

ODE TO A NIGHTINGALE

I

My heart aches, and a drowsy numbness pains
  My sense, as though of hemlock I had drunk,
Or emptied some dull opiate to the drains
  One minute past, and Lethe-wards had sunk:
'Tis not through envy of thy happy lot,
  But being too happy in thine happiness,—
    That thou, light-winged Dryad of the trees,
      In some melodious plot
  Of beechen green, and shadows numberless,
    Singest of summer in full-throated ease.

II

O, for a draught of vintage! that hath been
  Cool'd a long age in the deep-delved earth,
Tasting of Flora and the country green,
  Dance, and Provençal song, and sunburnt mirth!
O for a beaker full of the warm South,
  Full of the true, the blushful Hippocrene,
    With beaded bubbles winking at the brim,
      And purple-stained mouth;
That I might drink, and leave the world unseen,
    And with thee fade away into the forest dim:

261

Shades of Keats and Marvell

III

Fade far away, dissolve, and quite forget
  What thou among the leaves hast never known,
The weariness, the fever, and the fret
  Here, where men sit and hear each other groan;
Where palsy shakes a few, sad, last gray hairs,
  Where youth grows pale, and spectre-thin, and dies;
    Where but to think is to be full of sorrow
      And leaden-eyed despairs,
    Where Beauty cannot keep her lustrous eyes,
      Or new Love pine at them beyond to-morrow.

IV

Away! away! for I will fly to thee,
  Not charioted by Bacchus and his pards,
But on the viewless wings of Poesy,
  Though the dull brain perplexes and retards:
Already with thee! tender is the night,
  And haply the Queen-Moon is on her throne,
    Cluster'd around by all her starry Fays;
      But here there is no light,
    Save what from heaven is with the breezes blown
      Through verdurous glooms and winding mossy ways.

V

I cannot see what flowers are at my feet,
  Nor what soft incense hangs upon the boughs,
But, in embalmed darkness, guess each sweet
  Wherewith the seasonable month endows
The grass, the thicket, and the fruit-tree wild;
  White hawthorn, and the pastoral eglantine;
    Fast fading violets cover'd up in leaves;
      And mid-May's eldest child,
    The coming musk-rose, full of dewy wine,
      The murmurous haunt of flies on summer eves.

Shades of Keats and Marvell

VI

Darkling I listen; and, for many a time
  I have been half in love with easeful Death,
Call'd him soft names in many a mused rhyme,
  To take into the air my quiet breath;
Now more than ever seems it rich to die,
  To cease upon the midnight with no pain,
    While thou art pouring forth thy soul abroad
      In such an ecstasy!
  Still wouldst thou sing, and I have ears in vain—
    To thy high requiem become a sod.

VII

Thou wast not born for death, immortal Bird!
  No hungry generations tread thee down;
The voice I hear this passing night was heard
  In ancient days by emperor and clown:
Perhaps the self-same song that found a path
  Through the sad heart of Ruth, when, sick for home,
    She stood in tears amid the alien corn;
      The same that oft-times hath
  Charm'd magic casements, opening on the foam
    Of perilous seas, in faery lands forlorn.

VIII

Forlorn! the very word is like a bell
  To toll me back from thee to my sole self!
Adieu! the fancy cannot cheat so well
  As she is fam'd to do, deceiving elf.
Adieu! adieu! thy plaintive anthem fades
  Past the near meadows, over the still stream,
    Up the hill-side; and now 'tis buried deep
      In the next valley-glades:
  Was it a vision, or a waking dream?
    Fled is that music:—Do I wake or sleep?

Robert Lowell

Everything is real until it's published.
FLIGHT TO NEW YORK

I F W E M A Y assert with confidence so very soon after his death that Robert Lowell has attained the stature of a major American poet, it is important that we guard against making the claim for any of the wrong reasons. The difficulty arises out of the easy confusion of celebrity with achievement. On the whole, it's easier for fiction writers than for poets to become celebrities: their works can be filmed and televised; because they write prose, it is assumed by talk-show impresarios that they can probably talk; and then celebrity must furnish its own appetite for further celebrity, all of it benignly regarded by promoters and publishers and the public. Poets, on the other hand, though they may be regarded as *ipso facto* "strange," "passing strange," are only thought interesting if they have a conspicuous vice to exploit, or some aggrandizing aberration. And Lowell has undeniably been noticed for lots of reasons that are incidental, if at all related, to his literary attainments. Some have been impressed with the distinction of his family, his ancestral ties to Jonathan Edwards, to the early Pilgrim fathers, as well as to Harvard presidents, and an

264

ambassador to the court of St. James. Some knew he was important because his mental crack-ups received such notoriety; some knew him in terms of the political stances he took, often impetuously and courageously, beginning with his objection to this country's role in World War II, and continuing to the protests against our role in Vietnam. Finally, there is the undisputed fact that so soon after his death his biography has been written by the British poet Ian Hamilton, a certification of Lowell's clear importance, if one were needed. But it should be said that while none of these considerations is trivial or beside the point, they bear only indirectly on Lowell's singular accomplishments. Lowell himself made rather a mockery of the distinction of his family, and seems to have felt it rather an encumbrance than anything else. He was frequently appalled by his mental disturbances, and by their consequences. His political stances were always taken with seriousness and integrity and never simply in order to get his name or face into print. And this biographer, in distinct contrast with those of certain other modern writers whose weather eyes were cocked for the attention of posterity, was not officially appointed by him.

Lowell's biography was greeted with what may fairly be called rave reviews by Helen Vendler in the leading article in the *New York Review of Books*; by Richard Ellmann on the front page of the *New York Times Book Review*; and by Stephen Spender on the front page of the *Washington Post's Book World*. There is in this a rather poignant irony that is not likely to be lost on Mr. Hamilton, who is himself a poet. Of all the work of a lifetime dedicated to poetry, and abundant in its production, the only volume of Lowell's to receive front page notice in the *Times Book Review* was his last, *Day by Day*, reviewed there admiringly by Helen Vendler on August 14, 1977, less than a month before Lowell's death on September 12. Hamilton's book bids fair to be something of a best seller, and is firmly a book club selection; and, like the reviewers who are on record in praising it, I wish it every success. But he and I will not be alone in imagining that this book will be devoured by many who have no interest in poetry, and scarcely any knowledge of Robert Lowell's work.

The sort of prurience that is bound to contribute to the public's interest can be illustrated by an anecdote, true in its major outlines, and from which I have merely deleted the proper names. Some years ago, when Lowell was a firmly acknowledged celebrity, the editors of a popular magazine invited one of New York's leading intellectuals, a critic-author-editor of impeccable credentials, to lunch at one of the city's best restaurants to discuss some sort of possible article about the poet. The distinguished critic was intrigued by the emergence of this proposal from so unlikely a source, and perhaps engaged by the excellence of the restaurant. It was during the second, soothing martini that the editors began to make clear what it was they hoped the projected article would cover: they wanted to have as much in the way of particulars as could be managed about a) Lowell's girl friends and extramarital affairs, and b) his episodes of violence and incarceration in mental hospitals. The critic listened silently, savoring his drink, as these guidelines were laid out for him, and when they seemed to be quite through he asked the editors, "And how much space do you think should be devoted to the *poetry?*" The answer he received convinced him that, of their kind, these were real pros he was dealing with. "Roughly eighty percent of our readership," he was told, "hold B.A.s, and of those perhaps twenty percent have more advanced degrees. So I think you can safely assume that they will *know* the poetry, and you won't have to bother with it."

And indeed the biography, though sparing in both numbers and details (not a few women will doubtless be outraged to find their names omitted from the chronicle), makes it clear that Lowell's manic cycles almost always involved episodes of sexual adventurism. So much was this the case that at one time his New York psychiatrist, a woman, convinced that somehow Lowell's wife, Elizabeth Hardwick, had a deleterious effect upon the poet, and needed to be kept from him at all costs, nevertheless found herself so mystified by the urgency with which Lowell spoke of someone he was newly obsessed with (or so goes the story as I heard it) that, for all the therapist's hostility to Miss Hardwick, she phoned her to ask, "Who is this Gerta he talks about now all the time?" Miss Hardwick replied truthfully that her husband was talking about the author of *Faust*.

Hamilton's book deserves praise for many things, but I think chiefly for being astonishingly fair to all the major figures in the story he has set out to tell—not in itself an easy task, given a tale so congested with pain and cruelty, infidelity, wildness, and violence—but he is also to be congratulated on his usually respectful and intelligent dealings with the poetry, though he sometimes lapses into unfortunate generalizations and crude conjectures, as shall appear. But he is very keen, subtle, and knowing, for example, about Lowell's poem "Home After Three Months Away," indicating with great care the stratified, geological layers of reference that work down through the poet's entire biography. He is even more helpful, and helped in his turn by the painter Sidney Nolan, in the unravelling of an all but impenetrable poem, "The Misanthrope and the Painter," which seems defiantly hermetic and private. (It's impossible to tell whether the poem was meant to be cryptic, reserved for the understanding of the initiate, or was not sufficiently worked out.) And if Hamilton is sometimes hasty or careless in his dealings with the poetry, it must be added that in the portraiture of his subject he has somehow contrived to omit or gloss over some of Lowell's most endearing characteristics, especially his animated sense of fun, and his lively pleasure in the humor of others. Some of his taunting letters—to Peter Taylor, for example—were written in the spirit of outrageous jest, and are retailed in this book with a straight face, and without any indication that they could mean anything but what they seem literally to say. But in his honest dealings with his large cast of characters, and in his valuable comments on the poetry, Hamilton has done, I think, rather greater justice to Lowell than has been done to Byron by most of his biographers, some of whom, like Peter Quennell and Harold Nicolson, appear not really to be interested in the poetry at all.

The Byron comparison, while not to be pursued with Euclidean precision, and not Hamilton's but mine, is a fair one in some respects. Both poets were public figures and involved in the political events of their time; both were capable of devastating expressions of scorn for their opponents; both were powerful and handsome men; both were crippled, each in his own way; both were astonishingly attractive to women; both were aristocrats by inheritance (somewhat shabby aristocrats) and democrats by generous instinct; both were the subject of scandalous gossip during and after their lifetimes; and both were poets of acknowledged international stature, who *found themselves famous* quite early in life. It may be added that both were bedeviled by strict and relentlessly Puritan consciences and Calvinistic anguish. Hamilton reports that Lowell's nickname, Cal, was meant to stand for Caligula (as Lowell himself acknowledges in a poem) and Caliban. Robie Macauley has told me that it also stood for the Calvin in Calvin Coolidge. While there was something strikingly Julio-Claudian about Lowell's huge head, the Calvin of Geneva, a dim but satanic presence in the poem called "Children of Light" ("Pilgrims unhouseled by Geneva's night,/They planted here the Serpent's seeds of light; . . ."), has, I think, a legitimate part to play in the poet's psychic genealogy.

The nickname of the mad emperor was curiously prophetic because it was assigned to, and adopted by, Lowell before his madness had yet exhibited itself in any forms graver than eccentric recklessness and untidiness. Later, of course, the news of his periodic breakdowns spread with amazing speed, penetrating without difficulty to even the most remote recesses of the world. News, for example, of his Salzburg collapse reached me somehow in provincial Ischia, and I remember passing it on to Auden, expecting from him some grunt of commiseration, at the very least. I could not have been more astonished by his response. He regarded Lowell's whole tortured history of crack-ups as pure self-indulgence, and undeserving of any sympathy. It took me many years to come to even a partial understanding of this chilling reaction, and I can only guess that it may have been due to Auden's medical fascination with Georg Groddeck, Homer Lane, and other psychosomatic theorists who believed that virtually all illnesses are *willed*, as well as to a parental inheritance of clinical detachment, and the fact that there was no history of madness in his immediate experience. In fairness it should be added that he may have been at least partly right: Hamilton quotes Jonathan Raban's account of the dolphin binge (the buying of little glass or plaster dolphins) Lowell went on during the writing of *The Dolphin*, a binge that clearly represented a huge exertion of will power ("So the obsession," Raban reports, "was with dolphins—it never got into great men. Which was a triumph") directed toward avoiding a crack-up, and which, in this lone instance, worked. But Auden's lofty, condemnatory tone was to exhibit itself again when Lowell later, in *The Dolphin*, published poems of unprecedented intimacy, with details and even language frankly rifled from private conversations and correspondence, chiefly with his abandoned wife, Elizabeth Hardwick, but with others, like Allen Tate, as well. Hamilton quotes from a letter to Lowell by William Alfred, who had just met Auden for the first time: "He spoke of not speaking to you because of the book. When I said he sounded like God the Father, he gave me a tight smile. I write to warn you." Alas, in both these cases Auden sounds less like the Ancient of Days than like a prim

Robert Lowell

English nanny with a rigid sense of decorum. In fact, Auden is permitted to voice his objections in one of the book's sonnets, called, with some point, "Truth":

> The scouring voice of 1930 Oxford,
> "Nothing pushing the personal should be published,
> not even Proust's *Research* or Shakespeare's *Sonnets*,
> a banquet of raw ingredients in bad taste. . . ."

Undeniably, as Lowell's best and most admiring friends forced themselves to point out to him before publication, the book would be excruciatingly painful to Elizabeth Hardwick. In this regard Elizabeth Bishop wrote Lowell an agonizing letter, urging him not to publish the book, and saying: ". . . *art just isn't worth that much.*" And Stanley Kunitz must have raised objections no less strong and direct, as he indicated in a memoir published in the October 16, 1977, *New York Times Book Review*, because Lowell wrote to him as follows:

> About your criticism. I expect to be back in New York for a week beginning the 21st of May, and hope to unwind over drinks with you. Dolphin is somewhat changed with the help of Elizabeth Bishop. The long birth sequence will come before the Flight to New York, a stronger conclusion, and one oddly softening the effect by giving a reason other than new love for my departure. Most of the letter poems—E.B.'s objection they were part fiction offered as truth—can go back to your old plan, a mixture of my voice, and another voice in my head, part me, part Lizzie, italicized, paraphrased, imperfectly, obsessively heard. I take it, it is these parts that repel you. I tried the new version on Peter Taylor, and he couldn't imagine any moral objection to Dolphin. Not that the poem, alas, from its donnée, can fail to wound. . . .

Lowell appears wonderfully unaware that a poem that cannot fail to wound must have at least some moral objection to it. Anyway, the biography reports on these terrible debates and dilemmas without passing judgment, though at least one review that I have seen matches Auden's in righteous indignation.

The problem is not easily solved, nor does solution lie in some considered compromise between Auden's snooty evasions and Lowell's ruthless candor. Somehow Lowell must have clung to a fuddled conviction expressed in the line I have chosen for an epigraph: "Everything is real until it's published," whereupon, I think he may have felt, it becomes art, which is beyond the real but nearer the truth. Whatever theorizing or rationalizing may have lain behind this attitude, it took no account of the human pain it would engender. But Lowell's sense of the transformations wrought by art, removing its matter from the realm of the literal, is wonderfully documented. Jonathan Raban is quoted as observing that Lowell's revisions were usually

> a kind of gaming with words, treating them like billiard balls. For almost every sentence that Cal ever wrote if he thought it made a better line he'd have put a "never" or a "not" at the essential point. His favorite method of revision was simply to introduce a negative into a line, which absolutely reversed its meaning but very often would improve it. So that his poem on Flaubert ended with Flaubert dying, and in the first draft it went "Till the mania for phrases dried his heart"—a quotation from Flaubert's mother. Then Cal saw another possibility and it came out: "Till the mania for phrases enlarged his heart." It made perfectly good sense either way round, but the one did happen to mean the opposite of the other.

While it may be argued that there is a considerable difference between, on the one hand, tampering with the words of Flaubert's mother, and, on the other, appropriating the most intimate domestic communications of an abandoned wife with whom the poet lived in great happiness for many years, and who is the mother of his daughter, I think two other points must also be made. First, that any poet who habitually treats words and facts "like billiard balls" is likely to be convinced of their transmutability into a realm that is immune and indifferent to the literal. And, secondly, there is in this revision of the Flaubert poem an allegory of what Lowell must have felt about himself: if to others it appeared that his heart had dried, to the artist, to Lowell/Flaubert, it was clear that his heart was enlarged by the very act of finding words, by the very mania for phrases that so obsessed them both. It is a self-granted absolution of the sort Auden granted to Yeats, and to all who give life to language—in the first version of the final part of his famous elegy.

> Time that is intolerant
> Of the brave and innocent
>
> . . . .
>
> Worships language and forgives
> Everyone by whom it lives;
> Pardons cowardice, conceit,
> Lays its honors at their feet.

This is not a justification—the book is full of instances of Lowell's personal cruelty, attested to by Xandra Gowrie at some length, and in Hardwick's declaration that at certain times for the poet "the deep underlying unreality is there, the fact that no one else's feelings really exist . . ."—it is merely an attempt at an explanation.

In an essay called "Fifty Years of American Poetry," Randall Jarrell says, "Lowell has always had an astonishing ambition, a willingness to learn what past poetry was and to compete with it on its own terms." This driving ambition and sense of competition was with him from the first, and plays its role in other realms besides poetry. Hamilton quotes the first draft of "Waking in the Blue," then titled "To Ann Adden

(Written during the first week of my voluntary stay at Mc-
Lean's Mental Hospital)," from which these lines are taken:

> The bracelet on your right wrist jingles with trophies:
> The enamelled Harvard pennant,
> the round medallion of St. Mark's School.
> I could claim both,
> for both were supplied by earlier,
> now defunct claimants,
> and my gold ring, almost half an inch wide,
> now crowns your bracelet, cock of the walk there.

And in a letter of tribute and admiration addressed to Theodore Roethke, Lowell says, "I remember Edwin Muir arguing
with me that there is no rivalry in poetry. Well, there is."
This keenly competitive instinct accounts in some ways for his
wholesale appropriations of The Western World's Great Poetry, all converted into what someone has called "Lo-Cal" in
the volume called *Imitations*. But it also exhibits itself in somewhat more covert ways. For example, the most ambitious
poem in *Lord Weary's Castle* is probably "The Quaker Graveyard in Nantucket." This poem is deservedly admired, studied,
and commented upon by astute critics, who have located prose
passages in Thoreau, as well as more conspicuous references
from Melville, that are woven carefully into the fabric of the
poem. It first appeared in what amount to two installments,
in the Spring 1945 and Winter 1946 issues of *Partisan Review*,
and longer by a great deal, when those two installments are
assembled, than would appear in the final, careful pruning of
the poem as the text we now know. Lowell's editing of his own
poem was brilliant and right in every way; everything he
eliminated was excessive, and even sometimes rather shabby,
and so it is not entirely out of order to wonder why such material had ever been included in the first place. The answer
seems to me clear. If the two original installments are brought
together, they come to one hundred and ninety-three lines of

poetry, which is precisely the number of lines in "Lycidas."

In that chapter of Eileen Simpson's fine book of recollections, *Poets in Their Youth*, in which she focuses on Lowell, she records the matching excitement and enthusiasm both Lowell and John Berryman felt about Milton's poem. Describing a visit to Lowell and Jean Stafford in Maine, she writes:

> After Mass Jean repeated what she had said the previous evening; John and I mustn't think of leaving as originally planned. We must stay, Cal said. How could John even consider going when they hadn't discussed "Lycidas"? . . .
>
> The days of our visit, which stretched from a weekend to two weeks, fell into casual order. Although neither Cal nor John was supposedly working, there was never a time when they were not working. After breakfast and a good long recitation:
>
> > Bitter constraint, and sad occasion dear,
> > Compels me to disturb your season due;
> > For Lycidas is dead, dead ere his prime,
>
> and explication of "Lycidas," which they had no trouble agreeing was one of the greatest poems in the language (though there was the usual push/pull over the Three Greatest Lines), . . . Cal went up to his room.

A moment's reflection ought to make clear why this paradigm meant so much to Lowell when he came to write "The Quaker Graveyard." Here was one of the world's indisputably great poems, a marine elegy, formidable in its overt and hidden debts to its classical predecessors, distinguished for its striking outburst of moral indignation, the superlative work of a young but limitlessly ambitious poet, who not only composes a masterpiece, but ends by announcing that he looks to even greater undertakings in "pastures new." As a model of substance, of congested and densely packed style, of concealed prophecy and covertly declared ambition, nothing could have served Lowell better.

But Milton, rebel and symbolic regicide, and "Lycidas," trumpet voluntary of independence and ambition disguised as a pastoral elegy, served Lowell in an even more intimate and psychologically far more important way, being bound up with his primal act of rebellion against his father, who had written a prudish and insinuating letter to the father of a girl young Lowell regarded as his fiancée. The letter was eventually turned over to the poet, who went home and knocked his father down, an event remembered again and again in a series of poems that have been examined with great sensitivity and understanding by David Kalstone in his book *Five Temperaments.* Hamilton furnishes two versions, one from *Notebooks 1967–68,* and the other an unpublished poem, written about 1956, and now in the Houghton Library at Harvard, from which these lines are taken:

> I hummed the adamantine
> ore rotundo of *Lycidas* to cool love's quarrels,
> and clear my honor
> from Father's branding Scarlet Letter. . . .
> "Yet once more, O ye laurels"—
> I was nineteen!

In his excellent chapter on Lowell, David Kalstone quotes Randall Jarrell thus: "If there were only some mechanism . . . for reasonably and systematically converting into poetry what we see and feel and are." That somewhat wistful yearning of Jarrell's took on the quality of a ravenous appetite in both Berryman and Lowell. And it is true that lyric poetry in our days has conceded vast territories to the writers of fiction, of which the impelling narrative drive is merely the most obvious advantage to the novelists. By its concentration, its narrowly focused point of view, its determined elimination of anything but the absolutely pertinent, its inviolably single tone, the lyric has elected to exclude all the contingent, chancy shifts of event, character, atmospherics, the alterations of time and consciousness that are the chief textures of our lives, and the vital substances of our very sense of reality. Novels are omnivorous, capable of assimilating everything, whereas the lyric has, since the Victorians, become more and more emaciated. Lowell's commendation of Elizabeth Bishop's volume *North & South* and *a Cold Spring* makes his own craving clear: "Her abundance of description reminds one, not of poets, poor symbolic, abstract creatures—but of the Russian novelists." And of Anne Sexton's first book he wrote, ". . . an almost Russian abundance and accuracy." Hamilton indicates how admiring and competitive Lowell felt about Berryman's *Dream Songs*, which were performing feats everyone assumed were denied to poetry. In Lowell's own words of 1964: "The Scene is contemporary and crowded with references to news items, world politics, travel, low-life, and Negro music. . . . By their impertinent piety, by jumping from thought to thought, mood to mood, and by saying anything that comes into the author's head, they are touching and nervously alive. . . . All is risk and variety here. This great Pierrot's universe is more tearful and funny than we can easily bear." And Frank Bidart, recalling Lowell as a teacher in the Spring 1977 issue of *Salmagundi*, a salute to Lowell's sixtieth birthday, writes, "One day in Robert Lowell's class, someone brought in a poem about a particularly painful and ugly subject. A student, who was shocked, said that some subjects simply couldn't be dealt with in poems. I've never forgotten Lowell's reply. He said, 'You can say anything in a poem—if you *place* it properly.' "

Out of this appetite and ambition came *Notebooks 1967–68*, reissued in 1970 in a "revised and expanded edition," and ulti-

mately enlarged into *History* and *For Lizzie and Harriet*.
From that vast richness I want to single out two versions of
an unrhymed sonnet about Sir Thomas More.

> Hans Holbein's More, my friend since World War II,
> the gold chain of *S's*, the golden rose,
> the plush cap, the brow's damp feathertips of hair,
> the slate eyes' stern, facetious twinkle, ready
> to turn from executioner to martyr—
> or saunter with the great King's bluff arm on his neck,
> feeling that friend-slaying, terror-ridden heart
> beating under the fat of Aretino—
> some hanger-on saying, "How the King must love you!"
> And Thomas, "If it were a question of my head,
> or losing his meanest village in France . . ." Or standing
> below the scaffold and the two-edged sword—
> "Friend, help me up," he said, "when I come down,
> my head and body will shift for themselves."

This poem remained unaltered in the revised and enlarged
edition of *Notebook* that came out in 1970. And for the moment I wish only to offer a guess that Aretino may have suggested himself because, besides being fat, like the king, and
something of a womanizer, again like the king, and a poet, as
the king was, too, his portrait by Titian hangs in New York's
Frick Collection, directly across the room from Holbein's More.

> Holbein's More, my patron saint as convert,
> the gold chain of *S's*, the golden rose,
> the plush cap, the brow's damp feathertips of hair,
> the good eyes' stern, facetious twinkle, ready
> to turn from executioner to martyr—
> or saunter with the great King's bluff arm on your neck,
> feeling that friend-slaying, terror-dazzled heart
> ballooning off into its awful dream—
> a noble saying, "How the King must love you!"

And you, "If it were a question of my head,
or losing his meanest village in France . . ."
then by the scaffold and the headsman's axe—
"Friend, give me your hand for the first step,
as for coming down, I'll shift for myself."

This is the 1973 version from *History*. Before any comment on
the differences, it may be worth remarking on the similarities,
provided by Lowell's two main sources: the Holbein portrait
and the first biography of More, written by his son-in-law,
William Roper, the husband of More's favorite daughter, Mar-
garet. Lowell makes use of two passages in Roper, which are
worth quoting here.

> The King, allowing well his answer, said unto him: "It
> is not our meaning, Master More, to do you hurt, but to
> do you good would we be glad. We will therefore for
> this purpose [an arduous and dangerous embassy to
> Spain] devise upon some other, and employ your service
> otherwise." . . .
> And for the pleasure he took in his company would his
> grace suddenly sometimes come home to his house in
> Chelsea to be merry with him. Whither on a time, un-
> looked for, he came to dinner to him; and after dinner, in
> a fair garden of his, walked with him by the space of an
> hour, holding his arm about his neck.
> As soon as his grace was gone, I, rejoicing thereat, told
> Sir Thomas More how happy he was, whom the King had
> so familiarly entertained, as I never had seen him do to
> any other except Cardinal Wolsey, whom I saw his grace
> once walk with, arm in arm. "I thank our Lord, son,"
> quoth he, "I find his grace my very good lord indeed; and
> I believe he doth as singularly favor me as any subject
> within this realm. Howbeit, son Roper, I may tell thee I
> have no cause to be proud thereof, for if my head could

win him a castle in France (for then was there war between us) it should not fail to go."

And, later, this:

And so was he by Master Lieutenant brought out of the Tower and from thence led towards the place of execution. Where, going up the scaffold, which was so weak that it was ready to fall, he said merrily to Master Lieutenant: "I pray you, Master Lieutenant, see me safe up and, for my coming down, let me shift for myself."

These passages are so well known, as is indeed the whole Roper text, that we may be astonished at some of the liberties Lowell has chosen to take, and a few I find either unfortunate or inexplicable. More's own terse, nearly jaunty gallows humor, being far more off-hand than either of Lowell's more cumbersome versions, is by just so much the more felicitous. And since Roper makes it clear that it was he himself who remarked with awe and joy upon the King's benevolent intimacy with More, made the observation directly to More himself, and he to whom More gave his shrewd reply, we must wonder why Lowell provided a nameless hanger-on in the first version, followed by a nameless noble in the second. I am not persuaded that he gains anything by either choice; instead, he loses a sense of the intimacy and candor of the statement: what one confesses, regarding the moral character of a monarch, to a family member one trusts will be quite different from what one might divulge to some courtier—and More was a prudent man.

What next puzzles is the retained line in which More is said to be "ready/to turn from executioner to martyr. . . ." Obviously, More has no executioner's part in Roper's biography; those accusations were raised against him by Foxe, and later by Froude, among others, and have lately been revived by Jasper Ridley and Alistair Fox. What is strange, however, is to find them voiced by one who had chosen More as his patron saint, and who clearly knew More as the firm, mild-mannered, and compassionate man he is represented as being in Roper. And for this puzzle I will venture a conjectural answer.

With a sound instinct for drama and a self-lacerating honesty, Lowell identifies himself with both the king and the saint; and he is too cagey to reduce these wily antagonists to anything so allegorically simplified, or so crudely doctrinal, as The Good and The Bad. Opposed they are to one another, king and saint, but curiously alike in their divided inward selves. And not only do they resemble one another: in their determined opposition they are destined to enact the poet's personal torment. Fated by history to irreconcilable positions, they are also fated identities of the poet, More being able to be both intransigent fanatic and meek victim; Henry being able to be both benevolent patron and friend-slayer, whose "terror-dazzled heart" can go "ballooning off into its awful dream," presumably of lunatic omnipotence; the saint being able to "feel" the crazed heart of the king, in part, perhaps, because they are somehow alike, and are both linked to the poet, one by being his patron saint, the other by being like a famous licentious poet (now suppressed) as well as in other, more heart-rending and body-rending, ways. The conversion of Roper's "castle" to "the meanest village" merely insists on Henry's ruthlessness, though it misses the overtones of a chess game, implied in More's comment. But the charges of no less ruthlessness against More are revived for the sake of the divided symmetries of the poem, which is terrifying in its awareness of the hideous cost of greatness. As for its relation to Lowell, Hamilton tells us, ". . . it always unnerved him to make enemies of friends."

Some years ago John Malcolm Brinnin had toyed with the idea of writing a biography of Lowell, and at that time he had a number of long talks with me. Once, he asked me point-blank whether I thought Lowell was in any way an anti-

Semite, and after a moment's thought I answered flatly, "No."
I would still answer that way now, though there are those who
might feel entitled to think otherwise. Of Lowell's final lecture
at the University of Cincinnati, when he was in perilous mental shape, Hamilton quotes Elizabeth Bettman as saying that
he talked about "Hitler, more or less extolling the superman
ideology. . . ." This was neither the beginning nor the end of
Lowell's fascination with "great men" who were characterized by their "ruthlessness." But my own experiences with him
were not only free of this particular dementia (though I was
with him in several of his manic periods) but rather the reverse. Once, in his gentlest manner, Lowell asked me whether
I was a believing Jew. For reasons that might not bear a too
critical inspection, I said I was. He then said, "That means
you think the Messiah is yet to come," and I assented. He asked
whether I thought it might not be possible for the Messiah to
be born, unrecognized, right in this country, and in our time.
Given his pronounced excitement about the topic, together
with my by now slightly informed sense of the symptoms of
his illness, I was able to bring the whole conversation to a quiet
conclusion by remarking that I thought it would be extremely
difficult for any modern man to trace his ancestry irreproach-
ably back to the House of David.

Writing of what we may call (if we disregard the early, pri-
vately printed, limited edition of *Land of Unlikeness*) Lowell's
second book, *The Mills of the Kavanaughs*, Hamilton remarks,
"It is immediately noticeable . . . that the book is a clamor of
distraught, near-hysterical first-person speech, and that almost
always the speaker is a woman. The men in the book are
usually under attack. Thus, the rhetoric of 'Thanksgiving's
Over' and of large sections of the title poem, can, not too fan-
cifully, be heard as a fusing of two rhetorics—the enraged,
erupting aggression of *Lord Weary* somehow loosened and
given new spitefulness by echoes of letters Lowell had been
getting—throughout 1947—from Jean Stafford, and echoes

281

too (we might reasonably speculate) of the 'adder-tongued' invective that she used to pour into their quarrels."

As a description of the poem "Thanksgiving's Over" this is seriously off course and regrettable; and I am not concerned here with questions of biographical or autobiographical veracity, nor with the genesis or sources of Lowell's work. Instead, I want to indicate what strikes me, and furthermore, I would like to claim, must have struck Lowell himself, as a remarkable, over-arching design to his poetry, a thematic recapitulation or recurrence that resonates from the early work to the very latest with hollow and mordant overtones. It expresses itself, early and late, as a domestic drama of a bitter and terrifying kind, and early exhibits itself in "Thanksgiving's Over." The poem bears a headnote which reads,

Thanksgiving night, 1942: a room on Third Avenue. Michael dreams of his wife, a German-American Catholic, who leapt from a window before she died in a sanatorium. The church is the Franciscan church on 31st Street.

Though the note says "Michael dreams" in the present tense, the whole poem is retrospectively cast in the past, giving it the sinister effect of a nightmare that cannot be exorcized or forgotten.

THANKSGIVING'S OVER*

Thanksgiving night: Third Avenue was dead;
My fowl was soupbones. Fathoms overhead,

* I have used here the greatly shortened form of the poem as it appears in *Selected Poems.* In its original there was, admittedly, more vituperation, a good deal of it seemingly justified by dramatic context, on the part of the nameless and demented wife, who is the chief speaker of the poem. Her oscillations between hallucinatory piety and unbalanced acrimony offer not a little in the way of illustrating the poet's growing disenchantment with his adopted Roman Catholic faith. But for all the dead woman's tirades, as well as her craziness, the poem still follows the outline here presented.

Snow warred on the El's world in the blank snow.
"Michael," she whispered, "just a year ago,
Even the shoreleave from the *Normandie*
Were weary of Thanksgiving; but they'd stop
And lift their hats. I watched their arctics drop
Below the birdstoup of the Anthony
And Child who guarded our sodality
For lay-Franciscans, Michael, till I heard
The birds inside me, and I knew the Third
Person possessed me, for I was the bird
Of Paradise, the parrot whose absurd
Garblings are glory. *Cherry ripe, ripe, ripe . . .*"

Winter had come on horseback, and the snow,
Hostile and unattended, wrapped my feet
In sheepskins. Where I'd stumble from the street,
A red cement Saint Francis fed a row
Of toga'd boys with birds beneath a Child.
His candles flamed in tumblers, and He smiled.
"Romans!" she whispered, "look, these overblown
And bootless Brothers tell us we must go
Barefooted through the snow where birds recite:
Come unto us, our burdens' light—light, light,
This burden that our marriage turned to stone!
O Michael, must we join the deaf and dumb
Breadline for children? Sit and listen." So
I sat. I counted to ten thousand, wound
My cowhorn beads from Dublin on my thumb,
And ground them. *Miserere?* Not a sound.

There is enormous drama here, and a complication of settings
in time. Michael as dreamer or meditator sets the scene, but
even as he does so it is in retrospect, and chiefly in order to
allow the remoter voice of his now dead wife to recall something still further in the past. She speaks reminiscently, and,

on the whole, reverently, though perhaps somewhat insanely
with regard to her possession by the Holy Ghost, and with
only a passing touch of bitterness or recrimination when men-
tioning "This burden that our marriage turned to stone!"
though what is presented on the one hand as a touching and
innocent piety is ironically undermined by an allusion to a
Flaubert tale of credulous simplicity. Here the dead woman
says,

> I heard
> The birds inside me, and I knew the Third
> Person possessed me, for I was the bird
> Of Paradise, the parrot whose absurd
> Garblings are glory. *Cherry ripe, ripe, ripe.* . . .

This confusion of parrot and Paraclete seems grotesquely to
recall a similar confusion regarding a stuffed bird, a parrot, in
Flaubert's *Un Coeur Simple* and to remind us that the word
simple is honorific in a religious context but contemptuous in
a worldly one. The cry (*Cherry ripe, ripe, ripe*) is a well-
known London street cry (weirdly echoed later in "our burden's light—light, light") which is also, in this poem, a bird
cry, an especially apt conflation to suit Saint Francis among
the slums and gutters of Manhattan. Most of the poem is given
to the patient, enduring, suffering voice of the dead woman,
who concludes with a question and a plea:

> O Michael, must we join the deaf and dumb
> Breadline for children? Sit and listen. . . .

That request to Michael by his dead wife is not a request to
listen to her. It is a plea to listen to the divine voice.

> So
> I sat. I counted to ten thousand, wound
> My cowhorn beads from Dublin on my thumb,
> And ground them. *Miserere?* Not a sound.

Divinity does not vouchsafe its voice to him, offers no mercy. And the only things that linger in the silence are the defunct syllables of anguish by a defunct wife. Though not explicitly accusatory, they are the words of one driven to madness and suicide, and they are also the words of one who can hear a divinity which to her husband is dumb. And possibly deaf. The poem leaves us wondering whether it is God or Michael who is unhearing. That muteness, that blank uncommunicative silence would reappear just as accusingly in poems Lowell wrote near the end of his career.

They are unrhymed sonnets, like the poem about Thomas More, and they appear, side by side, bearing the same title, in the volume called *For Lizzie and Harriet*. The poems are called "No Hearing," and they concern themselves with the pain and blankness that attends the end of love and marriage. Their common title seems worth a moment's consideration, not only because it bears upon that silence with which "Thanksgiving's Over" concludes, but because it appears twice as a refrain in George Herbert's penitential poem, "Deniall." In considering the possibility of some connection, I mentioned the matter to the critic David Kalstone, who replied as follows: "I think you're absolutely right about the Lowell poems. It isn't beyond him to repeat the title because it occurs twice in the Herbert poem. The 'silent universe our auditor' is, I suspect, an accidental glance at the 'silent ears' of 'Deniall.' But most of all it's the tone, the quoted, intervening voices . . . 'Skunk Hour' revisited in a more moving key. . . . Cal knew Herbert very well. First on his own and then because Herbert was such a favorite of Elizabeth Bishop's. When EB left Castine [Lowell's home in Maine] after a troubled visit to the Lowells in 1957, Cal gave her a two-volume family Herbert which had belonged to RTSL I [i.e., Lowell's grandfather]. 'Skunk Hour' [dedicated to Elizabeth Bishop] was written within a few weeks."

I want to quote the Herbert poem both for its beauty and its relevance.

Robert Lowell

DENIALL

When my devotions could not pierce
Thy silent eares;
Then was my heart broken, as was my verse:
My breast was full of fears
And disorder:

My bent thoughts, like a brittle bow,
Did flie asunder:
Each took his way; some would to pleasures go,
Some to the wars and thunder
Of alarms.

As good go anywhere, they say,
As to benumme
Both knees and heart, in crying night and day,
Come, come my God, O come,
But no hearing.

O that thou shouldst give dust a tongue
To crie to thee,
And then not heare it crying! all day long
My heart was in my knee,
But no hearing.

Therefore my soul lay out of sight,
Untun'd, unstrung:
My feeble spirit, unable to look right,
Like a nipt blossome, hung
Discontented.

O cheer and tune my heartlesse breast,
Deferre no time;
That so thy favours granting my request,
They and my mind may chime,
And mend my ryme.

Robert Lowell

The blankness of life, the bleak, heedless, unresponsive silence—these, in Lowell's poems, are not relieved by even the possibility of prayer, and the disorder and dissolution of which they tell is worldly, secular, and irreparable. I have time here to attend only to one of them.

NO HEARING

Belief in God is an inclination to listen,
but as we grow older and our freedom hardens,
we hardly even want to hear ourselves . . .
the silent universe our auditor—
I am to myself, and my trouble sings.
The Penobscot silvers to Bangor, the annual V
of geese beats above the moonborne bay—
their flight is too certain. Dante found this path
even before his first young leaves turned green;
exile gave seniority to his youth. . . .
White clapboards, black window, white clapboards, black
       window, white clapboards—
my house is empty. In our yard, the grass straggles. . . .
I stand face to face with lost Love—my breath
is life, the rough, the smooth, the bright, the drear.

This is a dense and rich poem about impoverishment, and its first line ("Belief in God is an inclination to listen") connects it intimately and directly with "Thanksgiving's Over" from a much earlier period in the poet's career. The poet here is able to acknowledge that "our freedom hardens" us, and is itself imprisoning and isolating: "we hardly even want to hear ourselves . . ./the silent universe our auditor—" And then comes a line that appears in the text in italics: "*I am to myself, and my trouble sings.*" The line is at least a spiritual echo of details in "Skunk Hour" ("I hear/my ill-spirit sob in each blood cell") but rendered conspicuous by being italicized, the line appears to declare itself a quotation, or at least an allusion to some text outside Lowell's own corpus. I freely acknowledge that he may be quoting something I don't know and can't identify, but I'm prepared to make a wild guess nevertheless, and my guess is that this line is a parodic inversion of the refrain as it first appears in the first stanza of Spenser's "Epithalamion": "So I unto myselfe alone will sing,/The woods shall to me answer and my Eccho ring." Here, in Lowell's poem, which is the opposite of the marriage hymn Spenser composed for his own blissful marriage to Elizabeth Boyle, we have a line which is the reverse and negation of Spenser's, a grim and bitter finale: "I am to myself, and my trouble sings." The Penobscot River, the migrating geese, have their destinations and destinies, about which they have little or no choice. Dante's destiny, which involved his passage through Hell, was marked out for him when, at the age of nine, he fell in love with the only woman he would ever love, the Beatrice who would someday guide him to Paradise. Neither Dante, the river nor the geese are as free as Lowell is, but they move to ends which are not only ordained but desirable. In contrast, Lowell sees his life and his future spelled out in black and white: "White clapboards, black window, white clapboards, black window, white clapboards—" a litany that ends with "my house is empty." And the poem ends with the same absence, the same solitariness that was dramatized in "Thanksgiving's Over." Here the poet says: "I stand face to face with lost Love—my breath/is life, the rough, the smooth, the bright, the drear." The poem becomes a small allegory at the end. Breath is indeed life for us all, but for Lowell it is also the allegory of the harsh, irreconcilable inconsistencies of life; the poor, run-of-the-mill, everyday infernos and paradisos that possess us like the random motions of atoms; the ordinary man's secular (rather than divine) comedy, which, unredeemed and unremarked by God, and played out beneath a heaven that is both deaf and dumb, seems for that very reason more like tragedy than comedy.

In one of his longest letters, composed on and off between the 14th of February and the 3rd of May, and written to George and Georgiana, his brother and sister-in-law, in 1819, John Keats remarked:

> A Man's life of any worth is a continual allegory—and very few eyes can see the Mystery of his life—a life like the scriptures, figurative—which such people can no more make out than they can the hebrew Bible. Lord Byron cuts a figure—but he is not figurative—Shakespeare led a life of Allegory; his works are the comments on it—

If I began with a deceptively easy comparison of Lowell with Byron, I hope you will allow me to amend that judgment, and to assert that if it is no more plausible to compare him with Shakespeare, he is, first of all, clearly and singularly, Robert Lowell—which, as a poet, is not a bad thing to be; and that through his constant moral and artistic endeavor to situate himself in the midst of our representative modern crises, both personal and political, he has led, for us—as it were, in our behalf—a life of Allegory; and his works are comments on it.

Houses as Metaphors:
The Poetry of Architecture

THE FIRST thing you see as you enter the exhibit of The Treasure Houses of Britain at the National Gallery of Art is a mammoth photomural depicting an elevation of the great North front of Blenheim Palace, reproduced from *Vitruvius Britannicus*. "Colossal" is the word Pevsner applies to the building, and no one looking at that picture, let alone visiting the building itself, can fail to be astonished, and inclined to meditation. Blenheim was the gift of a grateful monarch to the First Duke of Marlborough for his decisive victory over the French in 1704. It was twenty-three years in the building, as a consequence of which the Duke was able to enjoy only the briefest occupancy before his death in 1722; Blenheim was not in fact completed till five years later. There is a patent irony in these bald facts which the scale of the building itself only emphasizes. It invites reflection on the monuments of many kinds by which human beings hope to recall themselves to the mind of posterity, and it summons memorials of our mortality, cenotaphs, inscriptions, and the grand prose of Sir Thomas Browne, who wrote: ". . . to subsist in bones, and be but Pyramidally extant, is a fallacy in duration. . . . Generations passe while some trees stand, and old Families last not three Oaks. But man is a noble Animal, splendid in ashes, and pompous in the grave."

Mortuary reflections occurred to the contemporaries of Vanbrugh, Blenheim's architect. It was a convention of epitaphy to pray that the earth, below which a man was buried, would lie upon him lightly, in the pious hope of an easy resurrection. Such a hope, for example, is expressed in *The Maid's Tragedy*, by Beaumont and Fletcher, in these lines:

> Lay a garland on my hearse of the dismal yew,
> Maidens, willow branches bear, say I died true,
> My love was false, but I was firm from my hour of birth;
> Upon my buried body lie lightly, gentle earth.

By contrast, some nameless wit composed an epitaph for Vanbrugh that goes:

> Lie heavy on him, Earth, for he
> Laid many heavy loads on thee.

Blenheim, in fact, provoked other lyric effusions. There is a poem variously attributed to Pope, Swift, and the Rev. Abel Evans that may be cited. It presents two speakers, one of them a sort of tour guide or professional commender, perhaps the Duke himself, and the second the innocent visitor. Let me advise you in advance of an allusion to a symbolic lion and cock. This refers to a stone sculpture by Grinling Gibbons, mounted on the clock tower, and representing the British lion overpowering the emblem of the French—*Gallia*, the Latin for Gaul, signified by *gallus*, the Latin for rooster.

> See, here's the grand approach,
> That way is for his grace's coach;
> There lies the bridge, and there the clock,
> Observe the lion and the cock;
> The spacious court, the collonade,
> And mind how wide the hall is made;

Houses as Metaphors: The Poetry of Architecture

The chimneys are so well designed
They never smoke in any wind;
The galleries contrived for walking,
The windows to retire and talk in;
The council chamber to debate,
And all the rest are rooms of state.
"Thanks, Sir," cried I, " 'Tis very fine,
But where d'ye sleep, or where d'ye dine?
I find, by all that you've been telling,
That 'tis a house, but not a dwelling."

These lines may lead us to some general considerations of what we mean, and have meant, by "house." And this will involve not only what dictionaries can tell us, but what we can learn from that curious genre of poems about houses, and what some architects themselves have written. Rome furnishes an instructive account of how quickly a modest and unpretentious dwelling can take on preposterous grandeurs. A house, or *domus*, had as its main feature an *atrium*, an unroofed central court, around which rooms were arranged in a more or less stereotyped order. The imperial palace in Rome began modestly under Augustus with a traditional *domus*, but things didn't remain that way long. After the fire of 64 A.D. had cleared the ground, Nero built his fantastic *domus aurea*, or "golden house," artificially landscaped, with a central lake on the site of the future Colosseum, and an architecture of magnificence and magnification was launched. It is not surprising that the Latin poets, in particular, Martial, Juvenal and Horace, should have seen in houses the moral emblems of their owners, and recognized buildings as highly symbolic creations. Horace never ceased to be grateful to his patron, Maecenas, who either gave him or was instrumental in getting him his Sabine farm, and Horace, in a number of poems, attributed his own character in its best aspects, as well as the quality of his poetry, to the life of retirement from public affairs he enjoyed in that country retreat, a sentiment not unlike that to be expressed later by Andrew Marvell in behalf of Lord Fairfax in the poem called "Upon Appleton House." Horace, in fact, seemed delightfully uncertain whether his merits had won him, or been induced by, his habitat, but he found himself, in a famous ode beginning *integer vitae*, to be miraculously invulnerable to the most terrible perils of existence. A modern version of that poem goes this way:

A blameless, upright life, an unblemished conscience,
Plus the fact that clearly I'm not on anyone's shit list,
Neither the Fed's nor any of my neighbors',
    Bolsters me, Hanson,

More solidly than a Saturday Night Special;
Whether footslogging through Brooklyn at four AM
Or risking the gloom-filled catacombs of the subway,
    Nothing alarms me.

For when catastrophe struck at Three Mile Island
I was miles away, singing about my Mabel,
Mating my rhymes, while even the liquid coolant
    Turned radioactive.

Things were quite tense in eastern Pennsylvania:
Would the milk, the air, the bloodstreams all grow radiant,
Women give birth to prodigies, their husbands
    Drop by the wayside?

You could set me anywhere—on a desert island
Without a TV set and no Man Friday,
Condemned to a steady diet of bark and berries
    And frittered star-fish,

Or banish me to the Thracian wastes of Sodus,
Where, rumor tells, the local men spit hailstones—
And you'd find me engrossed in innocent, flowing numbers,
    Measuring Mabel.

Houses as Metaphors: The Poetry of Architecture

The Oxford English Dictionary offers nineteen definitions of the word "house," including the squares in a chess board; and it also makes clear the striking ambiguity so rich and important to the poetry on this subject: that the word applies alike to the edifice and to the family or dynasty who built it, an ambiguity that figures prominently in the title of Poe's "The Fall of the House of Usher." Since the house and its inhabitants are linked by the double meaning of the word, it should not surprise us that the visible monument can so easily be construed as a cypher or cryptic device by which to represent something about the character of the owner, and country house poetry makes as much of this connection as possible. But it is a connection fraught with uncontrollable moral overtones, and literary pitfalls. Before addressing them, however, let me turn to the words of a would-be architect, and a particularly literary one, Sir Henry Wotton. He was the English ambassador to Venice for over twenty years, serving in behalf of both Elizabeth the First and King James, and he wrote a superb poem in tribute to James's daughter, Elizabeth, a poem beginning "You meaner beauties of the night," on the occasion of her marriage to the Elector Palatine. That wedding was also celebrated by the presentation of masques by Ben Jonson and George Chapman for which costumes and settings were designed by Inigo Jones, an architect Wotton may well have come to know during the time they both spent in Italy. It seems to me quite possible, incidentally, that the same marriage may be celebrated in Shakespeare's *The Tempest*. Be that as it may, Wotton's treatise, *The Elements of Architecture*, was written in the hope of obtaining a post as court architect when he returned penniless from abroad. He was disappointed in this hope, possibly because it was reported to the grave and comparatively humorless King James that Wotton had defined an ambassador as "a good man sent to lie abroad for his country." Instead, in spite of his fine essay, he was appointed provost of Eton, a post which he held until his death in 1639.

Houses as Metaphors: The Poetry of Architecture

He was, by the way, a friend of John Donne's. He writes, beginning with an echo of the Roman architect, Vitruvius, as follows:

"In architecture, as in all other operative arts, the end must direct the operation. The end is to build well. Well building hath three conditions: Commodity, Firmness, and Delight." (Let me interrupt to say that these three qualities correspond to what, in a modern translation, Vitruvius calls "convenience, durability, and beauty.") Wotton's first general topic is "The Seat, and the Work." He continues, "Therefore, first touching situation. The precepts thereunto belonging do either concern the total posture (as I may term it) or the placing of the parts; whereof the first sort, howsoever usually set down by architects as a piece of their profession, yet are in truth borrowed from other learnings; there being between Arts and Sciences, as well as between men, a kind of good fellowship, and communication of their principles." (Let me interrupt once again, apropos those "other learnings" to which Wotton refers, as distinct from purely architectural considerations, to note that Vitruvius says regarding the education of an architect, "Let him be educated, skilful with the pencil, instructed in geometry, know much of history, have followed the philosophers with attention, understand music, have some knowledge of medicine, know the opinions of jurists, and be acquainted with astronomy and the theory of the heavens.") In connection with the principles of architecture, Wotton continues,

"For you find some of them to be merely physical, touching the quality and temper of the air; which being a perpetual ambient, and ingredient, and the defects thereof incorrigible to single habitations . . . doth in those respects require the more exquisite caution: that it be not too gross nor too penetrative; nor subject to any foggy noisesomeness from fens or marshes near adjoining, nor to mineral exhalations from the soil itself. Not undigested for want of sun, not unexercised for want of wind: which were to live (as it were) in a lake or standing pool of air, as Alberti, the Florentine Architect, doth ingeniously compare it.

"Some do rather seem a little astrological, as when they warn us from places of malign influence; where earthquakes, contagions, prodigious births, or the like, are frequent without evident cause. . . . Some are plainly economical, as that the seat be well watered, and well fuelled, that it be not of too steepy and incommodious access to the trouble of both friends and family, that it lie not too far from some navigable river or arm of the sea, for more ease of provision, and such domestic notes.

"Some again may be said to be optical; such I mean as concern the properties of a well chosen prospect: which I will call The Royalty of Sight. For as there is a lordship (as it were) of the feet, wherein the master does joy when he walketh about the line of his own possessions, so there is a lordship likewise of the Eye, which being a ranging and imperious, and (I might say) an usurping sense, can indure no narrow circumscription, but must be fed, both with extent and variety. Yet on the other side, I find vast and indefinite views which drown all apprehension of the uttermost objects condemned by good authors, as if thereby some part of the pleasure (whereof we speak) did perish. Lastly, I remember a private caution, which I know not well how to sort, unless I should call it political. By no means to build too near a great neighbor, which were in truth to be as unfortunately seated on the earth as Mercury is in the heavens, for the most part ever in combustion or obscurity, under brighter beams than his own."

Let me note, first of all, that "combustion," as it is used here, is an astronomical term, defined as the "obscuration of a planet or star by proximity to the sun." And what Wotton indicates by this, as he calls it, "political principle" has to do with the very edgy moral question of pride, competitiveness, emulation and vanity that can never be quite divorced from the country house enterprise. Mark Girouard tells us that by the nineteenth century four-fifths of the acreage of Great Britain, including Scotland and Wales, was owned by less than seven thousand people, the great majority of whom were country house owners. They had control of both the House of Lords and the House of Commons, as well as their own houses and they were a force of considerable power. And the power was exhibited in the houses their families had built.

Not all buildings are calculated, in Wotton's winning term, to "delight." Some are specifically designed to intimidate. Such, for example, was the case of the imperial palace of Byzantium in the 10th century, as we find in a report by Liudprand, bishop of Cremona, who served as ambassador of the Frankish Emperor, Berengar, and which report, I suspect, in his wide and unorthodox reading, Yeats must have come across. Liudprand writes:

"Next to the imperial residence at Constantinople there is a palace of remarkable size and beauty which the Greeks call Magnavra, the letter "v" taking the place of the digamma, and the same being equivalent to 'Fresh Breeze.' In order to receive some Spanish envoys, who had recently arrived, as well as myself and Liutefred, Constantine gave orders that this palace should be got ready and the following preparations were made. Before the emperor's seat stood a tree, made of bronze gilded over, whose branches were filled with birds, also made of gilded bronze, which uttered different cries, each according to its varying species. The throne itself was so marvelously fashioned that at one moment it seemed a low structure, and at another it rose high into the air. It was of immense size and was guarded by lions, made either of bronze or of wood covered with gold, who beat the ground with their tails and gave a dreadful roar with open mouth and quivering tongue. Leaning upon the shoulders of two eunuchs I was brought into the emperor's presence. At my approach the lions began to roar and the birds to cry out, each according to its kind; but I was neither terrified nor surprised, for I had previously made inquiry about all these things from people who were well acquainted with them. So after I had three times made obeisance to the emperor with my face upon the ground, I lifted my head, and behold! the man whom I had just before seen sitting on a moderately elevated seat had now changed his raiment and was sitting on the level of the ceiling. How it was done I could not imagine, unless perhaps he was lifted up by some such sort of device as we use for raising the timbers of a wine press. On that occasion he did not address me personally, since even if he had wished to do so the wide distance between us would have rendered conversation unseemly, but by the intermediary of a secretary he enquired about Berengar's doings and asked after his health. I made a fitting reply, and then, at a nod from the interpreter, left his presence and retired to my lodging."

It should scarcely come as a surprise to find the architectural enterprise identified with the sin of pride. The association is as old as the story in the Book of Genesis of the Tower of Babel, and things have not much altered in our latter days. In all of poetry there is perhaps no more decisive and eloquent exhibit of this connection than at the beginning of Milton's *Paradise Lost*. The rebel angels, now cast out of heaven, reassemble in hell, and their first act of revenge is architectural, and a complex act of overt pride; they build the palace of Pandemonium, an extravagant parody of heaven (including artificial stars) as well as of classical architecture. To get this done efficiently, they divide into teams; and since in hell they must begin from scratch, the first team become miners.

> Thither winged with speed
> A numerous brigade hastened: as when bands
> Of pioneers with spade and pickaxe armed
> Forerun the royal camp, to trench a field,
> Or cast a rampart. Mammon led them on,
> Mammon, the least erected spirit that fell

Houses as Metaphors: The Poetry of Architecture

From Heav'n, for ev'n in Heav'n his looks and thoughts
Were always downward bent, admiring more
The riches of Heav'n's pavement, trodden gold,
Than aught divine or holy else enjoyed
In vision beatific. By him first
Men also, and by his suggestion taught,
Ransacked the center, and with impious hands
Rifled the bowels of their mother Earth
For treasures better hid. Soon had his crew
Opened into the hill a spacious wound
And digged out ribs of gold. Let none admire
That riches grow in Hell: that soil may best
Deserve the precious bane. And here let those
Who boast in mortal things, and wond'ring tell
Of Babel, and the works of Memphian kings,
Learn how their greatest monuments of fame,
And strength, and art, are easily outdone
By Spirits reprobate, and in an hour
What in an age they with incessant toil
And hands innumerable scarce perform.
Nigh on the plain, in many cells prepared,
That underneath had veins of liquid fire
Sluiced from the lake, a second multitude
With wondrous art founded the massy ore,
Severing each kind, and scummed the bullion dross.
A third as soon had formed within the ground
A various mould, and from the boiling cells
By strange conveyance filled each hollow nook,
As in an organ from one blast of wind
To many a row of pipes the sound-board breathes.
Anon out of the earth a fabric huge
Rose like an exhalation, with the sound
Of dulcet symphonies and voices sweet,
Built like a temple, where pilasters round
Were set, and Doric pillars overlaid

299

With golden architrave; nor did there want
Cornice or frieze with bossy sculptures grav'n;
The roof was fretted gold. Not Babylon,
Nor great Alcairo such magnificence
Equalled in all their glories, to enshrine
Belus or Serapis their gods, or seat
Their kings, when Egypt with Assyria strove
In wealth and luxury. Th'ascending pile
Stood fixed her stately height, and straight the doors
Op'ning their brazen folds discover wide
Within, her ample spaces, o'er the smooth
And level pavement: from the arched roof
Pendent by subtle magic many a row
Of starry lamps and blazing cressets fed
With naphtha and asphaltus yielded light
As from a sky. The hasty multitude
Admiring entered, and the work some praise,
And some the architect: his hand was known
In Heav'n by many a towering structure high,
Where sceptered angels held their residence,
And sat as princes, whom the supreme King
Exalted to such power, and gave to rule,
Each in his hierarchy, the orders bright.
Nor was his name unheard or unadored
In ancient Greece: and in Ausonian land
Men called him Mulciber; and how he fell
From Heav'n, they fabled, thrown by angry Jove
Sheer o'er the crystal battlements; from morn
To noon he fell, from noon to dewy eve,
A summer's day; and with the setting sun
Dropped from the zenith like a falling star,
On Lemnos the Aegaean isle. . . .

In his edition of the poem, Douglas Bush notes that "the architectural details range from classical temples and the temple of

Jerusalem described in First Kings to St. Peter's in Rome and
the architectural devices in Stuart Masques; the total effect is
of excessive artifice and opulence which, in Milton as in Spenser, is associated with evil." You will have noticed specifically
the hellishness of the Doric order, and noticed that these fallen
angels exhibit not only the pride of builders but the envy and
emulousness of tourists, copying for themselves what they
have seen in the home of their betters. Gervase Jackson-Stops,
curator of the Treasure Houses show, writes straightforwardly,
"Rivalry, friendly or unfriendly, was obviously at the heart of
country house building." And there is a classical as well as
biblical precedent for associating architecture with a decline
in the estate of Man from a condition of perfection. Ovid reports in Book I of the *Metamorphoses*:

> The first millennium was the age of gold:
> Then living creatures trusted one another;
> People did well without the thought of ill:
> Nothing forbidden in a book of laws,
> No fears, no prohibitions read in bronze,
> Or in the sculptured face of judge and master,
>
> . . . .
>
> No cities climbed behind high walls and bridges;
> No brass-lipped trumpets called, nor clanging swords,
>
> . . . .
>
>   The innocent earth
> Learned neither spade nor plow; she gave her
> Riches as fruit hangs from the tree: grapes
> Dropping from the vine, cherry, strawberry
> Ripened in silver shadows of the mountain,
> And in the shade of Jove's miraculous tree,
> The falling acorn. Springtide the single
> Season of the year. . . .
> Season of milk and wine in amber streams
> And honey pouring from the green-lipped oak.

The Golden Age, according to Ovid, was followed by a series of declensions into stages of increasing imperfection, the first of these being the Silver Age, which gave birth to architecture, giving it at least the distinction of great antiquity. The sculptor Carl Milles has designed a fountain set in a court of the Metropolitan Museum in New York, with nude figures representing the various arts of mankind. The figure for architecture is the only one exhibiting pubic hair, because, as Milles solemnly observed, "it is the oldest of the arts." But its appearance as a symptom of decline from a sort of paradisal bliss is alluded to in a splendid poem by Richard Lovelace.

LOVE MADE IN THE FIRST AGE:
TO CHLORIS

In the nativity of time,
Chloris, it was not thought a Crime
    In direct *Hebrew* for to woo.
Now we make Love as all on fire,
Ring retrograde our loud desire,
    And court in *English* backward too.

Thrice happy was that golden Age
When Complement was construed Rage,
    And fine words in the Center hid;
When cursed *No* stained no Maid's bliss,
And all discourse was summed in *Yes*,
    And Nought forbade but to forbid.

Love then unstinted Love did sip,
And cherries plucked fresh from the lip,
    On cheeks and roses free he fed;
Lasses like *Autumn* plums did drop,
And Lads indifferently did crop
    A Flower and a Maidenhead.

Houses as Metaphors: The Poetry of Architecture

Then unconfined each did Tipple
Wine from the bunch, Milk from the Nipple;
    Paps tractable as udders were;
Then equally the wholesome jellies
Were squeezed from Olive Trees and Bellies,
    Nor suits of trespass did they fear.

A fragrant bank of strawberries,
Diapered with violet eyes,
    Was table, table-cloth and fare;
No palace to the clouds did swell;
Each humble Princess then did dwell
    In the *Piazza* of her hair.

This is only the first half of a delightful poem with a surprisingly naughty ending, even for Lovelace. But neither time nor the solemnity of my topic permits me to continue in that direction. I only ask you to take note of the last three lines as descriptive of a pre-architectural paradise freed from both the presence and symbols of pride. Shakespeare, on the other hand, uses the "building" metaphor quite differently, and rather more complexly. To build a house was a complicated task that involved estimating your own resources, choosing the proper time and place, selecting a suitable design, setting a solid foundation, and many other phases and stages that form a part of the project, chief among them being a calculated foresight, an ability to prepare now for what is to come later. It is therefore an apt metaphor for a projected military rebellion, and is used in just this way in the Second Part of *Henry IV*, in which Lord Bardolph, one of the plotters of the rebel action, declares,

        When we mean to build,
We first survey the plot, then draw the model.
And when we see the figure of the house,
Then must we rate the cost of the erection,
Which if we find outweighs ability,

What do we then but draw anew the model
In fewer offices, or at least desist
To build at all? Much more, in this great work,
Which is almost to pluck a kingdom down
And set another up, should we survey
The plot of situation and the model,
Consent upon a sure foundation,
Question surveyors, know our own estate,
How able such a work to undergo,
To weigh against his opposite. Or else
We fortify in paper and in figures,
Using the names of men instead of men,
Like one that draws the model of a house
Beyond his power to build it, who, half through,
Gives o'er and leaves his part-created cost
A naked subject to the weeping clouds
And waste for churlish winter's tyranny.

Even here, in this complex metaphor, the topic of rivalry, a mode of pride, is touched upon in the lines, "How able such a work to undergo,/To weigh against his opposite." On the primary level, "his opposite" refers to the opposition party of the king, and the question of whether or not the king's army can be defeated. But in terms of the house-building metaphor, "his opposite" must be an alternate, and rival house. And we are prompted to remember that "house" means both a building and a dynasty.

Latent though it be, so strong is the notion of pride as figured in the image of a house that the usual strategy is to deny or repudiate any such accusation. Victoria Sackville-West was for the whole of her life acutely aware that, had she only been born a male, she would have been in line to inherit the Sackville estate at Knole, which was denied her by the laws of primogeniture that pertain only to the male line. She remarks of Knole that it "stoops to nothing either pretentious or mer-

etricious. . . . It is, above all, an English house." One cannot
too much admire the modesty of this claim in view of the fact
that it describes a building that requires four acres of roof, and
contains a room for every day of the normal calendar year—
365 of them. But Vita Sackville-West was not the first to employ this strategy of denial and deceptive understatement. It
is vividly present in Ben Jonson's famous poem "To Penshurst," perhaps the first, and certainly one of the greatest, of
English Country House poems. Penshurst was the estate of the
Sidney family in Kent, owned by Sir Robert Sidney, Viscount
Lisle, brother of the great Sir Philip, and husband of Barbara
Gamage, whose portrait, with her children, is to be seen in the
National Gallery's show. Before reading part of the poem, let
me offer these annotations. "Touch" is a kind of black quartz
or jasper, whose full name, "touchstone," derives from its use
in testing the purity of gold or silver by rubbing them upon its
polished surface. A "lantern" is a small cupola, surmounting
an often domed roof to admit light. And the line about "his
great birth" refers to the oak tree planted to commemorate the
birth of Sir Philip Sidney.

> Thou art not, Penshurst, built to envious show
> Of touch or marble, nor canst boast a row
> Of polished pillars, or a roof of gold;
> Thou hast no lantern whereof tales are told,
> Or stairs or courts; but stand'st an ancient pile,
> And these, grudged at, art reverenced the while.
> Thou joy'st in better marks, of soil, of air,
> Of wood, of water; therein thou art fair.
> Thou hast thy walks for health as well as sport;
> Thy mount, to which the Dryads do resort,
> Where Pan and Bacchus their high feasts have made
> Beneath the broad beech, and the chestnut shade,
> That taller tree, which of a nut was set
> At his great birth, where all the Muses met.

There in the writhed bark are cut the names
    Of many a sylvan, taken with his flames;
And thence the ruddy satyrs oft provoke
    The lighter fauns to reach thy Lady's oak.
Thy copse too, named of Gamage, thou hast there,
    That never fails to serve thee seasoned deer
When thou wouldst feast, or exercise thy friends.
    The lower land, that to the river bends,
Thy sheep, thy bullocks, kine, and calves do feed;
    The middle grounds thy mares and horses breed.
Each bank doth yield thee conies; and the tops,
    Fertile of wood, Ashore and Sidney's copse,
To crown thy open table, doth provide
    The purpled pheasant with the speckled side;

And now there comes a passage meant to recall the lines in
Ovid that describe the paradisal Golden Age.

The painted partridge lies in every field,
    And for thy mess is willing to be killed.
And if the high-swollen Medway fail thy dish,
    Thou hast thy ponds that pay thee tribute fish,
Fat aged carps that run into thy net,
    And pikes, now weary their own kind to eat,
As loath the second draught or cast to stay,
    Officiously at first themselves betray.

What is being said here is that pike, notoriously savage fish
that, in contradistinction to other varieties, prey cannibalis-
tically on their own kind, have been so redeemed by Penshurst
and its paradisal site that, in a noble parody of religious self-
sacrifice, rather than await a second cast and drawing in by
the fisherman, they leap into his net at his first effort.

Bright eels that emulate them, and leap on land
    Before the fisher, or into his hand.

Then hath thy orchards fruit, thy garden flowers
>Fresh as the air, and new as are the hours.
The early cherry, with the later plum,
>Fig, grape, and quince, each in his time doth come;
The blushing apricot and woolly peach
>Hang on thy walls, that every child may reach.
And though thy walls be of the country stone,
>They are reared with no man's ruin, no man's groan;
There's none that dwell about them wish them down,
>But all come in, the farmer and the clown,
And no one empty handed, to salute
>Thy lord and lady, though they have no suit.
Some bring a capon, some a rural cake,
>Some nuts, some apples; some that think they make
The better cheeses bring 'em, or else send
>By their ripe daughters whom they would commend
This way to husbands, and whose baskets bear
>An emblem of themselves in plum or pear.

Let me take note of some of the structural points of the
poem. It begins with significant, and possibly defensive, disclaimers. Other houses may exhibit boastful ornamental features calculated to excite envy, and while those houses are
"grudged at" this house, free of pretensions, is not only admired but "reverenced." That word is important as a kind of
moral certification, but it also serves as the first hint that Penshurst enjoys a special providence. Its chief virtues are in fact
not man-made, but the providential ones of its situation:

Thou joy'st in better marks, of soil, of air,
>Of wood, of water; therein thou are fair.

A courteous bow is made to the Classical Age by the mention
of Pan and Bacchus and Dryads, and to Sir Philip, in whose
person "all the Muses met." But you will not have failed to
notice that this "house" is praised chiefly for its grounds, and

what the grounds provide. In this it imitates Horace, for whom the house was assimilated to the grounds, and the grounds to the moral character. And so we move to that plenitude and unending abundance of Nature in its munificent and paradisal aspect. It is a sort of Eden before the Fall, a Golden Age, and it may remind us, in its nourishing luxuriance, of these lines of Marvell's:

> What wond'rous life is this I lead!
> Ripe Apples drop about my head;
> The Luscious Clusters of the Vine
> Upon my Mouth do crush their Wine;
> The Nectaren and curious Peach
> Into my hands themselves do reach;
> Stumbling on Melons as I pass,
> Ensnar'd with Flow'rs, I fall on Grass.

And we may be reminded of yet another poem, this one frankly propagandistic, and calculated to encourage emigration of Englishmen to the New World. Much has been written about the mythology of our nation as a newly discovered Eden. And so Michael Drayton was able to write:

> And cheerfully at sea,
> Success you still entice,
>   To get the pearl and gold,
>   And ours to hold,
> Virginia,
> Earth's only paradise,
>
> Where nature hath in store
> Fowl, venison, and fish,
>   And the fruitful'st soil
>   Without your toil
> Three harvests more,
> All greater than your wish.

> And the ambitious vine
> Crowns with his purple mass
>> The cedar reaching high
>> To kiss the sky,
> The cypress, pine,
> And useful sassafras.
>
> To whose the golden age
> Still nature's laws doth give
>> No other cares that tend
>> But them to defend
> From winter's age
> That long there doth not live.

We may offer a further gloss on Jonson's word "reverenced" in connection with Penshurst: it not only represents a moral certification that its owners are not mean and stingy, but hints at an Edenic copiousness matched with a locale providentially free from the taints of vanity, avarice, and pride. And the poem then continues with a firm insistence that no man is deprived or made envious by this miraculous abundance, but, on the contrary, all those of the neighborhood, no matter how humble, are encouraged to emulate the effortless harvestings of divine bounty by bringing gifts of their own. And we may observe, furthermore, that either some or all of these features become canonical in the interesting, if limited, genre of Country House poems. The notion that the house is hedged about with a divinity securing its peace and comfort has both its classical and biblical origins, but its chief function is to allow the poet to offer hyperbolically extravagant praise while at the same time certifying, for all their wealth, the moral impeccability of the owners. Some of these same devices appear in two poems by Thomas Carew, which are less well known than Jonson's; the first is called "To Saxham," which was an estate belonging to Sir John Crofts. Note: a "volary" is an aviary.

Though frost and snow locked from mine eyes
That beauty which without door lies,
Thy gardens, orchards, walks, that so
I might not all thy pleasures know,
Yet (Saxham) thou within thy gate
Art of thyself so delicate,
So full of native sweets that bless
Thy roof with inward happiness,
As neither from nor to thy store
Winter takes ought, or Spring adds more.
The cold and frozen air had sterved
Much poor, if not by thee preserved;
Whose prayers have made thy table blessed
With plenty far above the rest.
The seasons hardly did afford
Coarse cates unto they neighbors' boards,
Yet thou hadst dainties, as the sky
Had only been thy Volary;
Or else the birds, fearing the snow
Might to another deluge grow,
The pheasant, partridge and the lark
Flew to thy house as to the Ark.
The willing Ox of himself came
Home to the slaughter with the Lamb,
And every beast did thither bring
Himself to be an offering.
The scalie herd more pleasure took
Bathed in thy dish than in the brook;
Water, earth, air did all conspire
To pay their tributes to thy fire,
Whose cherishing flames themselves divide
Through every room, where they deride
The night and cold abroad; whilst they
Like suns within, keep endless day.

Houses as Metaphors: The Poetry of Architecture

It should be clear that a keen moral sense is required in composing and qualifying such poems of praise, for they must exhibit suitable modesty while at the same time describing an enviable and uniquely favored house and family. The family must seem, if not to earn, then at least to deserve, its singular advantages by virtue of a certain noblesse oblige, and a sensitive magnanimity toward the less favored in the neighborhood. Here, again, is Carew, writing to a friend from Wrest Park, an estate in Bedfordshire. Let me note in advance Carew's specific repudiation of Corinthian columns, a severity or purity that consorts well with the opinions of Wotton, who wrote, "The Corinthian is a column lasciviously decked out like a courtesan, and therein much participating (as all inventions do) of the place where they were first born: Corinth having been without controversy one of the wantonnest towns in the world." This sexy reputation of Corinth was transmitted by, among others, the geographer Strabo, who reports that though Zeus, Apollo, Dionysus, Heracles, Hermes and Artemis all had shrines at Corinth, no cult was as popular as, or could complete with, that of Aphrodite, who had "a thousand temple slaves, courtesans, whom both men and women had dedicated to the goddess." Here now is a part of Carew's poem:

> Here steeped in balmy dew, the pregnant earth
> Sends from her teeming womb a flowery birth,
> And cherished with the warm sun's quickening heat,
> Her porous bosom doth rich odors sweat;
> Whose perfumes through the ambient air diffuse
> Such native aromatics as we use—
> No foreign gums or essence fetched from far,
> No volatile spirits, nor compounds that are
> Adulterate, but at Nature's cheap expense
> With far more genuine sweets refresh the sense.
> Such pure and uncompounded beauties bless

Houses as Metaphors: The Poetry of Architecture

This mansion with an useful comeliness,
Devoid of art, for here the architect
Did not with curious skill a pile erect
Of carved marble, touch, or porphyry,
But built a house for hospitality;
No sumptuous chimney piece of shining stone
Invites the stranger's eye to gaze upon,
And coldly entertains his sight, but clear
And cheerful flames cherish and warm him here;
No Doric or Corinthian pillars grace
With imagery this structure's naked face;
The lord and lady of this place delight
Rather to be in act, than seem in sight.
Instead of statues to adorn their wall,
They throng with living men their merry hall,
Where, at large tables filled with wholesome meats,
The servant, tenant, and kind neighbor eats.

It is not easy, in our imperfect world, to maintain the happy
fiction of a paradisal estate. Hence all the nervous attention to
the humbler classes, which, after all, would not even have existed in Eden. By the same token, some way had to be found to
disguise the presence as well as the very fact of the servant
class. William Beckford, the author of *Vathek*, hit upon an
unusual solution to this problem. Beckford was an unusual
man to begin with, having inherited a princely fortune, studied architecture with William Chambers and music with Mo-
zart. He was the builder of eccentric homes of vast and unlikely
proportions, and in order to spare himself the sight of men
laboring in his fields, he required his gardeners to mow the
lawns at night. This, of course, was done not with lawn-
mowers but with scythes and by lamp-light, so there was no
disagreeable noise to trouble Beckford's sleep. The Duke of
Portland, we are told,[1] fired any housemaid unfortunate

[1] These details are drawn from an article, in the October, 1985 issue of
Smithsonian, by Israel Shenker.

enough to meet him in his halls, but in more liberal establishments housemaids were simply required to face the wall when family or guests appeared. The intention was to foster the illusion that work was done as by magic, with servants unseen and unheard. Probably the latest version of this fiction occurs in the novels of P. G. Wodehouse, whose breath-takingly perfect servant, Jeeves, appears and disappears in what seem almost like ectoplasmic manifestations, always on hand when needed, never in the way when not, and often described as "shimmering" in or out of a room. It is always amusing to find critics praising Wodehouse by remarking wistfully that he portrays a blissful but, alas, departed era.

Let me reverse the usual, or Napoleonic, order of things by turning from the ridiculous to the sublime. Nothing can better illustrate the huge variety of implications of the word "house" than an examination of a biblical concordance. My own abbreviated one has, I think, more entries for that word than any other. And the word in its biblical usages has the widest possible applications and implications. It is used in the Book of Job to refer to the house of the dead: "For I know that thou wilt bring me to death, and to the house appointed for all the living." It is used by Jesus, in John's gospel, to refer to the Kingdom of Heaven: "In my Father's house are many mansions: if it were not so, I would have told you. I go to prepare a place for you." It is used in the Psalms, in remembrance of the vanity of the Tower of Babel: "Except the Lord build the house, they labor in vain that build it." But there is a particular use of the word that I want to call to your attention. It first appears in St. John's account of the expulsion of the money changers and the cleansing of the temple by Jesus. And it is then repeated by St. Paul in both his epistles to the Corinthians, the citizens of that wanton township. Here is St. John's text in the King James version.

And the Jews' Passover was at hand, and Jesus went up to Jerusalem,

313

And found in the temple those that sold oxen and sheep and doves, and the changers of money sitting:

And when he had made a scourge of small cords, he drove them all out of the temple, and the sheep and the oxen; and poured out the changers' money, and overthrew the tables;

And said unto them that sold doves, Take these things hence; make not my Father's house an house of merchandise.

And his disciples remembered that it was written [Ps. 69:9], The zeal of thine house hath eaten me up.

Then answered the Jews and said unto him, What sign shewest thou to us, seeing that thou doest these things?

Jesus answered and said unto them, Destroy this temple, and in three days I will raise it up.

Then said the Jews, Forty and six years was this temple in building, and wilt thou rear it up in three days?

But he spake of the temple of his body.

When therefore he was risen from the dead, his disciples remembered that he had said this unto them; and they believed the scripture and the word which Jesus had said.

A temple, church, cathedral, synagogue, basilica is a house of God, but in this singular passage that house is identified with the body of Christ. In St. Paul's letters it is further identified with every human body.

Know ye not that ye are the temple of God, and that the Spirit of God dwelleth in you?

If any man defile the temple of God, him shall God destroy; for the temple of God is holy, which temple ye are.

What seems to me especially interesting about these passages in which the body is likened to a temple is that they

314

make their appearance at very close to the same point in human history that the chief architect of Augustan Rome, Vitruvius, likened a temple to the human body. You are no doubt familiar with the celebrated drawing by Leonardo of a naked man, with arms extended and legs parted in what seems an awkward stride, inscribed inside both a circle and a square. This image is a diagrammatic representation of what Vitruvius writes in his chapter on the design of temples. Let me quote briefly from his text.

"The design of a temple depends on symmetry, the principles of which must be most carefully observed by the architect. They are due to proportion, a correspondence among the measures of the members of an entire work, and of the whole to a certain part selected as standard. From this result the principles of symmetry. Without symmetry and proportion there can be no principles in the design of any temple; that is, there is no precise relation between its members, as in the case of a well shaped man.

"For the human body is so designed by nature that the face, from the chin to the top of the forehead and the lowest roots of the hair, is a tenth part of the whole height; the open hand from the wrist to the tip of the middle finger is just the same; the head from the chin to the crown is an eighth, and with the neck and shoulders from the top of the breast to the lowest roots of the hair is a sixth. . . . The length of the foot is one sixth the height of the body; of the forearm, one fourth; and the breadth of the breast is also one fourth. The other members, too, have their own symmetrical proportions, and it was by employing them that the famous painters and sculptors of antiquity attained to great and endless renown.

"Similarly, in the members of a temple there ought to be the greatest harmony in symmetrical relations of the different parts to the general magnitude of the whole. Then, again, in the human body the central point is naturally the navel. For

315

if a man be placed flat on his back, with his hands and feet extended, and a pair of compasses centered at his navel, the fingers and toes of his two hands and feet will touch the circumference of a circle described therefrom. And just as the human body yields a circular outline, so too a square figure may be found from it. For if we measure the distance from the soles of the feet to the top of the head, and then apply that measure to the outstretched arms, the breadth will be found to be the same as the height, as in the case of plane surfaces which are perfectly square."

It is curious that these texts, sacred and secular, the first likening the body to a temple, the second likening a temple to the body, should articulate themselves at the birth of the Roman Imperium. And to these texts I should like to add a third. It is what we may think of as perhaps a Christianized version of Vitruvius. It comes from St. Augustine's *City of God*, and it describes Noah's Ark. Augustine writes,

"The actual measurements of the ark, its length, height and breadth, symbolize the human body, in the reality of which Christ was to come, and did come, to mankind. For the length of the human body from the top of the head to the sole of the foot is six times its breadth from side to side, and ten times its depth, measured on the side from the back to the belly. I mean that if you have a man lying on his back or on his face, and measure him, his length from head to foot is six times his breadth from left to right, or from right to left, and ten times his altitude from the ground. That is why the ark was made three hundred cubits in length, fifty cubits in breadth, and thirty in height. And the door which was given in its side surely represents the wound made when the side of the crucified was pierced with the spear. This, as we know, is the way of entrance for those who come to him, because from that wound flowed the sacraments with which believers are initiated. And the order for square beams in the ark's construction refers symbolically to the life of the saints which is stable on every side; for in whatever direction you turn a squared object, it will remain stable."

All religious and mathematical considerations apart, this analogy between architecture and anatomy is enormously suggestive. On the most elementary level it affirms the humanity of the architectural enterprise. It furthermore suggests that all of us, inwardly and perhaps unconsciously, know what perfect architectural proportions are, or ought to be, through some instinctive response of our own bodies; and that our anatomies, however imperfect or enfeebled they may be, are aware of the possibility of a perfection which constitutes a widely shared ideal. And I want to suggest that such notions as these, human and humane, have colored the thought of poets who have addressed themselves to praising houses. This seems to me particularly true of Andrew Marvell's splendid, complex and difficult poem "Upon Appleton House." This is how it begins, with disclaimers, just as Jonson did:

> Within this Sober Frame expect
> Work of no Forrain *Architect*;
> That unto Caves the Quarries drew,
> And Forrests did to Pastures hew:
> Who of his great Design in pain
> Did for a Model vault his Brain,
> Whose Columnes should so high be rais'd
> To arch the Brows that on them gaz'd.

The vaults and arches of architecture are here made the emblems of such pretensions as are conceived by the ambitious brain of a foreign architect, probably that of a Mannerist or Counter-Reformation Baroque artist, a brain that vaults or leaps beyond reasonable limit to create columns reared so high the eyebrows must arch to regard them. This is the kind of supererogatory builder who would empty quarries to create empty caves, which is to say, grottoes, thereby substituting one vacancy for another; and, in a lawless search for timber, leveling a forest. The next stanza goes on to observe that all other creatures but man observe suitable and due proportions in their dwellings:

> Why should of all things Man unrul'd
> Such unproportion'd dwellings build?
> The Beasts are by their Denns exprest:
> And Birds contrive an equal Nest;
> The low-roof'd Tortoises do dwell
> In cases fit of Tortoise-shell:
> No Creature loves an empty space;
> Their Bodies measure out their Place.

> But He, superfluously spread,
> Demands more room alive than dead:
> And in his hollow Palace goes
> Where Winds, as he, themselves may lose.
> What need of all this Marble Crust
> T'impark the wanton Mote of Dust,
> That thinks by Breadth the world t'unite
> Though the first Builders fail'd in Height?

Those first builders, of course, were the builders of Babel. Since they so conspicuously failed, the modern builders, who are the heirs of their ambition, desire to unite the world by the breadth or square footage of floor space rather than by the height of their erections. And now, in contrast, Marvell turns to the house of Lord Fairfax that he means to praise. It was at first a Cistercian priory, which, at the dissolution of Church lands, was bestowed upon the Fairfax family. A history of the house itself figures as a small segment of the poem which is 776 lines long, and which I can therefore deal with only in the most fleeting way. But it is necessary to point out that Lord Fairfax was a general of the Parliamentary army that defeated Charles I. And the house therefore becomes a complex emblem of a building once Catholic and now Protestant, be-

longing to a general once active and now retired. Its virtues
are emphatically modest and in a specifically religious context,
as, for example, in the next stanza, in which allusion is made
to the following text from St. Matthew: "Enter ye at the
straight gate: for wide is the gate and broad is the way, that
leadeth to destruction, and many there be which go in thereat;
Because straight is the gate and narrow is the way which leadeth unto life, and few there be that find it." Now for Appleton
House itself:

> But all things are composed here
> Like Nature, orderly and near:
> In which we the Dimensions find
> Of that more sober Age and Mind
> When larger-sized Men did stoop
> To enter at a narrow loop;
> As practicing, in doors so straight
> To strain themselves through *Heavens Gate.*

> And surely when the after Age
> Shall hither come in *Pilgrimage,*
> These sacred Places to adore,
> By *Vere* and *Fairfax* trod before,
> Men will dispute how their Extent
> Within such dwarfish Confines went:
> And some will smile at this, as well
> As *Romulus* his Bee-like cell.

This last line represents remarkable archeological knowledge
on Marvell's part. The Romans of Cicero's time could still see
standing in the southwest corner of the Palatine, beside the pa-
trician houses of what was then the fashionable quarter of the
city, a simple thatched hut. Its post-holes are still visible today.
It was called "The House of Romulus," and it was traditionally
described as the shepherd's hut that Romulus had grown up
in six centuries earlier. But we should never be surprised by
Marvell's exotic learning. A bit later he makes use of the in-

formation furnished by Plutarch that the sweat of Alexander the Great smelled like flowers. I want to quote one more stanza, the sixth of ninety-seven.

> *Humility* alone designs
> Those short and admirable Lines,
> By which, ungirt and unconstrain'd,
> Things greater are in less contain'd.
> Let others vainly strive t'immure
> The Circle in the Quadrature!
> These *holy Mathematicks* can
> In ev'ry Figure equal Man.

Commentators on these lines have invariably referred, correctly, to the mathematical impossibility of squaring the circle, and have gone on to remark, apropos the "holy mathematics," that "the circle symbolized perfection and the square variously virtue, righteousness, prudence, religion, and justice." All this is true, but I would want to argue that the equation of a perfect building to a perfect man is a Vitruvian idea that seems clearly to belong to this poem. I abandon it with reluctance, since it is a favorite poem of mine; but it would have commanded a lecture all to itself. So I turn instead to Alexander Pope. Apart from his fame as poet and translator, he was famous for his estate and his gardens at Twickenham, and he had very pronounced ideas about the laying out and care of such grounds. In the spirit of jest at the more absurd kinds of topiary work popular in his day, he once inserted in *The Guardian* a "catalogue of greens to be disposed of by an eminent town gardener." These included:

Adam and Eve in yew; Adam a little shattered by the fall of the tree of Knowledge in the great storm. Eve and the serpent very flourishing.

The tower of Babel, not yet finished.

St. George in box; his arm scarce long enough, but will be in condition to stick the dragon by next April.

A green dragon of the same, with a tail of ground ivy for the present.

N.B. These two not to be sold separately.

A Queen Elizabeth in phylyrea a little inclining to green sickness, but of full growth.

A quickset hog, shot up into porcupine, by being forgot a week in rainy weather.

A pair of giants, stunted, to be sold cheap.

Pope alludes in passing to this same topic in his celebrated verse epistle to Richard Boyle, Earl of Burlington, on the subject of the proper use of riches. The entire poem deals with morality, including artistic morality, and more particularly the morality of the privileged and wealthy. A good deal of fun is had at the expense of a rich and tasteless parvenu classically named Timon in a passage I want to read. I again take the liberty of supplying a few headnotes. Brobdignag is Jonathan Swift's land of giants, in *Gulliver's Travels*. Amphitrite is a sea goddess. And it was a convention of Roman fountain statuary to exhibit a recumbent god, leaning upon an urn from which water flowed, as a personification of a great river.

> At Timon's Villa let us pass a day,
> Where all cry out, "What sums are thrown away!"
> So proud, so grand, of that stupendous air,
> Soft and Agreeable come never there.
> Greatness with Timon, dwells in such a draught
> As brings all Brobdignag before your thought.
> To compass this, his building is a Town,
> His pond an Ocean, his parterre a Down:
> Who but must laugh, the Master when he sees,
> A puny insect, shiv'ring at a breeze!
> Lo, what huge heaps of littleness around!
> The whole, a labor'd Quarry above ground.
> Two Cupids squirt before: A Lake behind

Improves the keenness of the Northern wind.
His Gardens next your admiration call,
On ev'ry side you look, behold the Wall!
No pleasing Intricacies intervene,
No artful wildness to perplex the scene;
Grove nods at grove, each Alley has a brother,
And half the platform just reflects the other.
The suff'ring eye inverted Nature sees,
Trees cut to Statues, Statues thick as Trees,
With here a Fountain, never to be play'd,
And there a Summer-house, that knows no shade;
Here Amphitrite sails thro' myrtle bow'rs;
There Gladiators fight, or die, in flow'rs;
Un-water'd see the drooping sea-horse mourn,
And swallows roost in Nilus' dusty Urn.

For reasons complexly historical or sociological, the writing of Country House poems fell into abeyance in the eighteenth century. One of the reasons for this has to do with a change in the relationship between patron and artist, a change from which Dr. Johnson, for one, was to suffer. It is not that there were no patrons, and there were certainly plenty of artists, but with the coming of the Industrial Revolution, with the passing of the Enclosure Laws, the rich became richer and the poor poorer, and humane arts and crafts gave way through economic necessity to mechanical production in the Satanic mills of which Blake wrote, while the number of wealthy who were both morally sensitive and artistically cultivated diminished. Of all English art and architectural historians, none was more alive to the moral as well as the artistic effect of this change than John Ruskin. By the mid-nineteenth century he was able to write,

"It must be our work . . . to examine what evidence there is of the effect of wealth on the minds of its possessors; also, what kind of person it is who usually sets himself to obtain wealth, and succeeds in doing so; and whether the world owes more gratitude to rich or to poor men, either for their moral influence upon it, or for chief goods, discoveries and practical advancements. I may, however, anticipate future conclusions, so far as to state that in a community regulated only by laws of demand and supply, but protected from open violence, the persons who become rich are, generally speaking, industrious, resolute, proud, covetous, prompt, methodical, sensible, unimaginative, insensitive and ignorant. The persons who remain poor are the entirely foolish, the entirely wise, the idle, the reckless, the humble, the thoughtful, the dull, the imaginative, the sensitive, the well-informed, the improvident, the irregularly and impulsively wicked, the clumsy knave, the open thief, and the entirely merciful, just, and godly person."

Generally speaking, Ruskin's observations seem clear-eyed, unsentimental, and as true today as they presumably were when he made them in 1860. Yet there are nevertheless some modern country house poems, and they were written by the greatest poet of our century, William Butler Yeats. In a sense, they are farewells to the genre, elegiac reflections that a certain kind of society, and the houses and patronage that distinguished it, is gone, or is about to go. Such a poem is the one called "Coole Park, 1929." It concerns the home of Yeats's great patroness, Lady Gregory, who, though allowed to stay on as a tenant for the rest of her life, was forced, in 1927, to sell her house and land to the Forestry Department. But I want to draw your attention to a somewhat earlier poem, the first of a set of lyrics called "Meditations in Time of Civil War."

Yeats's imagination was thoroughly dialectical; which is to say, he invariably thought in terms of contrasts and oppositions, which, given the normal irony of human events, are abundant enough. He is not, however, primarily an ironic poet. He was alive to all the dramatic contradictions involved in the Civil War itself, and he was thoroughly aware of the discords in the structure of society diagnostically described by Ruskin in the passage I quoted a moment ago. He was, moreover, alive to the distinction between our dreams, ideals, or imaginative life, and the, as he called it, "foul rag-and-bone shop of the heart" where all those dreams begin. Part of the premise of this very poem is that, while greatness can be achieved, this can only be through violence and bitterness, a cost especially obvious in wartime. And wealth itself, which is famous for its capacity to corrupt, permits a special kind of virtue: it eliminates the fierce appetites of ambition. The image of a great fountain, so characteristic an adornment of the gardens of large estates, dominates the first two stanzas, and is more than merely a symbol of wealth and grandeur. It stands for the very vitality of life itself, and the dream of a paradisal condition in which men ought to live. But the age when such dreams were plausible seems, at the time Yeats is writing, in the midst of war, to have vanished. It is recalled here in a highly dated and stylized way by reference to "slippered Contemplation," and to "Childhood," both with upper-case initials, the sort of personified abstractions we might have encountered in the poetry of Marvell or Pope. Convinced as he was that such oppositions as I have described lay in the very nature of things, in destiny, in the pattern and design of history, and the life of the human soul, it would have seemed to Yeats perfectly comprehensible that (certain noble and enfeebled exceptions, like Lady Gregory, apart) it would take, just as Ruskin thought, someone of a tough, ruthless, and perhaps piratical nature to accumulate the sort of wealth that would make possible a great house and generous patronage. Yet even that ruthlessness would have been prompted by some Edenic or Arcadian dream of a perfect life from which its own ruthlessness would be excluded. It is in the nature of man to seek to become his opposite, his anti-self, but he can never completely achieve this end, and achievement always fails to satisfy, except in dreams. Yeats's poem, with which I close these remarks, itself closes on a set of rhetorical questions, an irresolution quite in keeping with the unresolvable problems it considers. But they hint at a further question, not quite articulated but certainly implied: Isn't it possible that Irishmen who have the resolution to fight and willingness to die if necessary for the renovation of their country could construct, out of the same resources of their character, an architectural dream of what would be the perfect life?

ANCESTRAL HOUSES

Surely among a rich man's flowering lawns,
Amid the rustle of his planted hills,
Life overflows without ambitious pains;
And rains down life until the basin spills,
And mounts more dizzy high the more it rains
As though to choose whatever shape it wills
And never stoop to a mechanical
Or servile shape, at others' beck and call.

Mere dreams, mere dreams! Yet Homer had not sung
Had he not found it certain beyond dreams
That out of life's own self-delight had sprung
The abounding glittering jet; though now it seems
As if some marvelous empty sea-shell flung
Out of the obscure dark of the rich streams,
And not a fountain, were the symbol which
Shadows the inherited glory of the rich.

Some violent bitter man, some powerful man
Called architect and artist in, that they,
Bitter and violent men, might rear in stone
The sweetness that all longed for night and day,
The gentleness none there had ever known;
But when the master's buried mice can play,
And maybe the great-grandson of that house,
For all its bronze and marble, 's but a mouse.

O what if gardens where the peacock strays
With delicate feet upon old terraces,
Or else all Juno from an urn displays
Before the indifferent garden deities;
O what if levelled lawns and gravelled ways
Where slippered Contemplation finds his ease
And Childhood a delight for every sense,
But take our greatness with our violence?

What if the glory of escutcheoned doors,
And buildings that a haughtier age designed,
The pacing to and fro on polished floors
Amid great chambers and long galleries, lined
With famous portraits of our ancestors;
What if those things the greatest of mankind
Consider most to magnify, or to bless,
But take our greatness with our bitterness?

ACKNOWLEDGMENTS (CONTINUED)

On page 15, William Carlos Williams's "The Red Wheelbarrow" is reprinted from *The Collected Earlier Poems of William Carlos Williams*, copyright 1938 by New Directions Publishing Corporation; reprinted by permission of New Directions Publishing Corporation.

On page 19, Robert Frost's "The Wood Pile" is reprinted from *The Poetry of Robert Frost* edited by Edwin Connery Lathem; copyright 1930, 1939, © 1969 by Holt, Rinehart and Winston; copyright © 1958 by Robert Frost; copyright © 1967 by Lesley Frost Ballantine; by permission of Henry Holt and Company, Inc.

On page 18, Wallace Stevens's "The Snow Man" is reprinted from *The Collected Poems of Wallace Stevens*, Copyright 1923, 1931, 1935, 1936, 1937, 1942, 1943, 1945, 1946, 1947, 1948, 1949, 1950, 1951, 1952, 1954, by Wallace Stevens; by permission of Alfred A. Knopf, Inc.

On page 25, Richard Wilbur's "Advice to a Prophet" is reprinted from his volume *Advice to a Prophet and Other Poems*, copyright © 1959 by Richard Wilbur; by permission of Harcourt Brace Jovanovich; first published in *The New Yorker*.

On page 27, et seqq., W. H. Auden's "In Praise of Limestone," "A Letter to Lord Byron," "A Lullaby," and "Good-bye to Mezzogiorno" are reprinted from *W. H. Auden: Collected Poems*, edited by Edward Mendelson, copyright © 1976 by Edward Mendelson, William Meredith and Monroe K. Spears, executors of the Estate of W. H. Auden; by permission of Random House, Inc., and the Estate of W. H. Auden.

On page 119, Elizabeth Bishop's "The Fish" is reprinted from *North & South*, copyright 1941, © 1969 by Elizabeth Bishop; copyright renewed 1968 by Elizabeth Bishop; by permission of Farrar, Straus and Giroux, Inc.

On page 132, Richard Wilbur's "On the Marginal Way" is reprinted from his volume *Walking to Sleep*, copyright © 1965 by Richard Wilbur by permission of Harcourt Brace Jovanovich, Inc.

On page 147, et seqq., the quotations from Haim Hillel Ben-Sasson's *The History of the Jewish People* are reprinted by permission of Harvard University Press; copyright © 1976 by George Weidenfeld and Nicolson Ltd.

ACKNOWLEDGMENTS (CONTINUED)

On page 223, the quotations from Ezra Pound's "Canto XLV" are from *The Cantos of Ezra Pound*, copyright 1940 by Ezra Pound; reprinted by permission of New Directions Publishing Corporation.

On page 277, the quotations from the two poems by Robert Lowell about Sir Thomas More, and "No Hearing" on page 287, are reprinted by permission of Farrar, Straus and Giroux, Inc.; from *Notebook 1967–1968* copyright © 1967, 1968, 1969, 1970 by Robert Lowell; from *Notebook, Enlarged Edition* copyright © 1967, 1968, 1969, 1970 by Robert Lowell; from *History* copyright © 1967, 1968, 1969, 1970 by Robert Lowell; from *For Lizzie and Harriet* copyright © 1967, 1968, 1969, 1970, 1973 by Robert Lowell.

On page 282, Robert Lowell's "Thanksgiving's Over" is originally from his *The Mills of the Kavanaughs*, copyright 1950 by Robert Lowell; renewed 1978 by Harriet W. Lowell; reprinted by permission of Harcourt Brace Jovanovich, Inc.

On page 325, William Butler Yeats's *Ancestral Houses* is from *W. B. Yeats, The Poems, A New Edition* edited by Richard J. Finneran, copyright © 1983 by Macmillan Publishing Company; reprinted by permission of Macmillan Publishing Company.

Anthony Hecht's first book of poems, *A Summoning of Stones*, appeared in in 1954. He is also the author of *The Hard Hours*, which won the Pulitzer Prize for poetry in 1968, of *Millions of Strange Shadows*, 1977, and of *The Venetian Vespers* in 1979. He is the translator (with Helen Bacon) of Aeschylus' *Seven Against Thebes* in 1973, and coeditor (with John Hollander) in 1967 of a volume of light verse, *Jiggery-Pokery*. He has taught at Kenyon, Bard, The State University of Iowa, New York University and the University of Rochester. He has been a visiting professor at Harvard, and is presently University Professor in the Graduate School of Georgetown University.